First and Last Love

FIRST AND LAST

RANDOM HOUSE

LOVE

Vincent Sheean

W YORK

to Madame Lotte Lehmann

Dearest Lotte,

In asking you to accept the dedication of this book, the autobiography of a listener, I am offering once again that gratitude which is your due as the greatest artist of them all. Even so, since music always was to you both a being and a becoming, you know that it is a little more complicated than personal tribute alone. You will accept the intention for what it is, including, as it does, all who worked with you in the general realm—and, quite possibly, those also who worked against you—whether they were great or small. Your associates and rivals, predecessors and successors, as well as every orchestra player in the Western world and every choral singer, are the objects of this gratitude, which Schubert expressed in the song you know too well to sing. This book is a way of saying that I thank you.

Vincent Sheean

ROME, 1956

Contents

First and Last Love

1 : The Chautauqua

Why does anybody listen to music? In every one of the most direct forms, those which came earliest to the race and stayed longest, it is for some practical purpose: as an accompaniment to singing and dancing, for instance, or to arouse martial ardor. It plays a part in primitive courtship, as it does in ritual ceremonies; it accompanies marriage and burial, the birth of the year and the gathering of the harvest. All these purposes have been served by some form of rhythm and tune for unknown ages; man came into history beating a drum. The kind of purposive music Plato and Aristotle discussed, even in their age of elevated culture, was not essentially different from that of their remotest ancestors, even though it had developed into differ- ent "modes" or sequences of tones. The music Plato approved and the music he disapproved was alike in one thing, that it was all designed to bring about some action, and he judged the "modes" entirely by the action to which they were likely to lead. "Martial" music was good and "lascivious" music was forbidden in the Re- public not for content but for result.

Listening in itself alone, as a form of the contemplation of beauty, came into the life of the Western peoples late enough to be called

distinctly modern, keeping pace with the development of instruments, styles, notation and harmony. There have been no more than
three or four hundred years of music in this sense, without a purpose, without a result in any practical manner easily discerned. Even
in this relatively short period of Western history, the habit of listening to such music was at first restricted to small, privileged societies, and no large public of listeners—content merely to listen without taking part and without performing a deed in consequence—has
existed until the last century and a half. It is indeed now, at this
moment, that the largest number of listeners yet known exists in
the Western world. (It is necessary to repeat the word "Western"
not only because our music is distinct, but also because non-Western
music, that of Asia and Africa, remains purposive to the present day.)

Some psychologists, William James for one, have felt that even
our most highly developed music, such as the symphony, should
leave with the listener something more than a mere impression of
beauty or stir of emotion—should result in some harmonious deed,
and the sooner the better. To listen passively seems, from this point
of view, inert and useless. Without arguing the point, it is easy enough
to see that the millions who today listen to music of every kind are
far indeed from any such puritanical view of it, and, if asked their
purpose, would in almost every case define it as pleasure alone. And
yet it is a form of pleasure so various and so progressive that X may
detest what Y enjoys, while both may detest today what they
enjoy tomorrow.

All these millions of listeners in every Western country derive
something higher, stronger and more complex than mere pleasure
from that music which most appeals to them, or so I believe. They
derive, first of all, the same imaginative stimulus from music as from
poetry, the opening of magic casements, the view of another world,
as well as a translation of the emotions of this one. Hope, love, despair and aspiration, along with dozens of less recognizable human
impulses, go into another dimension—the dimension of beauty—in
music as in poetry, and in so doing they bestow upon the listener
something akin to the catharsis Aristotle found only in tragedy. As
music itself became more expressive toward the end of the nineteenth century (a tendency temporarily arrested, it seems), the ca-

tharsis tended to become a principal rather than a concomitant experience, and "pure" contemplation grew less, but never disappeared; it is now again—as in the eighteenth century—a major part of the act of listening. Nobody could pretend that these or other elements in the act are the same with all music or with any one piece of music all the way through, for, in fact, it is a very complicated act.

And since it is complicated, it is clearly susceptible of a good deal of change and development. You could never expect a boy of ten to get the same pleasure from a Bach chorale as a man of forty; even though that pleasure might be equal in degree (depending upon boy and man!), it would still be different in kind. Life, then, must have something to do with it—not merely musical life or experience, but all of life, which in its own unpredictable complexity reaches out toward music, too—as it does toward poetry and painting—to embrace what once was far away or to illumine what once was dark. Any event with depth, radiation or result in a human life may determine an evolution; if you have lost a child, wept for a love or suffered for an idea, you will in every case have some different sensibility toward the music which (even if only in your own mind) bears some relation to these events. It is not static. Like everything else, it is a perpetual flux.

The act of listening now engages many millions of Western persons for an appreciable section of their time on earth. There are eighteen million listeners for a certain operatic broadcast, twenty-two million for a certain symphonic broadcast, in the United States alone. There are hundreds of thousands in every large city who go to concerts with a frequency which has become habitual and is on the increase. Among them are musicians and students, but the greater number consists simply of persons like you and me, who like to listen to music, who have grown up in it and dwelt in it without a thought of practical purpose or result. It is one of the most important ways in which modern Western man differs, not only from his contemporaries in other cultures, but from all of his own ancestors: for this act of listening is one of the few phenomena which may be called truly modern. It scarcely existed at all until about a century and a few decades ago; it has never existed, even in that brief time, on such a scale as it does today. We listeners are more modern than the atomic bomb, because that, at least, was quite accurately foreseen in the most ancient documents of mankind, whereas the act of listening, as we do it, was unimaginable until the recent past.

Music and its listeners grew together, of course, and both are extremely late when compared to any other important aspect of the intellectual and emotional experience of the race. Compare music to numbers, or to poetry or painting, or to building; count the size of an orchestra (even the greatest) a hundred years ago; count the size of an audience (even the greatest) a hundred years ago. Beethoven wrote for an orchestra of forty pieces at best. He is performed today by a hundred and ten. He was heard by a few hundred; in the concert halls of Western countries today he is usually heard by about three thousand persons at a time. The thing itself grew as its appreciation grew; it became more complex and its determination more profound; it asserted a distinct claim to the attention of the human soul, above and beyond language; the claim was granted. There thus arose the most distinctive characteristic of Western culture in the modern era—defining "Western" as everything from the Ural Mountains westward to the Pacific Ocean—which is its alternate creation of and response to a highly evolved musical utterance. Our poetry, painting, architecture and sculpture have their counterparts in Asia, but our music is peculiarly our own growth and has no counterpart anywhere. The music of Asia, constructed on totally different principles and never for the listener alone—never for the autonomous creation but always in connection with another art—cannot be regarded as belonging to the same phase of human experience. Whatever its merits, they are extraneous to the life of Western man.

Now, naturally, this great mass of listeners which has come into being is not always constant. We all know men and women whose interest in music is real but fitful, and others who, after years of almost obsessive devotion, have lost the desire to listen to any but a very few things. This is, so to speak, the beauty of the transaction, that it is perfectly free—you can take it or leave it. But there are others who cannot really take it or leave it for very long at a time— by which I mean that they begin to feel ragged and cold, somewhat bereft, if they do not occasionally hear something which speaks to them in the language they think highest and best. These are the lifelong listeners, of whom I am one. We are addicts in a sense, but we are more like addicts to poetry than addicts to opium: that is, our joy does not dull or dim or fade, but grows keener with the addiction; and, moreover, we are never content with the moment but go on questing with a never quenched desire. The modern time created us and certainly exploits us to the utmost—it is cruel even to print the amounts of money we must pay today to hear what we want—but only the modern time has evolved ways of keeping us in being, by the radio or the gramophone if by nothing else, so that our number is ever on the increase and our ears are never satiated.

These, the lifelong listeners, make up the central body of the musical public. It is noteworthy indeed how many we are. We are of all the possible degrees of musical education: some of us can read no music at all, some a little, some a good deal. Some of us are governed by instinct and some by intellect; some are "literary" and voluble, some very nearly wordless; we are argumentative and contentious, or silent and stricken; the truth of the listener who *is* one cannot, however, be concealed from any other. I knew a farmer in Maine who played the gramophone to his cows, as well as to himself, and his very notable taste in music was perhaps shared by them, as they gave a great deal of milk (so he told me) under this treatment; but my friend could not or would not discuss any of the details of his prolonged acquaintance with music. Others are all words, voice and judgment, praising here and condemning there as if each orphan of the Lord could wield the thunderbolt.

Obviously, something which developed so late in human history could take a good deal of explaining and has, to my knowledge, received little. Freud's general theory of sublimation applies to the whole of human culture, including mathematics, the sciences, politics, art, literature and everything else in which mankind has ever been engaged. By this theory, which is most cogently expressed in the nontechnical or literary essay called *Civilization and Its Discontents,* all the higher activity of man is stolen from his sexual life and is therefore a "sublimation" of it. To a mere reader the theory seems partly common sense, easily confirmed by observation, and partly fantasy. It is fantasy to apply the same rule of thumb to manifestations so different in place, time and character. Freud's philosophical writing—as distinct from his actual practice and his

technical work—professes faith in the great variability of human nature but puts at its base the same simplicity of origin. Music, therefore, may be in some way a "sublimation" of the sexual life, since he
says so; but why did it come so late in history and develop so slowly?
Why has it created such an enormous public, whereas most of the
other arts (except literature) must worry along with less than they
had in ages past? The theory of sublimation gives no clue to these
puzzles, and although it may readily be accepted in general, it
seems in particular to explain little or nothing. Other parts of the
Freudian system, more technical and less general, can be used in
the analysis of almost any composition, but the process answers no
larger question. Example: in *Tristan und Isolde,* Act II, the notable passage in which Tristan describes the land to which he is going
—*"Das Land das Tristan meint, die Sonne nie erscheint"*—it is fairly
simple to label words and music as the expression of Richard Wagner's longing to return to the womb. Having said this, what have we
learned? Certainly we have not learned what makes the passage beautiful or why generations of our public have listened to it with such
exaltation. For myself, at any rate, the glossary which Freud has
supplied for works of art may be perfectly true as technical analysis
but seems, on the whole, irrelevant. A technique evolved for the
treatment of disease can shed only a special light; it shows the part,
not the whole. I can never forget the footnote Dr. Freud—in the
modesty of his greatness—put to a certain passage in his *Psycho-
pathology of Ordinary Life.* It concerns the child whom he had been
psychoanalyzing, who afterwards died of a physical tumor on the
brain. Freud's tremendous place in modern thought has dazzled us;
his word tends to be law even in fields which were not his own; and
yet—and yet—if he had been able to psychoanalyze Beethoven or
Michelangelo or Shakespeare in life, is it at all likely that they could
have done their work?

One way of trying to understand the processes of life is to tell how
they came about, it seems to me. A walked down the street and ran
into B, who told him a story, as a result of which he robbed a bank
and went to Texas to live forever after. The bald narrative can
then induce its own reflections. In setting out what it is like to live
partly in music—in telling the story—what we fall into is a
kind of autobiography, with whatever pauses for reflection may be-

come imperative. We are all a little bit like those people in Che-
khov's plays who suddenly remember their childhood (in some detail) in the midst of a picnic or a family tea. Forgetting the learned
doctors and their theories, some clues may arise simply from a re-
consideration of the past. As a listener, not a specialist of any kind,
but merely one of those millions to whom music is a parallel life
and therefore part of this one, let me see if I can trace it out.

It seems to me that in my own case it began at the Chautauqua in
Pana, Illinois, almost half a century ago.

2

There was joy in our park during the month of August. Joy was not
unknown there at other seasons for those old and brave enough, but
in that long, long childhood which our northern climes encourage,
when a year is like a decade and a day like a year, the park came to
life only at Chautauqua time. It would drip and freeze or bud and
bloom without our knowledge at other times, since we lived far from
it and were forever being warned against the "tramps" who were
said to infest it. In August it was ours—it belonged to everybody in
the town and in very nearly the whole of Christian County, but
above all, as it seemed to us, to the children. Under its elms and
maples and over its magic lagoon we had a moment of sovereignty,
and since everything was very spacious, with an immense variety of
incident and activity, there was plenty for all.

And "all," as a matter of fact, is what it was: I do not remember
any acquaintance in our town who did not frequent the park during the enchanted period, and many of them actually moved into it
for that time, living in tents of such magnificence that I wondered
how they could return to their own houses afterwards. These tents
had floors and rugs and gay cushions and a tremendous number of
pennants of various colors indicating the colleges and universities where their young were now being educated or aspired to be
educated, or even indicating only favorite football teams and local
patriotisms. The tents lay in rows up and down one side of the park
and there was a great social activity between them. They were
rented by the bankers, lawyers and men of business from the
central committee (a community organism more or less contermi-

nous with everything else in the town) which operated the Chautauqua, and no doubt the rentals helped, along with single and season tickets of admission, to pay the expense of the undertaking.

But most of the town went to Chautauqua for the day only, and for
the night which ended (under protest) at nine o'clock. And the
whole county, as it seemed, came at some time or other—perhaps
not every day; perhaps only one day during the week or (later) two
weeks; but in sufficient numbers to create the sensation of immense comings and goings, difficult transactions and preoccupations
on the part of innumerable strangers. It was this—the invasion of
the world—that remained as a first and pervading impression, as if
our town and our park had suddenly become, in its brief hour, a
center of interest for the whole teeming prairie on all sides.

The Chautauqua itself, the reason or excuse for such a centrifugal
movement, was hazy in my mind during early childhood. That is,
the question, "What is a chautauqua?" did not even arise. It was a
condition of life in summer, in August. It was a crowd; it was excitement; it was a whirl of light and sound; it bore some relation to
what went on in "the Big Tent," which later became the Auditorium, but just as much to the picnic under the trees, the boat on the
lagoon, and, earliest of all, to the delirious adventure of getting lost.
(I used to get myself lost quite regularly and with supreme pleasure.) There were concomitants, such as Crackerjack and various
colored sodas, paper caps and small wooden clackers or whistles,
which were sold on the periphery of the park but were not, for
some adult reason, encouraged in the neighborhood of the Big Tent.
And there was something else not comprehended even faintly in
the mind of a child, but to be phrased long afterwards as the purely
social assertion—that which the French mean when they say *faire
acte de présence,* that which the Hindus mean when they go into the
streets for *tamasa:* the pleasure arising from the consciousness that
"I also am here, I am not to be excluded from or deprived of these
rude communal joys, count me in, too," or perhaps, most simply of
all, "Here I am." As I grew older this aspect of Chautauqua dawned
on me, rather slowly it is true, but long before I departed from my
native region I knew that many men and women went there in
defiance of fatigue or even boredom, just so as to assert, in deed if
not in word, their existence. It is no secret that half the audiences in

the world, even in great centers of our Western culture, are formed in just this way.

And our Chautauqua did certainly, in different ways and for disparate reasons, call into being a very large audience. I know now that it was not as large as we once supposed. We used to say "three thousand" or even "five thousand" people had gathered for the great occasions. It was customary to mention such large figures and our town's newspaper sanctioned them by print. However, when I consider that the Metropolitan Opera House in New York, an immense theatre, can hold even at present, with more seats than ever before, just 3,500 persons, my faith in the great numbers that once bedazzled us is somewhat shaken. The Big Tent and its successor, the Auditorium, had nothing like the seating capacity of the Metropolitan Opera House, and even though the throngs stood around it ten-deep or even twenty-deep, the total number of persons in the crowd on the greatest days was probably no more than about two thousand. Our town's inhabitants were never counted at more than five thousand when I was growing up, and of these many were what we called "foreigners" who did not greatly frequent the Chautauqua during their first years of Americanization. At that time the absence of the "foreigners" (mainly Hungarians and Slavs, I think) was ascribed to their actual foreignness, which made them impervious to the mellowing influences of cultivated entertainment; now, of course, I believe that they remained away because our innocent platforms, with their conjurers and lecturers and vocal quartets, had little of interest to offer them.

This made the crowds homogeneous, at least: the great, swarming, sweltering, good-natured and loud-voiced crowd of the Midwestern prairie, farmers who had driven in for the day and town dwellers on their annual outing. It had many of the aspects of those fairs—the county and, in the largest form, the state fair—which still draw vast multitudes throughout the Middle West, but the fairs were centrally and traditionally exhibitions of livestock, fruits, grains and other agricultural products, no matter how many "big shows" and "side shows" they might also provide in the way of subsidiary entertainment; whereas our Chautauqua was purely for the edification and diversion of the crowd.

The whole concept, as I eventually learned, came from Lake Chau-

tauqua in New York State, where beautiful surroundings had been
used as the setting for a summer festival of music and learning, with
courses of lectures, concerts, recitals and innumerable lesser manifestations of culture and delight. By the time our Chautauqua season
was in flower I suppose there must have been thousands of others, all
more or less the same, throughout the United States. Of this I was,
and remained, ignorant; ours was the only one I ever saw,
and in my childhood it was the only one of which I could have
certified the existence. By the time I was in high school it had become beyond any doubt the kindest, cleanest and sweetest part of
the year, the season of trees and flowers, when all the girls wore their
prettiest dresses and the moon shone bright. It was also—and as the
balance is cast, this is what it most definitively was for me—the birth
time and the birthplace of a lifelong passion for music and all the
kindred arts.

Our programs were various indeed. Music was only a small part
of the whole; the theatre, except for Shakespeare, was scarcely represented. There were numerous activities which never at any moment
engaged my attention, such as classes (or lectures with demonstrations) in gardening and folk dancing and the like. My memory of
such things, which took place in the morning, consists simply in having wandered there by mistake and wandered out again. There
were at times films of educational value (I suppose they were what
we now call documentary films) and there was also a certain amount
of devotional temperament on exhibition by Protestant divines
who explained the New Testament, counseled and prayed.

None of this made much difference to me except as a perception
of active life, of things going on, of persons being taught or exhorted or enlivened by other persons. The programs at Chautauqua
began at ten in the morning, if I remember correctly, and continued
with intervals for luncheon and dinner (called dinner and supper)
until about nine o'clock at night. Nobody was supposed to be present
at everything and nobody was. I took what was for me; I took what
I was ready for. What was for me, essentially, was what I have indicated, music and the interpretation of words as well as music;
what I was ready for depended upon the age I had reached at each
successive Chautauqua. It is to me a little astonishing that I can re-

member some things so distinctly, whereas most of it is forever lost behind the stern amnesia of time and space.

According to an impression too vague to be called memory, Mme. Ernestine Schumann-Heink once came to our Chautauqua, complete with *"Der Erlkönig"* and "The Rosary," but I am told this is my own imagination based on gramophone records.

Of the other great highlights in those earliest days, when I was a child busy getting myself lost, I can distinctly recollect two. One was a lady called Mrs. Maybrick, who had been acquitted in England of murdering her husband by the administration of arsenic. Her trial had been prolonged, had apparently engaged the attention of a great part of the civilized world, and had resulted in an acquittal because the charge could not be proved beyond a doubt. She may have been a perfectly innocent woman, and she was also (or was supposed to be) an American by birth, so it is regrettable to have to note that the principal interest in her was, not only in the ghoulish mind of a small boy, but also in the talk of our Midwestern adults, that she was a "murderess." Perhaps I had never heard the word before. I do remember listening to her intently and watching her hands as she drew on, and then removed, her long white gloves, and all the while thinking: "This is a murderess, and those are the hands . . ." I did not understand very much of what she was saying but I have ever afterwards, no doubt most unjustly, connected those hands of hers with the idea of a "murderess." Murder did not occur in Pana, Illinois, at least during the time when I grew up there, and this was one of the most dramatic possibilities presented to the avid imagination of a child by our Chautauqua culture.

Mrs. Maybrick may have impinged upon us when I was eight or nine years old. Her lecture was, I imagine, upon her "ordeal," and had some overtones of persecution and self-pity, although this I really do not remember. What I do remember beyond question is the hands and the long white gloves.

The other great attraction of my early Chautauqua years was William Jennings Bryan. It was only after many decades that I learned to regard with respect this true son of our Middle West. When I was a child there were no Democrats to be discerned upon the horizon. My parents and all relatives automatically voted Republican in every election of whatsoever category, from the most local to the most general. This had been true of the only preceding generation (my grandparents had come from Ireland in the middle of the preceding century). It was also true of everybody I knew, which is to say, every child, and the parents of every child. I never saw or heard of a living Democrat until William Jennings Bryan came to our Chautauqua. I had quaint notions, based upon the "donkey" and "elephant" symbols which the Republican and Democratic parties had adopted not long before. To us the Democrats, and particularly William Jennings Bryan, were comical inventions, and at a very early age I was subjected to a cascade of witty jokes, sayings of the people about them, things which then as now spread swiftly and insensibly from coast to coast in our wondrously co-conscious and circumscribed national society.

But Bryan's visit to Pana had elements of high instruction. For one thing, although there were hardly any Democrats in the town or its nearby farmlands, the greatest of all possible crowds turned out to hear him. They were streaming in all day long by every sort of conveyance—for this took place at a period when the older buggies and wagons and surreys were still in use, along with the newfangled motors—and it was easy even for a child to compute that no such crowd had ever gathered in our park. Ordinary curiosity about a personage so very well known to the whole people at that time was responsible for most of this, no doubt, but there was also a very lively anticipation of pleasure from hearing him speak, no matter what he said. He was known as "the silver-tongued orator" and for this quality in itself—a technical achievement I suppose, or a natural gift trained to astonish the hearer—he was esteemed by those who would never have given him their votes.

The great crowd was also extremely polite in its attention and lavish with its applause. The Great Commoner, as he was also called, might have been forgiven for thinking that he had here in our responsive populace a mass of devoted followers, but he knew better than that: he had been a quadrennial candidate for the Presidency since 1896, and this was (I suppose) 1909 or 1910. The great error of novices in politics—such as, to take widely differing examples, Herbert Hoover and General Charles de Gaulle—is the assumption that large and enthusiastic crowds mean political victory.

Bryan could never have made that error. But at least one small boy in his huge audience was astonished at his reception and never has forgotten it.

However, none of the tremendous notables (and there was one, real or false, in every Chautauqua season) meant to me what the itinerant performers of music and poetry did. There were "readers" of some kind in every Chautauqua and, by my somewhat lopsided recollection, what they read was always Shakespeare. There were also "scenes from" this or that play of Shakespeare's as performed in costume and scenery, both rudimentary, by two or three, and sometimes four, players. I well remember that the Forest of Arden seemed magic to me even on the rather bare platform of our Auditorium with a setting which left most of it to the imagination.

The music was, just the same, more revelatory and evocative, newer to my ears and more imperative to my imagination. For one reason, perhaps, my own mother liked to read scenes or speeches of Shakespeare in her deep, beautiful voice and I had heard them from the time I could hear anything. She could not carry a tune at all—I think she must have been what is called "tone-deaf"—and her attempts to hum or sing were always weird. Other children apparently expected their mothers to sing to them; I expected mine to "say something" and very often badgered her to do so even when she was not particularly in the mood. When she "said something" it was generally from a play of Shakespeare's, although she also knew by heart a very considerable number of other compositions, chiefly in verse, which she had learned either for the rhetorical and declamatory competitions of her own school days or had put into practice on her pupils when she, in her turn, began to teach school. Aside from Lady Macbeth's sleepwalking scene, always thrilling to a child without any necessity for comprehension, she knew a great many of the Shakespearean tirades for men (Hamlet, Mark Antony, Wolsey and others, including Henry V), which she rolled out with no attempt at "acting" save by the voice alone. I cannot remember her making any gesture at all when she did this, except the more or less compulsory movements of the hands as Lady Macbeth. She knew these speeches by heart, or had once known them completely by heart, so she seldom looked at the book, even when she had it open at the page. She also knew "Lochiel's Warning," a very great favorite of my childhood, and the Gettysburg Address and some Irish curiosities which she had memorized in her youth for the delectation of her own father, a passionate Irish patriot who had belonged to the Fenian Society and had fled to America to avoid the consequences. One of these Irish oddities, as I can remember very well half a century later, was Robert Emmett's farewell from the scaffold: "When my country shall have taken her place among the sovereign nations of the earth, then, and not till then, let my epitaph be written!" Patrick Henry came into this *galère* somehow, although I doubt if it was with much more than the peroration of his great speech in the church at Richmond ("Give me liberty or give me death!"). There was also, aside from the Gettysburg Address, a considerable amount of Lincoln in my mother's familiar repertoire, including the Second Inaugural and the letter (of disputed authenticity, I was later told) to Mrs. Bixby.

I have only named the things in which I can still recapture some sound, or at least a distant echo, of her voice. Actually there was more: she used to "read" or "recite" Rosalind and Ophelia too, for example, but of this no actual sound seems to be retained in my ears—I merely do know that she did. But even though I have not named all the poems and plays and speeches that became familiar to me in her voice, I have certainly named enough to indicate that the Chautauqua had nothing very astonishing to reveal in these respects. Indeed I did quite confidently suppose—and perhaps rightly—that my mother could do most of these things better than the professional "readers" who came to Chautauqua. She had made me familiar with a larger literature, and at an earlier age, than anything they had to offer.

It was not so with music. Here there was a completely unploughed field. School and church music were of the most rudimentary kind in my earliest days, and I had heard almost nothing else when I began, probably quite tentatively at first, to relish the offerings in the park.

I say "probably" because I do not actually know how slowly the thing took on, became major instead of minor, and assumed the proportion it has since maintained in my existence. I have an idea that the predilection was there in a marked degree to begin with, although nothing in either heredity or environment put it there. I also have an idea that it was inhibited pretty sharply, to begin with, by the Middle Western prejudice which kept music as the prerogative, or special domain, of unmarried ladies, and put a certain seal of singularity on any male, of any age, who felt its powers. Even a respectable married woman was more or less honor bound obliged to "give up her music," as they expressed it, on the thither shore of matrimony. The social convention seemed to imply that music was, in moderation—that is, some aptitude at the piano combined with some freshness of voice if not too seriously employed—a kind of adjunct or secondary weapon in the young lady's battle to get married; once she had won the battle it was of no further use. And the man upon whom she lavished her accomplishments—well, presumably he had never cared much for them anyhow; they had served to fill in the part of courtship which was passed under the watchful supervision of the family.

Something like this, at any rate, was the current attitude toward music in the small Middle Western town where I grew up. There were exceptions, rebellions and dissents. Musical performances at Chautauqua invariably attracted a large audience and a big part of it was male: how could such a thing occur if the social fiction had not been, already in the early part of the century, at odds with fact? Then there were individual deviations of the most startling character: a young man of German origin, the son of a leading merchant of the town, played the piano so well that his own teachers at school and college wanted him to go on to a concert career. He played with strength, velocity and skill, as I remember very well: he was certainly the first person I ever heard do so. The "big" Chopin polonaise, afterwards endemic to the juke boxes of a much later era, the *"Marche Militaire"* of Schubert-Tausig, some Liszt rhapsodies and other piano music of the kind would come thundering out from under his long, nervous fingers, and I was already, at a very early age, of the breed of listener who can happily hear—and urgently request—the same thing over and over. He did not have his concert career; he came home from school and took over, gradually, his father's big drug store, as was the duty of an only son; but I am sure, not only by instinct but by what I remember of the endless talk on this matter, that his surrender to the folkways and mores was a moral defeat from which he never did recover. And there actually

were some good musicians in the town, especially among the parish-
ioners of the German Lutheran Church: there were pianists, violinists and singers, few and far between, but they existed. It was near
the moment of my own departure before I learned of the musical
life which, within severe limits but in complete sincerity and devotion, could have been found. My own piano teacher—a lady of German origin who struggled with my laziness for quite a long time
later on—had skill, musicianship and a much more comprehensive
repertoire than might reasonably have been expected.

However, my lines did not lie among musicians, actual performers on any instrument; I record their existence so that our town
may not seem more Boeotian than it actually was. My own slowly
awakening instinct for music, or predilection for it, was that of a
listener only, and as such it was in the Chautauqua that it received its
nourishment-in-chief for a long time.

It was not the martial bands or the salon orchestras, even so; and
it was not the "popular" compositions (at that time "popular" did
not mean ragtime or jazz; it meant "Hearts and Flowers" and "Poet
and Peasant"), nor was it the better-known singers or other soloists,
of whom we had a few; it was actually the run-of-the-mill vocal
quartets and string players who left a real impress upon me. They
did not aspire to the sublime in any way, and I doubt if such an
audience as we supplied could have spurred them to unusual efforts,
but some of them (whose names I never knew or rapidly forgot)
were probably very good artists making money in the summer by a
tour of our yokelry so as to survive another winter in the cruel cities.
So I think now; at the time I never wondered who they were or
whence; I was taken up by the various and cumulative discoveries
they made possible. Among these I suppose the most decisive, the
most normative and enduring, was the "impure" form, the quasi-
musical and quasi-dramatic, the distinctly literary and indirect invention known as opera.

No doubt to begin with I did not in the very least grasp what an
opera was, and still less could I have understood its brands
and breeds, its wide varieties of style, motive and effect. I merely
found out that this was a kind of performance which appealed to
me beyond reason. I had lively curiosity from an early age, and our
public library (a Carnegie beneficence) was well stocked with

works of reference, so it was not long before I did acquire information far in advance of my actual musical experience, but the information was not an objective in itself—it was merely a form of preparation for the entrancing prospect, half-hope and half-dream, of future performances.

We never had a full opera at our Chautauqua, and even "scenes from opera," which did occasionally get put upon the platform, were sung without scenery or costumes. This imposed upon singers the necessity of reducing action, and above all gesture, to the irreducible; sometimes since, it has seemed that real performances in real opera houses might benefit by the same discipline.

The drama must have come to me, under these conditions, through the singing alone—that is, from the composer's own lyrico-dramatic utterance so far as it could be expressed by the singers who attempted it. They must have been quite good singers really, to have created a theatre by their voices, for they had little help otherwise. There was no flowing orchestra to sustain them; aside from a very few occasions when vocal and instrumental ensembles collaborated, the accompanying scores had to be played on the piano, with all its percussive insistence, its incapacity to suggest the peculiar qualities and varieties of other instruments.

Furthermore, by a perversity inherent not only in the operatic phenomenon but in me, as listening child and youth, the English texts invariably used in these performances were awkward and forever offering themselves to easy ridicule. The "Ha!" and the "Ho!" and the "Beware!" were bad enough, but the misplacing of accent, very often even of sense, and the general banality of language, made me uncomfortable from the start. I was also, by having acknowledged such a transpontine taste so early, subjected to all the gibes to which the subject lent itself, and was thus swamped by personal embarrassment whenever one of our youthful band (or their elders) undertook the easiest of parlor games, an operatic burlesque. I had to be pretty thoroughly adult before I learned to enjoy (as I very much did afterwards) that particular kind of fun.

The sense of being personally involved, and therefore shy on the entire subject of operatic absurdities, has never altogether left me. Perhaps the root cause is my vague and helpless feeling that if life had afforded me any opportunity to learn the trade, I should have fared better and explored my vein with more result as an opera composer than in any other way. Fared better internally, I mean: derived more satisfaction from the work done. The whole is a tissue of supposition. That is, I can no more explain my sense of personal connection with or even involvement in opera than I can the original impulse, whatever it was, that caused me to take to it so strongly in the unfavorable climate of our Illinois prairie.

There was a special cause or reason for discomfort at the English texts used in the operatic music I heard in those years. It was not only that I had a perhaps exaggerated regard for the English language and had written it indefatigably since my sixth or seventh year—millions upon millions of words in small blue-backed notebooks, long histories of imaginary countries and great flat scenes from dramas that never evolved, poems and narratives and declamations in every category—and it was not only that I had been familiar with the poetry of Shakespeare (in my mother's voice) before I could even read. It was also, and with ever increasing efficacy as an irritant in this respect, that I came early to foreign languages. The better I knew them the more I felt inclined to compare these inept English texts with their originals in Italian, French or German, with results which are easily imagined. By sheer accident a gentle and indefatigable Irish priest, Father Fox, had felt impelled to give me lengthy private lessons in French from about my eighth or ninth year. (The first lessons, exploratory and shorter, had begun even earlier.) Father Fox was from Maynooth but had studied at a seminary in Tours. His accent in French was naturally far better than his accent in English, it seems reasonable to assume; at all events, that part of it which rubbed off onto me in childhood has done very great service ever since, so much so that it is difficult for me to imagine what my life might have been without it. Father Fox was as patient, long-suffering and arduous in his labors as I was quick and lazy. He held me to it, recognizing that I really *did* want to learn the French language in the larger intent even though at the precise moment of the lesson I might be yearning to go out and play with a dog or climb a tree and eat an apple. He stuck to it. I no longer remember how many years he stuck to it, but in spite of myself he endowed me with a structural and syntactical basis in support not only of French but of other languages as well. I have since tried to teach a little French myself, notably to my own children, with the result that I can appreciate how hard he worked.

Italian arrived when I was ten or eleven and German when I was thirteen. The Italian was in part due to the curiosities and interests arising from the bits of opera I had already heard, I suppose. (The interaction seems obvious and must have worked both ways.) It was very largely self-taught and therefore ill-taught, up to the time when —at seventeen—I went to the University. I was always too lazy to do much in the way of systematic self-teaching. There were aids in the endeavor, just the same, and first of all an innate hospitality, or what then seemed a natural simplicity, in the Italian language. It came easily, openly, masking its ultimate complexities with a smile. Its vocalism appealed to me from the very first, and it never could seem wholly strange to a boy whose ears had been attuned to church Latinity. There was also the formidable grammatical apparatus built on another terrain by Father Fox: after years of French verbs, the earlier stages of Italian grammar had no terrors. On this, too, I could still consult Father Fox; he did not know the Italian language, but he knew grammar and could explain how it worked when he had the textbook before him.

The textbooks, by the way, were the product of the Sears Roebuck Company, the universal emporium and Areopagitica of Middle Western life. The vast catalogue of that immense mail-order house in Chicago was the indispensable book in every Midwestern house, and hours were spent upon it by persons not otherwise given to reading. Sears Roebuck made and sold everything imaginable both great and small. My chessmen, during an early but brief passion for chess, came from there—and so, I rather imagine, did the pipe organ in our church. On the farms every kind of outside machinery, as well as everything used inside the house, was likely to come from the same abundant source. It was natural, therefore, when the time came, for me to turn to that inexhaustible catalogue and pick out a grammar and dictionary of Italian.

The only Italian in our town, so far as I knew, was in the fruit store just off Main Street. His name was Pietro La Placca, which we (and he) transformed into Pete Plack and there was a sign over his shop to proclaim it. He did not speak very intelligible English but he could recognize Italian words in print, and when they were too difficult for him (for he was barely literate) he could identify them by my phonetic pronunciation and set me straight.

I went to Pete Plack, whom I knew just as every small boy in our town knew him, from having tried to steal his bananas and oranges. Pete did not like boys for this reason and it took me some time to overcome his resistance. My proposal was not uneconomical but at first he suspected it of being connected with the crime he most detested, the plot against his merchandise. I think it was the actual books, the grammar and dictionary, which vanquished him. He had a reverence for the printed word, especially in Italian. He agreed to let me come and work for him an hour at a time now and then in exchange for lessons from the book on how to pronounce his own language.

Now, of course, this was not an ideal introduction to the language of Dante. Pete Plack was a Sicilian to whom Italian was no more familiar than it was to me. He did, however, know how it ought to sound—as they say of a tune, he knew how it "went"—and he was not totally illiterate, for he used to spell out an Italian-language newspaper which came to him from Chicago. He knew nothing of grammar and could explain nothing, but it was not explanation I required, it was exemplification.

I got it—and *what* exemplification! I had to labor, quite often, to make him understand what single word I wanted him to pronounce, over and over, until I had succeeded in saying it afterwards in the same way. It was hard for him to get used to a single word and perhaps he was not even conscious of words singly, but only as part of the general flow: he had to "use it in a sentence." One single verb form, a participle for example, would puzzle him sadly and it would be most difficult to reduce him to a willingness to separate it from any conceivable context, merely to say it, over and over.

I then repeated, parrotlike, until the word sounded to my own ear more or less like his pronunciation of it. I never depended on his ear, after the first days, because it was obvious that he had none. He could not hear the differences or the progress, if any. Nevertheless he developed an absolutely inexhaustible patience in this exercise and perhaps he may even have enjoyed it. It was at least a change from bananas and oranges.

But I never worked on more than a word at a time with Pete,

because I distrusted his sentences even when I was able to understand them. It was easy enough to find out, by Caruso records then very current on gramophones, that Pete's treatment of final vowels was not good Italian. But I shall always feel sure that he had somehow the swing of it in his singsong way, and it is always easier to modify the swing of a language later on than it is to learn it academically with no swing at all and then try the native lyricism as an afterthought. Actually this must experientially be considered proved in my own case, because I entered the University convinced that my self-taught (and La Placca-taught) Italian was academically worthless and registered, as a result, in the most elementary Italian class. After listening to me read a little—for which he had detained me after class, suspecting, by an isolated word or two, some acquaintance with the language—Professor Ernest Wilkins, one of the best Italian scholars of the day, booted me forward three whole classes. The accent, in other words, was too good; I really did not know (could not have known) as much about the language as the accent indicated.

Accent is perhaps a musical aptitude—certainly it depends upon some mysteriously complicated transaction going on between the ear and the organs of speech. Why else is a Cockney completely unaware of his H's? Why are there so many good linguists who can know a language *à fond* and yet fail to approximate its spoken sound? Why are so many singers able to sing with the utmost conviction and effect in languages which they would be incapable of employing to order a decent meal?

German came third in this progression of tongues and never came so easily early or late as the others. I was thirteen when I began to study it and perhpas that is too late—it is obviously too late for most aptitudes, perhaps too late to acquire anything but information. The first teacher of German in the high school was a Lutheran pastor in whom we had to deplore a passion for Schiller which pushed us on too fast. In my third year the German language ran headlong into public prejudice and was abandoned; war with Germany was clearly at hand and the enemy language could not be taught in a public school. Aside from its bad logic, this decision was regrettable for my own sake; a continuity was interrupted; when I resumed German in college after the war I had forgotten too much, and neither in Germany nor Austria afterwards could I ever regain the lost ground.

Still, even in German, I acquired a passable accent fairly early and have never quite lost it, although my ignorance of the language is deep. This most of all—the acceptable, and therefore deceptive, German accent—leads me to think that the parrot aptitude for making a language sound right is independent of meaning and therefore not a faculty of intellect at all. I have made broadcasts in German to Germany, apparently without disaster, many times when I could not myself have written a single sentence of my own discourse in correct German.

This whole linguistic apparatus played a great part in my own life and may have determined many of its turns and twists, its meandering thither and yon, its deeps and shallows. What it had to do with the concerns which are the subject of this book can be guessed easily enough. It must have made opera more natural for me than it could ever have been otherwise, for surely language is as organic to opera as music itself, and these particular languages are connected in my mind because they arrived simultaneously, that is, during the same short but decisive term of years, in my consciousness; they dwelt there, *au pair*, in a maturing and fecundating and evolving relationship; the forms of their wedding, that is, in opera, oratorio, Kunstlieder and the Christian Mass, were all eventually forms of my own communion with the other world, the better world to which we accede, when we do, only by transcending this one.

And yet the process began, as I have said, in discomfort over English texts. The misery of this maladjustment tended to make me insensible to many or most of the arguments put forward for opera in English. I may accept the arguments as valid and agree, moreover, that translations nowadays are far better than the clumsy, ludicrous English used in my childhood. Even so, I still do not like Italian, French or German opera sung in English, and I have heard very little opera originally composed to English texts which seemed to me at the same time vocal, intelligible and musical, all three. (Purcell's *Dido and Aeneas* and, just lately, Benjamin Britten's *Turn of the Screw* are in that very small class.)

There were actually not many chances to hear music with its original words at Chautauqua, but there were some, enough to make me like them better than the ludicrous English that otherwise prevailed.

And very soon during years of more conscious and deliberate attention to music (I suppose between the ages of twelve and sixteen)
scores for voice and piano began to come my way, with both original
words and their translations affixed, so that it was easy enough to
compare them on the printed page. Furthermore, in the German
taught in high school, for so long as it was still taught, singing was a
part of the day's work. There are a number of Schubert songs which
we learned in school German and actually sang in class (*"Heiden-
röslein"* and *"Der Lindenbaum"* were among them, of course). The
calm, straw-haired woman who taught us those songs spent her summer holidays in Germany, was of German origin, tried to give us a
liking for German poetry and song, and actually wept when she told
us that German would be dropped from the curriculum in the next
year. Her name, which comes back to me suddenly, was Miss Alma
Liessmann, and although she did also teach us *"Deutschland über
Alles,"* I cannot see that it did us much harm; it is a fine song. Both
she and her predecessor, the Lutheran pastor, seem to have felt very
plainly the natural alliance of music and language.

The Chautauqua performers to awaken my curiosity about singing
were chiefly the "operatic quartets" who annually roamed the
country in summer. We had one or two a year and their programs
were what I liked best and remembered longest from the music in
the park. They were very mixed programs as a rule, only about half
operatic and the rest of a more popular nature, which meant, at
that time, sentimental English and American songs or the works of
such composers as Tosti. On rare occasions whole scenes were given
in costume and with, as I have said, rudimentary scenery: since the
quartets were vocally competent and not lacking in courage, the
suitable music (*Martha, Il Trovatore, Faust, Rigoletto*) was frequently performed, and indeed from one year to the next there was
no great change in it. The high point of such a concert, whenever the
singers were skilled enough to manage it, was the *Rigoletto* quartet,
and since this was also a favorite on every gramophone in the region,
it became familiar at some very early period. There were also solo
performances by each singer, often arias from the same or kindred
operas; there were certain almost inevitable duets (soprano-tenor or
contralto-tenor from *Il Trovatore*) and although I suppose not more
than a dozen different works were tapped for our delectation, these

were at least the tried and true, the ones which are most familiar because they are liked by most people.

How early in the game I began to tamper with this music myself, to sing at it or go over it at least in my head, I do not know: it must have been after my voice changed, reasonably speaking, although I am not at all sure that I did not make some stabs at opera music even before then. I used to pick out tunes on the piano before I could read the notes with any security, and whatever voice I had— and it never could have been much either before or after changing —was employed in the same cause. The cause, of course, was the satisfaction of my own curiosity. So far as I can remember, I never attempted to sing for the pleasure of others—I had no voice—but merely to convey to myself, or to that obstinate listener inside myself, what the things were like or what they were supposed to be. To this day I think it is the only proper way of learning a song's true meaning and content, although the noise produced in so doing might be disadvantageous to other ears.

A certain amount of singing, that is, in church and school, was normal for all the young in the community, but I probably enjoyed it more than most of us did. As a result of this interest, and of a naturally good ear, I could perhaps turn out a passable version of the tune and the time. Beyond this I doubt if I could ever go, but it was enough; all through these years, and in the college glee club afterwards, I was kept at it, and the various choirs, choruses and double quartets in which I warbled may have given me some insight into the difficulties of vocal performance.

Even so, and even though I did also work at the piano in my usual haphazard and lazy fashion for some time (perhaps two or three years?), it was never at any time in my mind that I could be or wanted to be a musician, a singer, or any kind of musical executant. If I understand what I hear somewhat better than I might have done otherwise, it is in part due to these various attempts (singing, piano, even, later, a brief fling at the violin), in which a sort of innate and irrepressible musical curiosity sought most of all a first-hand acquaintance with compositions, not a performance of them. They were not a "waste of time," if time can indeed be wasted; they were an expenditure enormously repaid thereafter in the enhancement of life. No doubt I could derive practically the same pleasures from *Die Meistersinger,* from the Beethoven Seventh Symphony and from the Verdi *Requiem* if I had never learned time-and-key signatures or the most rudimentary harmony or indeed if I could not tell one note from another, but I still think it has done no harm to have a bowing acquaintance with the way music looks on the printed page.

Even so, the Chautauqua, although it first presented me with the reality of performed music and thus bears a heavy responsibility, was most of all a period of rejoicing for the young. Whatever its intentions as education or culture, it was first and last a resort of pleasure, and the leafy maples, the soft grass, the moon of August and the stealthy boat on the dim lagoon were its happy language. We all waited for that magic season and regretted it when it had come to an end. I remember across the decades a girl I was with one day, walking along on the East Hill, as she critically inspected another girl across the street. "Mary's looking pretty tacky," she said, "but I suppose she's just saving her clothes for Chautauqua." The remark was not merely the tribute of one feminine nature to another, but more or less indicated the frame of mind of our town as I remember it.

For hitherto, in the attempt to dig out some origins of and early evolution of the musical mania, I have no doubt given an overserious and concentrated version of my own salad days. Language and music were by no means everything—they were the way the tree was bent, that is all, and for years even the inclination was hardly conscious. If I had aptitudes for language and an inclination toward music, it does not follow that I did not enjoy the more general pleasures of my age; and certainly it does not mean that I had comparable aptitudes for anything else. I was just as lazy, I suppose, as any other schoolboy, and stupider than most of them in such matters as mathematics and science. Games were not much in my line, but I played them, and there was a time when I was doing pretty well, for a season or two, at football. The only consistent peculiarity I presented, so far as I can remember, from my sixth year onward, was an exaggerated devotion to reading and writing; I was a "bookworm," and why it did not "stunt my growth," as they said then, I do not know; being a bookworm, I spent much more time alone than did my fellows; but I don't believe I missed many of the ordinary doings of a Midwestern childhood. We bobbed for apples in water at Hallowe'en, and pulled our girl cousins' pigtails, and went skating and drew candlelighted "street cars" over the snow; in my earliest days there was still the wonderful delight, now vanished, of the swift sleighride. The Christmas tree, the Thanksgiving turkey, my Aunt Mary's surrey with a fringe all around its square top, a huge old collie named Rex who allowed me to pull him to bits, and a large and lively cousinage scattered over the town —all these were the highlights of my existence. My own principal crimes from an early age were hiding and running away, both of them, I imagine, arising from some desire to be alone so as to read a book. I had a particular tree (a silver maple) to which I could repair, with a book and usually an apple or two, and become invisible at will for long periods. And later on, too, like every other boy in our town, I was busied with innumerable small jobs to earn money after school hours. All in all, it was not so unlike any other Midwestern childhood and youth, and its chief peculiarities, the growing concentration on books, language, writing and music, were for the most part secret, gradual, half-conscious, for I do not believe that I realized then or for a long time afterwards that such things were subject to discussion.

They were discussed in books, certainly. But books dealt with a world which seemed to have nothing to do with life in Pana, Illinois, so far as I could tell. In books everybody seemed to be either rich beyond belief or abysmally poor—that is, they seldom hit the recognizable conditions, the ones known to me. That is what gave them the quality of another world from the moment I had learned to read them. I read just about everything, novels, history, biography, essays, an enormous proportion of them from England, France, Russia or the New England states of our own country; there were remarkably few books about the great Midwestern prairie where I grew up, and those I knew (such as the stories of Mark Twain) were clearly of another period in time, so that they possessed another dimension of removal from my own condition. It was not, really, until the 1920's that there began to appear all those novels which (like the massive studies of Sinclair Lewis) actually did depict the recognizable society in which I was born; and by that time I was far away from it.

Books and music came together once in our high-school days in the

Shakespeare tercentenary. What a lively memory it left and how much still remains! We were sixteen; it was 1916; no doubt a decision at some higher level (The State Board of Education, or all the boards of education of all the states?) had made some form of Shakespeare festival or commemoration more or less obligatory on the three hundredth anniversary of his death. What we contrived in our school was called a "pageant," which meant that almost anything could be fitted into it by an effort. What I enjoyed most was the work of a chorus, actually a double quartet but called a chorus, which with an infinity of rehearsals prepared and performed a considerable number of Shakespeare songs in various settings. Our two sopranos each had a solo, and they were sweet-voiced girls (one of them a professional singer thereafter): they sang, respectively, "Orpheus with His Lute," as set by Liza Lehmann, and a traditional setting for "O Mistress Mine!" Together we sang "It Was a Lover and His Lass," in the setting by Sir William Davenant, and some less suitable music including, of all things, the Soldiers' Chorus from *Faust* at the very end. It seems to me that I also had to say something (verse, perhaps); I usually did; but that has departed from my memory altogether, while I remember vividly all the fun and hard work of those choral rehearsals and performances, including each person who took part, names and all, although I have seen none of them since. It is a common enough experience to marvel at what we remember and what we forget; all of us must be struck sometimes by the irrelevance of recollection and its strange, unpredictable spottiness. What I can most confidently say about my own memory, so powerful in some respects and so blank in others, is that it retains musical experience, even the trivial, better than details of "real" life. It is the simple truth that I remember even minor singers from opera performances of long ago, even from provincial or makeshift companies, and have never forgotten any even partially musical effort (such as those Shakespeare songs) with which I had any traffic; but whether I also bawled out some segment of *Hamlet* or *Macbeth* on the same occasion, or took part—perhaps—in some scene with others, I cannot remember at all. Thus it goes.

Many years later I saw the park again, and the lagoon and the trees. They were not really very big.

2 : The Shore of the Lake

Never a day goes by in Chicago, for most of its inhabitants, without some act or thought of appreciable importance which is determined by Lake Michigan. There are, it is true, monstrous great areas to the westward where no wind from the water can be felt, and yet even the dwellers in these wastelands must go for many of their pursuits, even if it is only a shopping expedition, toward the long, long shore. The lake rules. The city was strung out along it with an instinctive feeling for its power, even though the pressure of population drove a larger and larger bulge inland toward the Illinois prairie. And the lake, which makes the good weather and the bad, is the distinctive peculiarity of the city; it is hardly possible to think of Chicago without thinking of it. Other great cities are the children of rivers, and some of both the river and the sea; water-borne traffic stings them into being; but Chicago has embraced its lake far more than was economically necessary, stretching arms in both directions for air, for variety, for beauty. The lake is a Great Lake, and refuses to be imprisoned; it can muster an oceanic fury; it throws off the bitterest blast in winter that the temperate zones know, but it has settled into such a relationship with its metropolis now that they seem to face each other with the security of habit, wary but permanent.

Everything that made up my own life in Chicago during the years at the University and on occasions afterwards was near the lake or directly on it. The old opera house, the memorable Auditorium, was there facing our inland sea across Michigan Boulevard and the flat space where there is now a landing field. The coldest of all blasts seemed to come from that flat, open space by the lake, as many an opera singer fresh from Europe must have discovered in consternation: and our opera seasons, of course, were always in midwinter. Farther up Michigan Boulevard was Orchestra Hall, the home of the Chicago Symphony Orchestra; the Art Institute was across the boulevard, even nearer the lake; the big public library was higher up on the same icy expanse, near the beginning of the North Side.

And the University itself, the center of my own existence during those years, was near enough to the lake to share in the lakeside weather, even though many streets (and Jackson Park) lay between. A good many of the University students known to me lived near the lake, as did some of the most memorable of its teachers—Dean Lovett, for example, Dean of the College of Liberal Arts: Robert Morss Lovett, a Harvard man of the great days who taught literature as if it were a matter of passionate current interest like political elections or baseball. The Lovetts became friends early along in my college life (I was the holder of a scholarship in English Literature and thus directly of interest to the Dean), and I can remember the bitter sweep of wind at their hospitable front door on Jackson Park even now.

During those years, I doubt if anything took me far from a narrow band along the lake front. It was decades before I had even seen the immensity of the city behind that breezy edge. Revisiting Chicago now, and traversing the whole city to get from the airport, is to get a graphic proof of how little I knew when I lived there, and how the city was in fact for me a long, narrow band of light set against a continent of darkness.

Music at the University itself was not a major concern and there was no provision made for musical studies of any kind—not even those courses in "appreciation" which afterwards grew up more or less all over the country. A concert series in Mandel Hall—our chapel then—provided half a dozen symphony concerts every year and some solo recitals, all at "student prices," which were low enough for the poorest of us. There was a wealth of music at hand also in the great city itself, some of it almost equally accessible to students. It was, however, my misfortune that the kind of musical performance to which I had an early addiction, as if by fatality, was the most expensive. The addiction may not have been fully formed by the time I went to the University but I think it was—I think it already existed *in posse,* had not been openly acknowledged because I had never heard a whole opera all the way through, but it needed only that experience, perhaps with a repetition or two, to become fixed and irrevocable.

However, I have never been unwilling to forego a couple of meals (or a textbook!) for the sake of an opera. Even before I discovered various other ways and means, and even when my resources were at their most exiguous—in my freshman year, for instance—I managed to hear and see a good many of the most popular works which had been known to me before only in the Chautauqua excerpts. One of the very earliest was *Carmen,* in English, at the old Illinois Theatre, if I am not mistaken. I even remember the name of the mezzo-soprano who sang the part: Elaine de Sellem. I have never heard of this artist since, but I thought she was wonderful and I went back again. This was in some series of low-priced performances in English, and although it is *Carmen* that I distinctly remember, I have the vague impression that I did hear others as well, no doubt *Faust* and *Il Trovatore.* And it is certainly true that the companies performing opera at low prices were assured of my full support, to the extent of probably a dollar a week, then and thereafter. The first one, with the wonderful *Carmen,* happened to be a company singing in English. Most of them were Italian and sang everything in that language. Their vocal standards were fairly high, although orchestra, settings and general stage production were of no particular account. The artistic achievement in such a work as *Il Trovatore* must have been very low indeed, what with all the shouting that can be done in such work when singers are given a free field. But a great deal of luscious singing was poured forth, just the same, and in these small, traveling companies with their shabby stage settings and their sketchy orchestras, their powerless conductors and their general bad taste, you could get to know the works performed and imagine for yourself, if you had that kind of imagination, what they might be under other circumstances.

The basis of the repertoire for such small companies at the time was Verdi and some Donizetti, with the addition of *Faust* and *Carmen* sung in Italian. Puccini's works were still subject to a fee for the Ricordi firm in Milan, which was jealous of its copyright; just at that time, my freshman year in college, an extremely popular song called "Avalon" had been the cause of a lawsuit in which Ricordi claimed (and collected) damages: the tune was approximately that of the tenor arioso in the last act of *Tosca*. So Puccini was impossible for the makeshift companies. All of the late Verdi works, all of Wagner, and practically all modern opera was impossible for other reasons—too big, too complicated, too exacting. So my friends in the traveling troupes stuck to *Il Trovatore, Rigoletto, La Traviata, La Forza del Destino, Lucia di Lammermoor, Faust* and *Carmen*. There were slight variations when some singer of special gifts came along: a big contralto, for example. Such a one was Nina Frascati, who sang in one of those companies during one of those seasons: for her extremely opulent voice there were performances of *La Favorita*, a work I have never heard since. If the scenery was made up of bits from other operas, it did not matter in the least. The orchestra was mostly tum-te-tum and the chorus a feeble *"Andiam,"* but Frascati herself, an extremely unbeautiful lady with protuberant upper teeth, rolled out that honey-smooth Italian tone which I have always found irresistible. I sat very close (by some accident) at a performance of *La Favorita* and had an excellent view of Mme. Frascati's method with the conductor. She never took her eyes off him, because it was through him that she conducted the orchestra and indeed the whole opera. Her tempi ruled not only because she could at will drown out the orchestra and compel its obedience, but also because by frowns, nods and simple indications with the outstretched hand, she could enforce her will even when she was not singing. (Variations of the same technique are not unknown even in the greatest opera houses.)

It was probably with this singer that I made the discovery, important to any lover of opera, that the peculiar illusion of an operatic performance does not depend upon physical appearance. The singer was far from beautiful, as I have said. Her appearance must indeed have been remarkable to remain, as it does, cut into my memory. She had a big nose and phenomenally big teeth which stuck out at an angle of 22.5 degrees from her upper lip. She frowned a great deal at the conductor and visibly filled her whole organism with breath—a cataclysmic operation with that body—just before she was about to sing. When she was the gipsy mother in *Il Trovatore* none of this mattered, but from the lovely mistress of the King in *La Favorita* it was rather startling. And yet she did give a performance because she had a beautiful voice and knew exactly what she was doing. I have an idea that from then on I realized that for me the visual illusion, however desirable, could never be the main consideration or the chief hope in opera. The form itself, whatever it may be called—the "bastard form of art," the "irrational entertainment"—makes such considerations vain and foolish. One must either accept Mme. Frascati's buck teeth and ferocious frown or else not hear her at all, and I preferred to hear her.

What may be known of this singer on greater stages I have no idea. She did not appear in any of our big American companies, but only with this traveling troupe (her own, I think) for a year or two. That, however, means nothing much about her professional standing. Singers have easily passed from these small troupes to the big ones and there could hardly be a better groundwork of stage experience for a young artist. Lauritz Melchior spent years in a traveling troupe when he was a young man, singing small parts (he was a baritone then) practically every night, and usually in tents. Conversely, older singers famous in Italy, members of the Scala or the Costanzi, have come to America and sung in such troupes when they found their way barred in the big houses. Luisa Tetrazzini made her first American appearances in just such a troupe, in California. So perhaps Nina Frascati was famous or at least known in the great world of opera; it is too late to find out now. She is memorable to me because I learned from her the simple, fundamental lesson without which no sustained enjoyment of opera performances would have been possible: that is, you cannot hear with your eyes, whereas you actually can see with your ears.

Seeing with the ears, of course, is a prerogative of all who love music and, furthermore, according to the evidence, of the great musicians as well. Beethoven's "Pastoral" Symphony, even discarding all literary "program," is music seen as well as heard by the ears. It becomes a little more complicated in opera, with the whole of a theatre tradition at war with the composition itself. This war—this inherent impossibility of resolution to the problem—is what compels almost all great composers to try their hands at it: the permanent challenge can be ignored by few.

The Chicago Symphony Orchestra was the main purveyor of "pure music" for all of us. Its concerts at the University were never adventurous—we got Bach, Beethoven, Brahms, Tchaikovsky and Strauss—and there were no soloists. In the city itself, that is, at Orchestra Hall on the lake front, I heard a good many other concerts during those years, frequently with soloists, and frequently with music new not only to me (which was saying nothing) but to the whole of that audience. The orchestra's conductor was Dr. Frederick Stock, who, as a German, retired during the war years and came back afterwards to conduct until his death. I knew him a little (later on) and learned to appreciate his unassuming but absolute certainty about his own work. He was a very fine conductor, perhaps a great one, and in his long tenure of power over that orchestra he made it into one of the best in the world. His results were obtained with a minimum of physical frenzy. That part of his anatomy which was visible to the audience seemed, indeed, solid and stolid and almost immobile, but his control was absolute and I learned at some of his rehearsals years later that he was anything but stolid. It was immense good fortune for me to have made my first acquaintance with the symphonic literature, and with more or less all of it, from such an orchestra and such a conductor.

There were soloists of renown and accomplishment: piano, violin, voice, violoncello (at any rate, Casals). They could not come to the University for our fees, but sometimes I was able to hear them in Orchestra Hall or elsewhere. There was one pianist I remember as distinctly as I do Mme. Nina Frascati: it was Fannie Bloomfield Zeisler, who no longer made concert tours but occasionally played recitals in Chicago, where she was teaching. She was an aged lady with a humped back who trailed onto the stage of Mandel Hall (our chapel) looking as if she could not possibly get through a whole hour and a half at the piano. When she threw up her old head and began to play, these visual deceptions ceased to exist and the Chopin at the end of her program seems to have moved into my memory for good and all.

Such was the mixed bag of my first years as a listener. As may be seen, it was indiscriminate. I took an equal pleasure in *La Favorita* and the Beethoven Seventh Symphony, I believe. The pleasures may have been different in kind but they were equal and my appetite was insatiable, at least under these conditions. What might have happened if I had ever had to choose between *Carmen,* a symphony concert and a Flonzaley Quartet recital, all on the same evening, I do not know. The necessity of choice never arose. What did happen was that I went to hear whatever I could whenever I could, more or less without debate, and enjoyed it all. It was a long time before I learned *not* to enjoy a performance of music and sometimes, at really bad ones which I nevertheless sit through, I wonder whether I ever did.

2

The Chicago Opera Company was at the height of its glory in 1917-1921 and for several years afterwards. It was the child of Oscar Hammerstein's strange, willful dream as an independent opera impresario. He had so annoyed the Metropolitan in New York by the insolent rivalry of his Manhattan Company that they had paid him a million dollars, some years before (1910), to retire from the field. His principal artists, settings, costumes, conductors and copyright agreements—which included a considerable repertoire by living Frenchmen—were all taken over by the new Chicago-Philadelphia Company, giving performances for some weeks in Philadelphia, for some weeks in Chicago, and on Tuesdays at the Metropolitan in New York. This unwieldy arrangement came to an end after three years, and the unit, still essentially Hammerstein's, was transformed into the Chicago Opera Company, with the Auditorium as its home.

The Auditorium was a magnificent theatre for the performance of opera—a big, round, cupped hall in which the boxes were low and perfectly open; sound had little interference on its way. It was built so that the stage action was visible as well as audible from every part of the house. Its openness and roundness made it seem less vast then it was, and singers always loved it for its acoustical kindness to the voice. (There are such theatres in America: the Academy of Music in Philadelphia is another.) It had been an opera house for many years and during the time when Covent Garden in London and the Metropolitan in New York were substantially the same company under the same director, the Auditorium in Chicago also had its share in those seasons. (The company went to Chicago in autumn, then to the Metropolitan for the winter, then to Chicago again usually, and opened at Covent Garden in May.) That was in the 1890's and the early part of the 1900's. It was at the Auditorium, while Melba and De Reszke were singing the Garden Scene of *Roméo et Juliette,* that a maniac jumped onto the stage and tried to shoot Jean de Reszke. The episode is in all the books, but I have lately heard of it again from Miss Mary Garden, who, as a schoolgirl, was present at that performance.

The history of the wonderful old theatre was not known to me when I was in college. Its contemporary existence was quite enough. Although all tickets to the opera were expensive (even the cheapest of them), there were ways open to anybody who really wanted to go.

The first of these was made known to me by a written notice on the bulletin board at Cobb Hall: male students who wished to work as ushers for the Chicago Opera Company were to apply at such-and-such a place. I do not remember where we applied or what the conditions of employment were. Certainly we were unpaid. We must have had some instruction in how the seating ran and what our duties were: all this, too, I have forgotten. What I remember is a golden glow, a rare and exalted kind of excitement, which hung about the performances themselves, and some details, some fleeting pictures and echoing tones, from what took place on that magic stage.

We had to report well before the beginning of a performance (half an hour, probably) and we, the students, who were an undependable lot, had to be counted and assigned to designated blocks of seats. The chief ushers were, I suppose, never sure how many of us would appear for any given performance or if we would be presentable enough by opera standards to undertake the work. Most of these details have faded out by now: I remember that very few of the students came from the University of Chicago and sometimes I was the only one from there. The others came from Northwestern or from the musical colleges and I never knew any of them. There was one so-called "professional," or at least experienced, usher in charge of each block of seats and to this authority we, the students, turned in every difficulty.

I soon found that a girl called Rosa, who was in charge of orchestra seats on the lower left, had a kindly spirit and not only shared my wild excitement over the performances but actually knew a great deal about them. She was a student of singing and had been an usher in the opera house for two or three seasons: consequently she knew everything, had seen and heard every artist, had strong opinions—not to say prejudices—and in some mysterious way collected news, gossip and rumor from the very walls of the theatre. "Galeffi is a fine baritone but he isn't Ruffo," she would say with an edge of regretful decision in her low, slightly foreign voice. Such statements, indicating arguable opinion about individual singers, were thrilling to me because I had never heard them before and in quick imitation of Rosa I soon began to have opinions of my own to offer. The patter of the operagoer, the endless chitchat about singers, performances and plans, the anecdotes of the house—all that was new to me. Rosa was a superb guide to the novelty of corridor talk, and we spent the intervals between the acts in such exploration. With her long, dark face and her long, glittering earrings, her faintly foreign voice and her general air of knowing the world, Rosa herself rivaled the performers on the stage and made a more lasting impression on me than the majority of them. She may have been anywhere from seven to ten years older than I was and yet she seemed, in age, wisdom and beauty, in another dimension. I suppose she was of (perhaps) Italian or Spanish or Jewish origin, Something Mediterranean at all events, and her slightly "foreign" way of speaking was only that tinge or delicate infusion of Latinity which often comes upon the speaking voices of those who study singing: working, as they do, in foreign languages all the time, and insecure in their control of any language, even their English undergoes a change.

The actual work of the student usher in that house was finished soon after the curtain rose. Few of us could be trusted to seat people correctly in the dark: the latecomers were taken to their places by the "professionals" such as Rosa, furious at the intrusion but smoothly polite. "That woman!" Rosa would say. "Always twenty minutes late." Then she would sit on the step beside me and listen, so intently and motionlessly that there was nothing passive about it—it was a sort of active listening, the kind that can be felt as communication through the music.

There was much to deserve it. The principal conductor of the house was Cleofonte Campanini; and even at the very end of his career (he died in 1919), he was still one of the most remarkable of all conductors. German works had been dropped for the duration of the war and the repertoire consisted of Italian and French operas, both of the kind known to me (the old familiar fare of the traveling troupes) and of a new vintage. Amelita Galli-Curci, who had made her extraordinary debut about a year before I went to college, was at the peak of her vocal beauty and strange physical charm: a slim and startled young figure with a long, anxious face, *Italianissima*. She sang about twice a week, sometimes more, to feverishly excited and overcrowded houses. The principal dramatic soprano in Italian was Rosa Raisa, the owner of a voice which has probably never been surpassed in volume and intensity, although the violence of her temperament treated it with very little consideration. She also sang twice a week as a rule. And finally there was Mary Garden, a whole style and school of opera in herself, who began earlier and lasted longer than any of her contemporaries: she, too, sang twice a week during her annual period with the company. Thus it happened that these reigning sopranos, when they were all in Chicago at the same time, governed the repertoire for the entire week—two performances each for the six days, which made a normal week. (There were seven or even eight at times—Sunday performances in the afternnoon, were not only legal but popular in Chicago.)

Galli-Curci sang in *Lucia, Rigoletto, La Traviata, Il Barbiere di Siviglia, Dinorah, Lakmé, La Sonnambula,* and a number of seldom given show pieces for coloratura, such as *Crispino e la Comare,* by the Ricci brothers, which one would have to travel far to see or hear now. After my day there she also sang in *La Bohème* and *Roméo et Juliette.* The limitations of her list made no difference at all to her audience—it is the same with all great coloratura sopranos—and, but for the subscription system, which demands a different opera in each subscribed series (the Mondays, the Wednesdays, etc.), she could have gone right on with the same two or three operas for years. Campanini did his duty by the subscribers and dug up some tattered "novelties" from an almost forgotten era, but the subscribers did not really care what Mme. Galli-Curci sang so long as she strung out the lovely line of her melting, melancholy, and somehow uncertain voice. ("Uncertain" in that it had none of the sure, hard brilliance of the usual coloratura—and this very "uncertainty," for lack of a better word, this sense of a dying fall, was a great part of its irresistible appeal.)

Raisa sang *Aïda* (she could have sung it every night—her resources were equal to anything) and all the repertoire which is implied by the possession of an *Aïda* voice: *Norma, Il Trovatore, Un Ballo in Maschera, La Gioconda, Otello, Cavalleria Rusticana, Tosca, Madama Butterfly, I Gioielli della Madonna*—and the rest of them, up to and including the excellent *Tannhäuser* which was the last I heard (in New York and in German), a few years later, of that superb voice at its best.

And Mary Garden, of course, sang the works which were peculiarly her own, many of them written for her, many of them unimaginable with any other performer. Some came from the Opéra-Comique and some from the Grand Opéra de Paris, for she belonged successively to both those houses; and some of the most celebrated had been studied and first performed for Hammerstein in New York (*Thaïs, Le Jongleur de Notre Dame, Salome*). The masterpiece of her repertoire was *Pelléas et Mélisande,* but it was still regarded as "difficult" or "obscure" by the general public and was not given every year in Chicago or anywhere else. She had, as a rule, one quite new opera each year, an "American première" of something written for her in Paris, and such works were prepared with great care in décor, costume, ballet and stage direction, for she had discretionary powers over every production in which she appeared. Thus a treasure of time, money and talent would be expended upon the "Garden novelty" of the year, which could be depended upon to drop out of the list after another season. A "Galli-Curci novelty" could be thrown upon the stage without undue trepidation over its theatrical effect or its accessories, but Garden insisted upon as much care for each new work as if it had been *Pelléas.* Thus *Ghismonda,* by Henri Février, had a most wonderful and elaborate production during my last year in Chicago, and was off to the storehouse incontinently there-after. I have never heard a word about it since, in Paris or anywhere else.

So it went at the height of the season: our three great sopranos dominated and divided the nights and the afternoons. There were, of course, plenty of other luminaries. Titta Ruffo was singing in Chi-cago in those days, powerful and tempestuous, with a range and quality of voice beyond the dream of most baritones. It was Ruffo who had—just about this time—changed parts with his friend Caruso at some performance in South America without the audience becom-ing aware of it. The tenor sang baritone and the baritone sang tenor (was it *La Forza del Destino?*) for a good part of an act and nobody knew the difference. It could hardly be possible of any other singers, but with these two, so exceptional in range, there might be more in it than there is in some opera stories.

We had also, in a rather large number of works both French and Italian, the tenor Lucien Muratore, romantic in style, noble in ap-pearance, suited in every way to the works in which he performed. He would not appear in any others, giving evidence of intelligence by what he would not do as well as by what he did. He was Faust, Roméo, and Don José in *Carmen;* with Mary Garden in *Monna Vanna*—more play than opera, but a good play—he was a memora-ble Prinzivalle. At the period of which I speak none of the other tenors amounted to much; it was the age of Caruso and most of the Italians of the day could not surmount that difficulty. Perhaps some of them (Dolci, Crimi and others) were, in fact, better than we were ever able to admit at the time.

Muratore was married to the astonishing Roman beauty, Lina Cavalieri. She did not sing in the company (in fact, I never heard her sing) but she went to many performances, particularly when Mura-tore appeared, and I saw her really incomparable face and figure quite often and quite close. It was a breathtaking apparition. Once I was wandering, quite illicitly I suppose, and found myself near the passageway which led from the Auditorium Hotel to the Audito-rium itself—an immense convenience to singers who feared the Chicago winter: they could walk from hotel to dressing room without even getting a sniff of the lake breeze. As I stood there the door was opened and Cavalieri came into the opera house with a party of

friends, all talking French. I even remember her precise, her immortal words, and the light tone in which they were delivered.
"C'est par ici, je crois," she said.

Well, of course, I was only seventeen. But there is something of
divinity in the mere being of such as Cavalieri: the forms of life are
lifted and perfected in their physical here-and-now, making the
earth itself fair. I saw her again—even talked to her—in New York
and for the last time twenty years later in Paris, but she never lost
that astonishing intensification and enhancement, the abstraction,
the Platonic Idea, of physical beauty.

The stage of the Auditorium was deep and wide, but it had no
remoteness—the theatre was so built that you felt at times as if you
could reach out and touch the persons of the drama. It seems to me
now that I cannot remember any performance I saw there, fully and
all the way through. Nothing remains as a whole. There are fragments as vivid as today's sunset, and tones I can remember as clearly
as any I heard last week. Such a tone, for example, was Rosa Raisa's
declamation of *"Suicidio!"* in *La Gioconda*. I have an aural memory
also for Mary Garden's singing of the single word *"éternellement"*
in the scene before the looking glass in *Thaïs*. I hear various tones
of Galli-Curci's, especially from *La Traviata* and especially in the
long scene with the baritone in Act II. If there should be learned
gentlemen who say that it is impossible to remember a single tone in
this way (so as to hear it again more or less at will, and sometimes
against the will) for forty long years of a very crowded life, I can
only reply that this has been my experience. In the case of Mary
Garden I went on hearing her in New York and Paris for another
decade after I had left Chicago, so some of the many aural memories
I have of her voice (especially as Mélisande) may come from a later
time. However, this could not apply to *Thaïs*, which I never heard
again.

Muratore in the garden scene of *Roméo et Juliette* left an impression which has remained, too, but it is curiously combined—I do
not hear simply a tone, but I hear a tone which is mixed with the
slow and somehow very musical movements of a stage body. (He
began his stage life as an actor with Sarah Bernhardt.) When I think
of Ruffo it is of a frightening presence and some equally frightening tones—*Rigoletto,* nothing else, and perhaps I never saw him in

anything else. A charming and effective soprano named Yvonne Gall from the Opéra-Comique left a visual impression as Marguerite and as Juliette, but I cannot actually recall a single tone of her voice. In fact I see her most vividly in the dress of a peasant's wife in an opera (which I liked at the time) called *Le Chemineau,* by Xavier Leroux, but there is no aural memory connected with it at all.

The pictures that remain—without an accompaniment of tone: with merely the vague recollection of tone beneath them—are many. Montemezzi's opera, *La Nave,* with a libretto by Tito Ricordi based on D'Annunzio's play, had a production of the greatest splendor with an immense ship on the stage and Rosa Raisa emitting notes of an awe-inspiring power. Also Raisa wore a pink dress in Act II of *Tosca* which clashed with the sofa on which she sat. Garden's entrance in *Thaïs,* scattering roses, her cold fury of disdain in the last act of *Carmen,* and practically every move she made as Mélisande, all created memorable pictures—but, as I have said, much of my memory of Garden may come from a later period. The pictures that have clung from those early years in Chicago are vivid enough and numerous enough, but they are like a collection of old snapshots and it is not easy to be sure what they all were before the camera caught them.

My career as an usher at the opera house was not long—a few weeks—but during that time I heard everything that was to be heard, including the repetitions. Those hours in the darkness, watching the enchanted stage, had to come to an end. Not only was my college work suffering (I might have endured that) but the problem of laundry bills had become acute. Opera standards with regard to linen were very high, and I could no longer afford, it was quite plain, so many clean, white, starched shirts and collars. I ceased to report for duty. This was in the student's agreement and was partly why we were such unreliable workers: we were on the list and could come when we wished, but it was recognized at the start that we might be able to come only now and then or not at all. I went to every performance, night and afternoon, for quite a while, but when I stopped I stopped altogether.

There was another and even more appetizing way of hearing opera for nothing in the autumn of 1918 (the next season). Once I got into a uniform I could go to the opera with no more outlay than the five cents it cost to get there on the elevated railway and the five cents for return.

The war had overtaken the University: not only were many (or most) of the upper classmen in service, but also the War Department had taken over this and almost all other universities for the training of officers. I was only eighteen, but since I had already been in college for a year, with fairly acceptable grades or marks in my book, I had no difficulty enrolling in the cadet corps. (It was called Students' Army Training Corps—S.A.T.C.) We wore the regular infantry uniform and did regular infantry drill along with college work, most of it of a different kind from that which I, at least, had been pursuing as a civilian. The Armistice came very quickly (to our disappointment!) and by Christmas we were all out of uniform again, vaguely disgruntled at having seen nothing of the war.

However, the opera made up for the war. At the very beginning of the season I discovered that I could slip out after the final roll call, cross the Midway in the darkness, get to the Sixty-Third Street "El" Station and be at the Auditorium in a quarter of an hour. The last roll call, hastily performed in the cold and the dark at about seven o'clock (after our evening meal) was followed by a study period of two hours in Harper Library, to which we were marched in formation; afterwards we were marched back to barracks again but there was no further roll call. There were sentries everywhere, but they were students like ourselves, not very vigilant and easy to avoid. By the time the opera opened (early November) we had only been playing soldier for about three weeks and none of us took it too seriously except to moan over physical fatigue. (They did march us into a coma sometimes, especially on Saturdays.)

Subscribers to the opera season had pledged themselves to give their tickets free to any soldier or sailor who presented himself—first come first served and no questions asked. I was not the only soldier or sailor who got to the opera in this somewhat unorthodox way, as I discovered: many of us, possibly most of us, were absent without leave, but I never got over the feeling of wild adventure, desperate danger and abysmal guilt every time I escaped across the dark, snowy Midway to the lights of Sixty-Third Street, where I fully expected everybody I saw to recognize me as a fugitive from the study hour. Once inside the opera house, I felt perfectly safe—in fact I forgot the war, forgot my uniform and could have looked even a general in the eye without a qualm. I never did commit this military crime—A.W.O.L., absence without leave—except for the opera.

We lined up in the lobby of the Auditorium at an appointed desk and were given our tickets well before curtain time. And they were very often among the very best seats to be had in that admirable theatre—the best boxes, the best orchestra seats. I do not remember ever having been asked to sit above the boxes, and might have grown haughty about it if it had happened: so very quickly, after only a few performances, did we habituate ourselves to the best. In all probability it was the holders of the most expensive seats—the richest people in a very rich city—who decided at the last minute not to go to the opera. ("Let's stay home, Sally—my feet hurt.") Subscribers higher up in the house would use their seats whatever the weather or their own mood. Moreover, the opera management itself gave unsold seats to the soldiers and sailors. Thus there were plenty for all: I never got a bad one and was never turned away.

So again, for the space of almost two months, I became an assiduous operagoer. No escape from our war was possible by day, but every night except Saturday and Sunday, it was, or became, relatively easy. In later years, on visits, I sometimes sat in boxes which I had known well during this period of uniformed privilege: so far as I remember I never had the courage to tell their owners how I had availed myself of it.

And Rosa, the dark-eyed contralto usher, was not to be found this season. I assumed she had gone on to New York or elsewhere and I never saw her again. She was no longer required as cicerone: I had myself become very knowledgeable by this time, very willing to offer an opinion as an "old hand." The other soldiers and sailors, my companions in this windfall, were older than I and some were in fact musicians, which curbed me a bit. Again (as in the ushering episode) I never met anybody I knew, anybody from my own University. It was a solitary adventure from first to last.

Its rewards I have already discussed, but I think they were greater in this season than in the one before: I understood more, felt more, responded more; I had also examined voice and piano scores in the library and elsewhere; I had read a good deal on the general subject. The whole opera company engaged my partisanship by this time:

they had had a triumphant season in New York the preceding winter and I used to go to the big Public Library and look at all the reviews in the New York papers to see what "my team" had done. It was in distinctly a football spirit, as I remember, a form of local patriotism, but it did introduce me to the work of a good many New York critics, one of whom, James Huneker, showed more than a football interest. I proceeded immediately (as was my way in those days) to read every volume of essays he had published up to that time, not all of them on music by any means, and I think I was none the worse for it. What took me first to Huneker was his ability to put into words the very strange quality of musico-dramatic interest aroused by Mary Garden: I had felt the same kind of thing, obscurely and only half-consciously, and it was a liberation to find it expressed so well in public print. The strange pallor of Garden's voice, its total difference from those rich Italian instruments I had (like most people) instantly loved, had bothered me too, in all my adolescence and ignorance, so that I often wondered how such a voice could express so much, and whether I was wrong to think it did. When I encountered the cliché of the day ("Garden's wonderful but she can't sing"), I had no reply. I thought it was possibly true; I had no confidence in my own judgment. Huneker gave me at least one leg to stand on in my instinctive belief that this artist surpassed all others in expression on the musical stage.

Then, too, although I was not Mme. Galli-Curci's most fanatical admirer—partly because I quickly tired of her repertoire even as a boy—it was a great thing for our football team to see her taking New York by storm—mounted policemen quelling the mob, traffic held up for hours, and all the other phenomena of the excitement she aroused. Chicago had gone wild enough—at her debut the audience stood on the seats to cheer—but at least in Chicago it had not spilled over from the opera house into the streets. In the same way it was gratifying, although less astonishing, to read the tributes paid to the third star of our team, Rosa Raisa, whose singing exacted the admiration of every critic in New York.

When I was out of uniform it was not so simple to commandeer the best seats in the opera house. By this time I did occasionally get an invitation from the families of fellow students, but my own third (and final) resolution of the problem came through the *Daily Maroon*. This was the undergraduate daily newspaper, on which I had been a reporter in my freshman year and to which I was now, after our brief military episode, elected or chosen (I forget how) as critic of the theatre and music. It was actually more the former than the latter, but I distorted the emphasis as much as the editors would permit, and had first claim on whatever free tickets the *Daily Maroon* received. These were for second or third performances, never for first nights, but even so I doubt if any production at the Chicago Opera during 1919 and 1920 escaped me. Among these were a number of new works, for one of Campanini's principal aims was to keep his list alive and moving. I have already mentioned *Le Chemineau*, the Leroux opera which I saw several times and found charming, and *La Nave,* Montemezzi's work, which I remember for its grandiose stage setting; then there were Mascagni's *Isabeau,* which I can scarcely remember at all except for a vague picture of Rosa Raisa in blue brocade; and there was the *Trittico* of Puccini.

It was toward the end of my Chicago years and I went to *Trittico* more than once. I remember more about it than I do about the others (the "novelties"). For one thing, all three of the little operas composing the *Trittico* had and have today a valid reason for existence as representing aspects of the composer's talent, elements which demanded expression. The first one, *Il Tabarro,* a sanguinary melodrama, was Puccini in one undeniable mood; *Suor Angelica* was the Puccini with a mystical aspiration; and *Gianni Schicchi* was a rollicking outburst of Puccini's native wit and humor. Of these only the third is much performed today, which seems in some ways regrettable: the three have a connection by contrast and do belong together. At the first hearing I know I was much more taken by *Suor Angelica* than by the others.

Gianni Schicchi, probably Puccini's finest work, was slower to penetrate to me, although later on I fully surrendered. The fact, however, is plain: most of the "new" works I heard at the Chicago Opera—and whether strictly "new" or not, all were recent and all by contemporaries—the one of which I retain the most distinct memory is the Puccini *Trittico.* This is not from subsequent hearings: except for *Gianni Schicchi* once or twice, I never heard the

Trittico again. It sticks, I believe, because it was actually memorable and did (does) express the talent of a masterly theatre composer.

By this time, of course, that is after three and a half Chicago Opera seasons, Puccini was no stranger. *La Bohème, Tosca* and *Madama Butterfly* were all in the repertoire and I had heard them not once (I never heard anything once) but several times. My developing appetites, not yet disciplined or refined by any attrition of taste, had taken to Puccini in my freshman year with all the *gourmandise* of a child in a chocolate shop. I used to bellow *"Recondita armonia"* or *"E lucevan le stelle"* in the bathroom, and get dressed to the tune of Rodolfo's narrative. (In my fraternity house there was a record of John McCormack singing it, and I used to play it until the brothers threatened to scalp me—and, by intention or not, I was of course memorizing it.) For several years the frank, bold theatricalism of Puccini and his wonderful gift for short, tuneful outbursts of emotion captivated me; I pored over the scores and sang to myself whatever I could; there were not many Puccini performances in Chicago or afterwards in New York that I did not get into by hook or by crook. This greediness, this sweet tooth, lasted for years—until it was obliterated, like almost everything else, by the Destroyer and Avenger, Richard Wagner.

The fascination and the excitement of the opera did not deafen me to music itself, although there were times when this might have seemed almost true. I was hearing a good deal of "pure music" all the time both at the University and at Orchestra Hall, thanks to the *Daily Maroon.* How I held down so many jobs at once—for I was also the correspondent in the college for a city newspaper—baffles me now. College work did suffer, of course, although total failure came my way only, as I recall, in mathematics. Somehow I found time for symphony concerts and recitals, too, and as drama critic of the student paper, I must have gone a certain amount to the theatre, although I have forgotten that altogether.

Moreover, I probably enjoyed my own attempts at singing, at puzzling out opera scores, at trying over different scenes and arias, as much as I did true musical performances. I know I did a great deal of it. A girl known as "Tommy" Atkins (her name was Eleanor and she was a charmer) enjoyed ploughing through an entire opera, as I did, from beginning to end, ignoring the notes that could not be sung or played and whisking on merrily just as if everything had been in its right place. Tommy would sit at the piano indefatigably for three hours and more, eager and impatient of interruption. She sang all the women's parts and I all the men's, regardless of voice, except when there was a duet for men: in that case she sang the upper part and I the lower. The one we found most congenial to our talents and performed a considerable number of times was *Faust*. The upper notes were always beyond me and I indicated them by a yelp or, when strictly necessary, dropped them an octave. We had an unbelievable amount of fun doing this and one result has been that although I do not see *Faust* often (I cannot describe it as my favorite work) I find that an enormous number of the words and notes, at least for tenor and soprano, have lodged in my head to stay. It was the same with *Carmen,* although here Tommy was less happy because she enjoyed a higher range than the part permitted. Her mother, who had been a teacher of singing, used to intervene from time to time, coming in from another room to see what she could do. She never once said, as she had every right to do, that the noise was unbearable and we were murdering the music. She put it another way. "Dear me," she would say mildly, "how you do scream! Do you know you are ruining your voices?" This always made Tommy and me laugh: we cared less than nothing for our voices. We were enjoying ourselves in a way we understood, which was enough.

Tommy's mother once in a great while could be persuaded to sing, and then we were extremely attentive. She had a soft, exquisitely smooth soprano, not a concert voice but properly trained and produced, and she sang more or less all the song composers at one time—the scores were all over the piano and the house—but what she sang for us were some lyrics by Reynaldo Hahn.

At the fraternity there was a piano (never in tune) and some kind of phonograph or gramophone to which unknown benefactors had added a few records in addition to the immense collection of dance music and jazz songs. One record I played constantly was McCormack's from *La Bohème,* and there was one by Leo Slezak, too, which was worn to a wisp before I left—the *"Lotosblume"* of Schumann. When I got hold of a score, I used to pick it over at that toneless piano in hours when the fraternity brothers were all away at classes, as I should have been also. And then, of course, there were houses where music was played, the houses of friends, for a great many of my fellow students lived in Chicago, many of them not far from the University. Ruth Falkenau's mother—"Aunt Esther" I called her—played Chopin and Liszt and Schumann to me until she grew tired; I never did. When I got a chance, which meant when I found a willing victim to play the accompaniments, I used to try over some German songs (Schubert and Schumann), although I never at any time could really sing them; it was, just the same, a glowing pleasure to know those songs and the habit, good or bad, lasted. There are many *Lieder* which came to me thus early and have stayed as permanent guests. What I do to them when I try to sing them has nothing to do with how they sound in my own head.

If this period of avid absorption had been merely a gluttony, like a passion for apple pie, it would scarcely be worth the telling. And yet a great deal of what I have here related takes on the appearance of simple gluttony, an insatiable appetite. It would exhibit more of its own ultimate meaning if I could truthfully say that there was any intellectual or aesthetic growth, any augmentation of the inner resources, by means of all this preoccupation with music during my college years. I am afraid that the objective truth is quite different: my college work suffered and I squandered a great deal of time listening to music I cannot even recall, however vaguely, to my adult mind. The boy grew older, yes, in skin and bone and hair, with perhaps a little sharpening of the other faculties, but so far as I can see the boy remained a child where music was concerned—a child stricken with wonder and delight, but still, and more than ever, a child.

However, that may be the way musical experience proceeds, makes its print upon the film of our total experience: this also is possible. It may be that one must gobble up everything for a while, for rather a long while, before one knows what to accept and what to reject. Even preference, which shows itself early in all matters, may be difficult, half-conscious and unsure, as it often was with me. Preference may merely be an excedent, as if to say: I like everything but I like this a little more than that. I could and did listen to whatever came my way, vaguely liking some things more than others, but rejecting nothing. That wide-eyed voyage of discovery can only be undertaken once, and when we have really made our landfall—discovered our new world—we can never again survey the open sea in the same expectation of mountains and marvels. It is when we get onto dry land that we start to make maps.

3 : The Wine-Dark Sea

New York received its annual increment of youth from all parts of the nation, then as now, with a good-natured indifference amounting almost to hospitality. It was not difficult to find work or living quarters or an assortment of friends. There have been cruel exceptions: during the depression years (when I was not there) a very different mood was general. In 1921, in spite of the "recession" following after war, the good nature was more apparent than the indifference, and the Republican Government, newly returned to power after the eight years of Woodrow Wilson, had made its firm vow to the goddess "prosperity." Things were looking up; and in truth—such was the narrowness of my youthful experience—I never knew that they had (for a year or so) looked in any other direction.

There was much "growing older" to be done, and some of it was, I think, done at breakneck speed. As a young reporter I had every opportunity to lose innocence in all directions, to experiment, explore and try to navigate. My life in the University had been, after all, fairly cloistered, when viewed from the fine free air of the City Hall Park in New York. I had been frugal, perforce, and abstemious by custom, because everybody else was; early to bed and early to rise because those were the conditions of life; inordinately curious in literature and music but substantially ignorant of life. A few months as a reporter on a New York newspaper changed all that.

The country as a whole was undergoing the profound but purely social revolution caused by the national prohibition act. (Consumption was not prohibited: only manufacture and sale.) This had come into effect on January 1, 1920, and within the year it had begun to alter the manners, customs and social attitudes of a whole people. In the illicit traffic that immediately came into being there was every temptation toward the corruption of public officials (especially the municipal police) and lawlessness among the outlawed dealers; all this grew to a climax during the decade and brought about the repeal of the law in the end. I was not to see all this except from afar, but I saw the significant and extremely vigorous beginnings. More intimately, more personally, I saw how practically everybody of whom I had any acquaintance took pleasure in flouting the law, and how speedily it became fashionable to drink cocktails made with bad gin and Scotch whisky which had never seen Scotland. There were dozens of other effects, too—a great alteration in the customs of the women was first of these—but what came first for me was the discovery *in propria persona* of what the nation as a whole was also discovering.

It was not altogether the hours spent in the comfortable, illicit back rooms around Park Row and City Hall Park—then still the center, for a little longer, of the city's newspapers—in the company of other reporters. It also involved an intensive cultivation of all the Italian restaurants with their floods of common red wine, now released from all taxation or control. We called it "red ink" and I, an enthusiastic neophyte, consumed more than my share of it that year. I may have taken to the Italian restaurants partly as a means of practicing the Italian language (for I did that a lot, I know) and partly because they were cheap. At all events, my consumption of spaghetti and other forms of *pastasciutta,* as well as of "red ink," was greater during those months in New York than it ever was in Italy afterwards.

And opera talk, too. The Italians were ever full of it, and many or most of them had a tendency to break into song at intervals as part of the general character assumed (like spaghetti and red wine) in the operation of a restaurant. These were open restaurants; policemen often came into them; our only concession to legality was to drink our wine from thick, white coffee cups, pouring it from pots of the same deceptive ware.

"Red ink" and spaghetti did not lead me to the Metropolitan Opera House; I would have gravitated there by nature; but they are all associated in the jumble of those early explorations. It was Caruso's last year at the opera house; the French had never amounted to much there; the Germans had been obliterated by the war; it had therefore become primarily an Italian opera house in the minds of many people. Caruso fell ill before the season had gone far and I never had an opportunity to hear him sing, except on his records, wherein the voice is preserved better than any other we know, even today. But I was not long making my way to the Metropolitan, just the same. The price of "general admission" (standing room) was then one dollar, and the space available was nearly always crowded, but I made my way in a good number of times before I discovered a better entrance.

The press agent of the Metropolitan was W. J. Guard, "Billy," who had been with Hammerstein at the Manhattan and had contributed much to the success of that enterprise. I had occasion as a reporter to go and see Mr. Guard a number of times—I think it was about some marital or other difficulties of Miss Geraldine Farrar—and although I never had occasion to write a word about music, I had the traditional notion that "the press" as a whole could claim (as of right) free admission. When I put my case to Mr. Guard, he said he would "pass me in," that is for standing room, whenever I came, providing there was not too much of a crush. I thus got on the "free list" unofficially, although I doubt if my name ever appeared on it: Mr. Guard was always in his office on the Thirty-Ninth Street side of the house and he always pressed the button—or made the nod of the head—which admitted me by that door. To this day I prefer it and use it, the "back door" so to speak, no matter how much I may have paid for my tickets: when I go in that door I am coming home.

Without Caruso the Metropolitan might have been, in theory, severely embarrassed. He sang there twice a week, twenty-five weeks a year, to invariably crowded houses. Half the operas performed included him among their principal performers even when they did not depend upon him altogether. But the opera house never ceased to make money throughout the 1920's up to the Wall Street crash, and in fact it made more money after Caruso than before. The phenomenon is general, not particular: any institution of the kind, offering a chance for conspicuous expenditure and display, could always make money if astutely managed during a decade of "boom times," when there was money to burn. The Metropolitan was astutely managed. Giulio Gatti-Casazza had a shrewd sense both of what the public wanted and of what it would stand for—its demand, saturation point, endurance and intolerance. It wanted good shows and "starry" performers without too many repetitions: it would stand for poverty of imagination and insight when it came to production and cared little about orchestral performance; it could not and would not tolerate anything "highbrow." *Pelléas and Mélisande* was intolerable: *Tosca* sung by Farrar, Caruso and Scotti was the ideal. Upon these principles it was possible to make money by opera, as Gatti-Casazza did, because the money was there if you knew how to get it.

I came in, therefore, on a period of commercial management which differed sharply from what I had seen in Chicago. The opera there was conducted on the assumption, common to opera management throughout the world, that a deficit was inevitable and that there was no use trying to prevent it. In Chicago a number of rich citizens who happened to like opera, Mr. and Mrs. Harold Mc-Cormick chief among them, paid the annual deficit without public complaint. In Europe, as I was soon to find out, the State itself was most often the benefactor of the opera, although there were also municipal companies and some operated (like the Scala in Milan) on a special plan: all provided for a loss. Only the Metropolitan was actually operated at a profit until, in the 1930's, the aftermath of the Wall Street crash ended its deviation from the rule.

In a company like that in Chicago many works deficient in general appeal could receive a few performances before going to the warehouse and oblivion. At the Metropolitan nothing could be given unless it met certain minimal requirements in popular interest: it was supposed to be good for at least the performances subscribed in advance (five at full prices and a sixth at a lowered tariff), and if it was really good it should have some profitable extra matinées, outside the subscription, as well as showings in Philadelphia, Brooklyn and other cities. Gatti-Casazza could thus quite easily get a dozen performances out of one standard opera or one new production in the course of a season, and frequently did. Campanini was lucky in some cases if he got three.

Well—those were the housekeeping details. They never interested me much and in those days I was barely aware of them. What drew me into the house was the performances which, in spite of much lackadaisical work on the part of mediocre conductors, managed to sustain a good level. As is always the case at the Metropolitan (even now), some of the principals were invariably interesting. It was hardly possible for Antonio Scotti to do anything wrong at that time, and moreover his voice was still resonant and full of juice. Adamo Didur was a basso of high quality; Pasquale Amato was still singing; the English soprano, Florence Easton, gave beautifully exact and proportioned representations of everything she attempted to do; the entrancing Lucrezia Bori was then at her very best in the *lirico spinto* parts, and the great contralto Margaret Matzenauer, having declared herself a soprano as well, was equal to the demands of everything from Isolde to Azucena and back again. Rosa Ponselle, velvety voice and controlled emotion (too controlled for me at times), was beginning her reign in the Italian dramatic parts.

Those were some of the talents at Gatti's command during the first two seasons I spent (so to speak) in the crowded shadows behind the orchestra seats. But a more remarkable one in many respects was that of Miss Geraldine Farrar, whose personality had made a great impression on the American public for the past fifteen years. Her personality was more remarkable than her voice by the time I heard her. The voice had grown wiry thin in all its upper reaches and it never could have had much to offer in the lower part. By compensation there were wonderfully expressive tones still at her command in the middle voice, and she actually did have something to express. She was not always good—a spoiled darling of the public, with flowers scattered over her wherever she went, and by some accounts a capricious termagant to those who opposed her, she had no single-minded aesthetic purpose and thus could not become a great artist. She had made films, some of them very bad, had conducted a good many of her personal and professional quarrels in public, had pushed out her repertoire in all directions without regard for her special gifts, and was quite capable—as in Leoncavallo's *Zaza*—of an exhibitionism which had nothing to do with play, music, character or the lyric theatre in general. She almost seemed to be winking at the audience as a circus clown does. She liked silks, satins and trains, and she wore them; even the village maiden in *Faust* had acquired a train by the time I saw her, and the dresses for *Madama Butterfly* must have cost a fortune. Her famous Carmen was a soprano, of course, and she used all the customary soprano substitutions of notes as well as some (if I mistake not) which were all her own. And yet, much as I dislike a soprano in a part which is not only mezzo or contralto in music but also by character, I think even now that Farrar's Carmen was one of the very best I ever saw or heard.

Her last two seasons at the Metropolitan were my first two, and I heard her often: she was, like Caruso, an all-season singer (twenty-five weeks) and sang twice a week except when indisposed. Such contracts do not exist any more and did not exist even then for any but Farrar and Caruso.

It may be asked by an attentive reader (if such there be) why I heard Farrar so often and admired her work if, as I said a while ago, she "had no single-minded aesthetic purpose and thus could not become a great artist." According to my view, great artists are rare, rarer on the lyric stage than on any other, and a singer may be tremendously famous, highly gifted and invariably interesting, as Farrar was, without being one. The element of self-surrender—nowadays usually called, I think pretentiously, "dedication"—is the test of a great artist. What distinguishes the truly great from the others, whatever their interest or fascination, is simply this: the surrender of the self to the character in all its aspects, so that there is not a single moment on the stage when the artist (even with nothing whatever to do) is not merged into the musico-dramatic creation. According to these ideas, Geraldine Farrar was an artist intermittently in every part but never a great artist in any. You cannot wink at the audience if you have given your soul to God and receive it back again in the form of one of his creatures. Some such transaction is implicit in the finest characterizations I have seen and heard in opera, for nothing else will ever explain them.

Caruso died in Naples in August, 1921, of an illness they called pleurisy which lingered on after his attack of the preceding autumn. Throughout the last half of the 1920-1921 season, which was the part I heard, his illness had been minimized; the Metropolitan seemed to think he might be cured and would return to sing. He was a good deal better when he left for his holiday in Italy that summer, and the sudden relapse followed by his death was a shock to New York.

The grief of the city at large seemed to me queer indeed, since it was paraded by an infinity of strangers—persons who had never heard Caruso sing and cared nothing for his life's effort in reality: it was the result of what we were beginning to call "mass suggestion," I suppose. The whole city seemed plunged into mourning, and actually the words overheard in the streets and in public conveyances were mostly about the departed tenor. Practically every Italian one saw was in tears or dissolved into tears at a word. There were pages about him in the newspapers. It appeared that he was a national hero not only to the Italians but also to the Americans. I was myself sad and personally aggrieved as a child might have been. What it came to was a sense of deprivation: "Now I'll never hear Caruso!"

The death of the tenor spurred the Metropolitan into engaging a number of new singers of high importance for the next season (1921-1922), which was my last there for some years. Mme. Galli-Curci was the first of these: she opened that season in *La Traviata*. Maria Jeritza of the State Opera in Vienna made her debut in Erich Korngold's opera *Die Tote Stadt* on November 17, 1921, and Fyodr Chaliapin returned to the United States, after an absence of eleven years, in *Boris Godunoff* (December 9, 1921).

These dates I have extracted from the records, for the sake of neatness, but every one of those performances is securely graven in my memory. Galli-Curci was by no means a stranger to New York after her triumphant visits with the Chicago company, but her lovely tone and melancholy grace were as effective as ever.

Jeritza was a blonde beauty with a fresh, strong voice, an eager awareness of the public, a sort of all-out unreserve in singing and acting, which quickly gave her the same kind of popularity in New York which she had had for seven or eight years in Vienna. In *Die*

Tote Stadt, at her debut, I thought she was wonderfully beautiful. (There is a scene in that forgotten work where she is a framed portrait on the wall and then comes to life.) There was not a trace of subtlety in her voice or acting, but what she had to give was given so lavishly, so honestly and *de bon coeur,* that no audience could resist her in those years. The one thing I did not particularly like was her Tosca, with which she threw New York into wild enthusiasm two weeks after her debut. In the second act Mme. Jeritza, by accident or design—the story goes that it was by accident—fell to the floor in her tussle with Antonio Scotti and sang the *"Vissi d'arte"* from the prone position, gazing piteously at the conductor. It was like Columbus with the egg; it was simple but nobody had thought of it before; the house was in a delirium of joy. For the next decade or so there was hardly a Tosca left in the world who dared to sing the arioso right end up.

The third of the international idols who came to the Metropolitan in the year after Caruso's death was Fyodr Chaliapin. In this case there was no room for discussion: the man was obviously a supreme artist, a "creator" if ever there could be such a thing on a stage. Mussorgsky's Boris, the Boris of history, the suffering sinner Boris, the abstract and the specific Boris were all one, they were all Chaliapin's Boris: and this was so splendidly tragic, so augustly true and beautiful, that it left one at the end of the performance stricken with the awe of a religious experience, mitigated by exhaustion. The exhaustion I mean is a special sensation of almost ecstatic emptiness, exactly what I understand by the "tragic catharsis" of Aristotle, which "purges" us by pity and terror. It has come to me more undeniably through music, and through certain performances of Shakespeare's plays, than in any other way, but it is rarely so overwhelming as it was when I first saw and heard the Boris of Chaliapin.

At this time Chaliapin was getting toward fifty but had lost none of the round, ringing power of his incomparable voice. It was a voice capable of almost any variety of expression, emphasis or suggestion. Except that he was a basso by decree of nature, it would have been impossible to assign limits to his musical and dramatic power. When that Gargantuan voice was reduced to a whisper, it could still be heard in the remotest part of this or any other house. With such an unequaled endowment he combined an infallible sense for stage action in the representation of character. For this he never had an equal, so far as I know, except Mary Garden. Neither could have created character in this way—*lived* character, *been* character —in the ordinary theatre, with its totally different demands, but in the lyric theatre, where everything up to and including the innermost soul of the personage is a function of music, they were the first and so far the only examples of their kind. Garden's original resources must have been far less imposing, physically and materially speaking, than Chaliapin's, but with them she had evolved the same power of "creation," as it is called, on the opera stage. Her Mélisande and his Boris—to which I added in later years Lehmann's Marschallin—were spun from within like the spider's web, and the beholder had nothing left to do but to marvel and, perhaps, to weep.

For Chaliapin's first performance the Metropolitan, correctly estimating the rise of public interest, had raised its prices. (His fees were the highest ever, $3,000 a night after this, but only the first performance brought augmented prices.) I was determined to get into the house and to sit down for once, and repaired to the opera on the first day of the open sale to see what I could do. It was a test of patience and fortitude even to get to the box office and, when I did, the only good seat left from which I could be assured of both hearing and seeing was in a box. It cost eleven dollars. I paid it, although it was certainly a large part—probably about one-third—of my weekly wage. This extravagance is one I have never regretted and never will.

Chaliapin's late career, which began on that night, was unlike any other. It had all the surroundings and consequences which we are accustomed to associate with reigning tenors (like Caruso) or prima donna sopranos (like Melba). Yet he was a basso, probably the only one in history who received such attention. He was a childlike creature by temperament—I knew him later—and I have no doubt he enjoyed every minute of it. He had retained his youthful powers, I think, precisely by means of this childlike temperament, which did not permit him to worry or even to think except about the ferociously serious business of the "creation." Where the "creation" was concerned he was adult in the extreme, fanatically concentrated and incapable of compromise. Each of the great "creations"

—not only Boris itself but Basilio in *Il Barbiere di Siviglia* and all the others—was the work of years, but once it was fixed, it had the permanence of sculpture or architecture. He was a member of both companies, the Metropolitan and the Chicago Opera, through the 1920's, singing also at Covent Garden and the Paris Grand Opéra besides giving concerts in his own style, without a fixed program. (A book was distributed in lieu of programs; from this book he chose what he wished to sing and announced it as he went along.) Out of all these activities he must have made several fortunes, all of which he spent. Opera singers often collect a court about them, when they can afford it, and Russians have a reputation for unthinking gregariousness. Chaliapin's traveling circus, which he took with him all over the world, was enlarged by the doubling of these qualities. He also is quoted as having said more than once that he "didn't know" how many children he had. With this largeness of spirit he could hardly have been expected to keep track of money. When I knew him in Salzburg and Paris he was over sixty but he still had the irresistible charm (and also the smile) of a gifted and unself-conscious child. He once explained to me the whole Russian Revolution in a nutshell. *"Ces Bolcheviques, vous savez,"* he said, *"ils sont fous."*

The coming of so many new singers of renown to the opera company was bound to have some effect upon the fortunes of Miss Geraldine Farrar. She had been for some years in the position of *prima donna assoluta,* unofficially speaking—she could almost have called the Metropolitan what Melba called Covent Garden, "my opera house." She was not yet forty; she was beautiful, at least on the stage (I never saw her anywhere else), and her talents were still highly appreciated. When she took her bows flowers were thrown at her from all parts of the house. When they came pelting down from the highest gallery I often thought they threatened some slight danger to the singer herself, not to speak of the men in the orchestra pit. She had a particular following of young girls who were known as "Gerry-flappers," great throwers of bouquets and standers at stage doors, a sort of ready-made claque for whatever she did. The public had by no means wearied of her, and, what is more, her performances during this last season actually improved: the furore over Jeritza had induced her, perhaps, to take a little more care than she had troubled to take before. I was present at her last *Tosca,* which I greatly preferred to that of Mme. Jeritza. I was not much given to judgment in those days but it seems to me now, in retrospect, that she was a more interesting artist—except, perhaps, in sheer physical body—than Jeritza could ever hope to be. After that last *Tosca* it was announced that Miss Farrar would retire from the Metropolitan at the end of the season. It has since become known that Gatti-Casazza had offered to renew her contract for half as many performances a season (that is, twelve weeks instead of twenty-four) and she preferred retirement. "Twenty dervishes may sit upon a carpet," says the Persian proverb, "but the whole world is too small for two Shahs." Farrar had not squandered her money as so many singers do, and had therefore (from the bourgeois point of view) no reason to fear retirement. She made her actual farewell not in that last *Tosca* I saw, but in Leoncavallo's *Zaza.*

This year, which saw so much coming and going among the singing artists, also was the last in New York for Mary Garden. She continued to sing elsewhere until 1930: I heard her a good many times in Paris and Chicago. But the Chicago Opera Company, of which she was general artistic director for that one year (1921-1922), had decided to stop giving its annual season in New York. If all the accounts of the matter are to be believed, no fortune, however great, had sustained losses of the kind the McCormicks had been paying for the Chicago Opera. The deficit during Mary Garden's year of management was said to have been roughly one million dollars. She had undertaken the task at Mr. McCormick's request, but had never concerned herself with money matters: she was given a free hand and she used it. Her understanding was that she was to give them a lavish season.

There is no other instance on record of a prima donna soprano actually directing a big, international opera company. There probably never will be another. (Mme. Germaine Lubin at the Paris Grand Opéra had, under Nazi occupation, the name without the game.) Garden was not only singing twice a week herself but she planned the entire season, engaged singers, commissioned new works and, I have no doubt, had a wonderful time. She certainly engaged a great many more singers than were needed and as a result some of

them collected their full contract payments for one or two performances. Some, it is said, never sang at all and were paid just the same.
The fact that there are only seven days in a week (and only six in
New York!) was apparently forgotten. Out of six days, if two were
allotted to Garden and two to Raisa, as was necessary in this company, only two others were left over for a dozen international divas
to share among themselves.

Even so—whatever the damage—it was a remarkable opera season.
I went as often as I could and reveled in the originality of the arrangements. An opera might be given once only—two performances
was rather a long run—and a singer might make a debut which was
simultaneously a farewell. These singularities are most often the
prerogatives of failure: we tend to think that a singer who sings
once only must have something wrong and an opera not repeated
must have failed to please. Not at all: Garden conducted her whole
season through a tootling of success like the triumphal scene in
Aïda. There was simply too much of everything to get it all in, but
overwise it was highly relished and usually praised to the skies.

The thing I remember best out of it was Garden's own *Salome,*
which had not been given in Chicago while I was there. It had been
seen first in this very house, Hammerstein's Manhattan Opera: for in
this, its last New York season, the Chicago company had left the
Lexington and taken over the theatre which had been, essentially, its
birthplace. Thus Garden was enabled to make her New York farewell—it was on February 25, 1922—on the same stage which had
seen her resounding debut fifteen years before.

Salome, revived for this last season, was a memorable evocation
which may not have been, note for note, what the composer put on
paper, but beyond any doubt conveyed his whole intention better
than any subsequent performance I have seen. Garden's vocal powers
were no longer able to subdue the music and perhaps they never
had been. One of the New York critics had written, after her first
Salome thirteen years before, "Of course she cannot sing one note of
this music." That was the kind of wild nonsense in which the critics
of the time delighted; actually she could sing most of the notes even
in 1922. What is more, the middle part of the voice was perfectly
suited to the music and gave the young Judaean princess not only

youth but perversity—an accomplishment quite outside the possibilities of those heroic sopranos (all Brünnhildes at heart) who usually sing the work.

Garden also provided the first New York performances (to a total of two) of Serge Prokofieff's *Love of Three Oranges,* which she had commissioned him in advance to write for her season. It was not liked by the New York critics then, although the same critics have since heaped praise upon it. It was the most popular of operas in Moscow in 1927, when I was there, but by ill luck or bad management I have never yet been able to hear it except in fragments.

When I left New York for Europe that spring, I had already heard about as much opera, I suppose, as most people hear in a lifetime. My tastes were still extraordinarily inclusive but they were beginning to sort themselves out into some order. I had heard Wagner for the first time, although I believe it was in a manner more dutiful than enraptured. The Metropolitan had produced both *Lohengrin* and *Tristan und Isolde,* in English for fear of war patriots, and the Chicago Company had produced *Tannhäuser* in German. I had heard them all more than once. In fact I heard two Isoldes in those English performances at the Metropolitan, Mme. Margaret Matzenauer and Miss Florence Easton. Mme. Matzenauer's noble performances, then and later on, were too monumental for me. I well understand and have already expatiated upon the peculiar and separate demands of style on the lyric stage, its subordination to the music in which it has its origin, its radical differentiation from any kind of acting for the spoken drama. Even so, I might say of Mme. Matzenauer what my friend Margaret Webster has said of a present-day soprano whom she tried to direct at the Metropolitan: "This is *la donna immobile.*" Matzenauer, looking magnificent or ferocious as the case might be (she had both expressions), stood up and sang. Sometimes she also sat down and sang. Without expecting from her anything like what is called "acting" in the spoken drama, or even the kind of creative impersonation of which lyric drama is capable (Chaliapin, Garden), I did expect the singer to suggest, at the very least, the character. Matzenauer did not. Easton, our other Isolde, did: she was in fact a very good artist, but the English language bothered her a great deal more than it did Matzenauer, because she was an Englishwoman and cared something about it. Later on when I heard Easton's Isolde in German, I came to know what she could do with it. She never had the great tumultuous flood of tone to give—only two in my lifetime, Leider and Flagstad, have had it—but she was a fine singer of the best German school (all her formation and early experience were in Germany). She would have been eminently satisfactory as one's fifth or sixth Isolde, but not as one's second, especially when the first had been Matzenauer.

Every young man with a passion for music-drama ought to have a really great Isolde for his first experience of that work. Granted, there are not many, and for years upon years at a time there are not any, but we speak of what ought to be rather than what is. My own relentless and, as I see it now, wholly inevitable progression into Wagnerism might have been somewhat expedited (and the progression out of it thus accomplished a little sooner!) if my first interpreters of the principal parts had been more suited to their tasks. As it was, only one principal (Rosa Raisa in *Tannhäuser*) in the whole lot had anything like the grandeur of a Wagnerian concept. These things, at whatever stage of our own or Wagner's development we look at them (even *Tannhäuser* and *Lohengrin*), are the results of a Titanic parturition and dwell in a Titanic world. To see them as I did first in both our opera companies was to get a false start into that new world through which, at whatever cost, almost every musical pilgrimage seems to go. The young man who, having survived the variety of musical experience here outlined (and more, besides, that needs no telling), took ship for France in the spring of 1922, was not in the least a Wagnerite: he was in fact so little a Wagnerite that he felt and said, as almost everybody does sometimes, that he preferred to hear Wagner played by a symphony orchestra without voices. He was a little more adult, musically speaking, than he had been a year and a half before on his arrival in New York, and a few ideas were beginning to sprout where once there had been only appetites.

2

Willem Mengelberg, then about fifty, had returned to New York in the preceding year to conduct the New Symphony Orchestra, which was rebaptized the "National" Symphony Orchestra for a year and taken then into the Philharmonic in April, 1921, to form the "Phil-harmonic-Symphony Society of New York." There was still in ex-istence the New York Symphony Orchestra—Walter Damrosch's founded by his father—so that at the time I arrived on the scene there were three orchestras demanding the attention of the same pub-lic. After 1921 there were two, and after 1928 only one, the Phil-harmonic.

None of these orchestras, in 1921 and 1922, could compare to the one I knew, the Chicago Symphony. All were beset by guest con-ductors, money troubles and a certain staleness or *routinière* quality arising from a lack of either energy or talent in their resident con-ductors which no "guest" could ever cure.

Mengelberg came into New York like a cleansing wind. He had electrical energy, driving will, blazing talent of an inexplicable vari-ety, and no patience whatsoever. He had been and remained con-ductor of the Concertgebouw in Amsterdam (he was there for forty years in all) where perhaps his high tension, being familiar, was ac-cepted as a normal condition of life. It was not so in New York. Long periods of complacency in repertoire and performance are characteristic of New York's musical life, throughout its range, but this satisfied and well-fed quietude explodes every once in a while into something like a revolution. Toscanini's tour with the orches-tra of La Scala di Milano in the previous year had upset all possible complacency: the Italian orchestra was far better than anything New York had heard since Mahler left in 1911. In the ensuing rearrange-ments Mengelberg blew in, at first with the "New" or "National" or-chestra, and gave such performances as the moribund Philharmonic (under Josef Strusky) could not emulate. The two orchestras were then combined and, under Mengelberg, the Philharmonic began its swift ascent to the preëminence it achieved a few years later under Toscanini and held as long as he remained there.

Mengelberg was the first "great" conductor I ever heard—using "great" not only as a description of his best performances but also as a suggestion of the general esteem in which he was held, his man-ner and style and also his fame: he was what some call a "prima donna conductor." For Wagner, Tchaikovsky and Richard Strauss he had a special gift, for the second and third more even than for the first: and his demands from the orchestra were absolute—as imperious, I should think, as Toscanini's, although he was unable to obtain from it the constancy of perfection in all styles which made it unique while Toscanini had it.

At all events it was, in 1921-1922 (Mengelberg's first with the two orchestras combined), a rousing experience. At one bound the Philharmonic, lax and fading, was jerked into life again and delivered itself of some performances which converted one's spine into a sort of electromagnetic field. I have never enjoyed the Tchaikovsky symphonies so much as I did then—or the Strauss tone poems when I could hear them. They seemed to yield their secrets at Mengelberg's behest—particularly *Ein Heldenleben*—although it may be said that their secrets are neither numerous nor arcane. The normal repertoire was present, of course, in Mozart, Beethoven and Brahms, but it is the later composers I remember from Mengelberg's first season and associate with him. I heard him do the same things afterwards, on several of my scattered New York visits. He did not actually leave the orchestra even when Toscanini came, and shared it with him until 1930: but no later Mengelberg performance ever aroused me to the same pitch of excitement. For all things there must be a first, and for Tchaikovsky and Strauss the early are probably the best hearings. (I had heard the same Tchaikovsky and Strauss in Chicago without the same perturbation, but they were not Dr. Stock's most congenial composers.)

The Stadium concerts had already come into existence (since 1918) and I made my acquaintance with that easy way of listening to music on some hot nights of the 1921 summer. Easy, that is, in their being out-of-doors and at that time not too crowded; you could move about, pick your own place and change it at will, smoke a cigarette, come late or leave early if necessary—in fact, do as you please. The Philharmonic was not always at its best in the Stadium and the open air is perhaps not ideal for stringed instruments, although I should have thought the savage overheating of Carnegie Hall in winter might be worse. It was wonderful just the same to be able to go there and listen in the relative coolness by the river at a season when New York in general has no music at all.

These remarks about the Philharmonic and Mengelberg refer to a stage in which I was, I believe, gradually changing my base of operations not from one form to another at all, but to a broader and more permanent field which is in fact music itself, general, abstract and particular. That is, I was and remained an opera enthusiast, originally without rhyme or reason, and only gradually, by dint of much frequentation, came to understand in some slight degree what I was hearing. These five years of listening to opera had been accompanied, just the same, by a slow and steady opening up of other musical doors. I had heard a fair amount of symphonic music in Chicago, and recitals as well (piano, violin, chamber music) without undue disturbance of my central nervous system. It was not until Mengelberg that the orchestra came into being for me with its full authority, its seductive magic, its limitless range—the power and the glory. It was only a beginning, but to have perceived it at all and to have set forth on this trail was enough through the next ten or fifteen years to transform all musical experience. Mengelberg was what might be called a forerunner of Toscanini. To hear an orchestra, merely to *hear* it as it can be heard under the ministrations of a master, is to begin to think, in all the larger forms, orchestrally; it leads even to thinking of literature and life itself in terms not disparate as before, but entwined and interdependent. At that time I had never examined an orchestral score—even in the miniature form I afterwards knew best—but I believe it is not too far-fetched to say that for me some start was made in 1922 toward an awareness of the great foundation, that which, in depth and breadth, actually sustains the multiform architectonic structure of beauty in music.

3

Paris, Venice, Milan and Rome were a heady mixture in that year of 1922. I stayed in Venice for some months before going to Rome in—as it happened—October. This was the year and the month in which Mussolini, having tried the strength of his *squadristi* and found the State powerless against them, held his last Fascist Congress in Naples and decided to march on Rome. This event—the *Marcia su Roma*—took place October 22, 1922, when I was in the train from Rome to Paris. My knowledge of Italian, skimpy though it really was, surpassed that of almost all the other young journalists available just then, and seemed more useful under the circumstances than it might have seemed a month before; I found myself with a

job. In the kind of journalism it thrust me into, music certainly had
no place: the preoccupation was political all the time, morning to
night, with France, Italy, Spain and even Germany as our area of interest (although our Berlin office could usually, except in a great
crisis, account for Germany without any help from Paris). I doubt if
I heard any music at all during most of my first year in Europe: in
the beginning (summer and early autumn) there was none to hear,
and after that there was too much to do. To a considerable extent
my aesthetic interest may have moved itself along to the art galleries:
that was certainly true during my first months in Italy. But the addition of a new interest did not really drive out the old. It was simply a matter of time—the long hours and in general the pervading
quality of this kind of journalism seemed to occupy all the time
there was.

Little by little, after a few months, I began to drift back into the
habit of listening to music when I was able to do so. It was nothing
like the pertinacious pursuit of everything which had been my lot in
Chicago and New York. It began to be selective, too much so, for I
made some rather disconcerting discoveries. For one thing I found
out after some desultory trials that I really did not like either the
orchestras or the singing in Paris. The orchestras were exceedingly
lax, even when they contained excellent musicians. A great many
players in the orchestras were also teachers; many had other outside
jobs to augment their incomes; and some, perhaps, were simply lazy.
At all events the system of "substitution" for rehearsals was in full
control. A player who could not or would not get to a rehearsal sent
a substitute and no questions were asked. (When Cortot formed his
orchestra later, he abolished the system and achieved a result.) Thus
a performance, given by first players, was often ragged, disunited,
uneven to a degree, because the leading musicians had never rehearsed the work with their conductor. Quite regardless of tone, in
which the French strings and brasses could never really please my
ear, the sheer carelessness of such performances seemed to me dis-
graceful. Until I went to Paris I had never heard a bad orchestra or a
distinctly bad performance of a whole program from beginning to
end. No doubt a music lover born and bred in New York and never
leaving it would spend his life thinking that the kind of Beethoven
and Brahms heard from the Philharmonic was normal and ordinary.

Germans are in the same case; they seldom hear downright bad performances, bad all the way through. Only an Englishman, perhaps, would have been more or less at home in a Paris concert hall in the early 1920's, although even the English have vastly changed since then.

Opera was worse. Here there was not only a threadbare repertoire, bad orchestra, ramshackle scenery and a deadening routine of style and tradition, both at the Opéra-Comique and at the Opéra, but there was the further startling discovery that I did not like French singing. Why? Actually it seemed to me, after a few years in Paris, that the French *could* not sing. But I had heard a good many French singers in America and liked them—beginning with Mary Garden, who, although born in Aberdeen, was a product of French training and a child of the Opéra-Comique. Many other singers, especially in the Chicago Opera, were French: Muratore, Vanni-Marcoux, Yvonne Gall, Geneviève Vix. Why was I so disconcertingly upset by the singing I heard at the Comique and the Opéra?

A good deal of it must have been due to the general standards, which were very low when I first went to Paris. That is, the management and the conductors did not expect much of their singers. The public, which had nothing else, was easily satisfied and—as the word goes—"never knew the difference." (I think the public always knows the difference, but there are times, and this was one, when it has no choice.) Singers did not trouble to give their utmost care to a performance: success was more easily attained by extracurricular activity, clothes or jewels, Parisian notoriety. Of a certain manager at the Comique it is said that no soprano ever reached the stage for the first time without passing by his bed. Both at the Opéra-Comique and at the Paris Grand Opéra it was customary, as it is today, to permit "qualified" singers to perform leading parts upon payment of a fee. Only a few years ago the fee at the Paris Grand Opéra for a celebrated American soprano was three hundred dollars a night— that is, from her to them, not from them to her: it is more, much more, than they pay even the best of their own singers.

These conditions are never favorable to quality in performance. But beyond that was something even deeper in the quality of the French voices and in their method of singing. The language itself has a recurrent nasality which, when used by poets with a knowing ear, gives wonderful results. Think of: *Les sanglots longs des violons de l'automne.*

The three nasals are used like musical instruments and although two are technically identical they are in fact quantitatively different, the *on* nasal being necessarily much longer in *longs* than it is in *violons.* The three nasals make a dominant chord which is resolved in the beautiful open tone of *automne.* The beauty of this verse could never be reproduced in any other language.

But the nasals, a resource to poetry, are a curse to singing—so much so that all the best French teachers of singing have adopted a "modified" version of them, by which *an,* for example, as in *"les neiges d'antan"* would be sung with the slightest possible nasality, almost like *aw.* In high notes for soprano or tenor it is physically impossible to pronounce a nasal at all, and if it were pronounced it would be unbearably ugly. The high C for tenor in the garden scene of *Faust* is a case in point. The line is: *Où se devine la présence d'une âme,* etc.

The high C comes on the nasal second syllable of *présence* and cannot be pronounced: the tenors "modify" it to a sound rather like *aw* with a very slight nasal cover.

Normally French singers are quite unable to make this modification throughout, although nature forces them to do so on high notes. Nor is it desirable for them to de-nasalize their language altogether and change its character. In the result the nasals invade their vocal method and more or less take over—like bad money driving out good. The impression received by the ear, listening for sound alone without regard to sense, is of a pervading nasality in the vocal emission. It sounds as if the voice were placed firmly in the antrumsinuses and pushed out through the nostrils, with all the resonance deriving from the bones of the nose and around the eyes. A very high note, by this method, comes precisely from the place where the bridge of your glasses sits (if you wear glasses); that is, from between the eyes and just above the bridge of the nose.

Well . . .

I did not like French singing and I reminded myself of Charlemagne's remark, that his French singers sounded like old wagons over cobblestones, and I wished sometimes that they did. The reasons why French singers sounded better in America were numerous:

they tried harder, took more care, to begin with. Then they were often the only French singers in an international cast, which gave their own styles certain advantages, certain disadvantages, but invariably distinction. Furthermore, by simple economic pressures it was the best French singers who came to America as a rule, the Muratore or the Vanni-Marcoux (those two being half-Italian anyhow) or the Plançon or Calvé. It was not of them that I was thinking: such artists were scarcely ever heard at the Opéra or at the Comique in my experience, although all were products of those houses.

The run-of-the-mill French singer is at his Frenchest in vocal method when he is performing in a cast which is entirely French. The results when four or five mediocre artists of this sort collaborate upon a routine performance of *Carmen* or *Manon* at the Comique, *Faust* or *Samson et Dalila* at the Opéra, were such as to discourage me for a long time from attendance at such festivals. To this day I have to be pretty sure of what I am going to hear, who is singing, who is conducting, and what is the relative newness or oldness of the production, before I enter either of those houses. Sometimes their new productions are prepared with reasonable care for musical and dramatic representation, and a new production (at least at the Opéra) is likely to be quite generous or even interesting in such matters as décors, dresses and ballets, the extramusical elements. Ordinary repertoire in all my early years was generally treated with the contempt which, quite possibly, it deserved.

I did not mind missing ordinary repertoire very much, although in capitals where opera is well produced and sung (Rome, Milan, Berlin, Vienna and New York) I have generally gone to hear it gladly and still do. But I really did resent the routine treatment given at the Comique to *Carmen*. This work which, along with *Pelléas et Mélisande,* is the glory of the house, ought to be kept in apple-pie condition. It should never be allowed to deteriorate into a slapdash and perfunctory charade with tattered settings and abject costumes, a casino orchestra with a cast which is thinking of something else and has to be reminded by the prompter (very loudly) of what opera is being performed. That has been the state of *Carmen* at the Comique in almost every attempt I have made to hear it since 1922. For the house's acknowledged masterwork this is shabby treatment indeed.

There are, of course, exceptions. During the 1920's, later than my first visits to the Comique, Mme. Ninon Vallin honored the house by some performances in *Carmen*. She was an artist and her Carmen, although a soprano, was excellently thought, felt and sung. It was the best I ever heard at the Comique; moreover, it hoisted the conductor and other singers onto a plane to which they never otherwise aspired. Even with Vallin, however, the stage looked like something thrown out of an abandoned warehouse. Another good Carmen of a little later on was Renée Gilly, a daughter of the Algerian baritone Dinh Gilly, and in this case, too, the routine was shattered. She had a genuine mezzo-soprano voice and, although she was too fat for Paris, she did look and act like a gypsy. Gilly's bold and bitter, sluttish way of playing the part carried the performance which was otherwise deplorable.

A regeneration took place at the Grand Opéra de Paris twelve or fifteen years after my first acquaintance with it, and I shall have occasion to say so in the right place, but it was in no better condition than the Comique when I first went there. Its *Faust, Roméo et Juliette, Samson et Dalila* and *Thaïs* went on their eternal rounds, relieved by a little Verdi and Wagner—*Rigoletto* and *Tannhäuser*— from time to time, just as the Comique's eternal repertoire was relieved by a dosage of Puccini. In neither house was it safe to trust the announcements; operas were changed at the last moment and there were no refunds; if the lights went out or half the score were cut (both of which I have seen) the audience might yell its lungs out, but there was no redress.

So Paris was almost a musical desert for me, and it was not until some later developments (Cortot's orchestra; Mme. Germaine Lubin at the Opéra, to name only two) that I was able to derive any real pleasure from performances there. Garden's Mélisande in the summer of 1926 was a glaring exception to all Paris rules.

The years 1922-1925, my only active years in journalism (that is, in regular employment), took me hither and thither, to the occupation of the Ruhr, the Rhineland "separatist" war, to Rome, to Madrid, to Rome again, to Morocco, and for one interlude (spring, 1924) to London. The little music I was able to hear was everywhere better than in Paris. In the intervals of dodging bullets —or vanquishing boredom: it was one or the other in the Rhineland—I heard *Figaro* for the first time in my life. It was at the opera house in Düsseldorf and was played by the company from Cologne. The sheer loveliness of the music needed no gloss and I knew at once that this must be a source of never ending delight. Although my own ignorance of the work and of Mozart's operas in general was complete and I thus had no standard, I could hear and see the exquisite care with which every note had been prepared, the wonderfully apposite but restrained stage direction, the fresh, pretty settings and dresses. Nothing so good as this *Figaro* would have been possible in the Paris of that day or, I suspect, any other, because these agreeable voices (none great or famous) were beautifully styled and blended. No sight or sound was ugly and the evening was, I have often thought since, one of the most satisfactory I have ever spent in an opera theatre. One's first *Figaro* comes only once, and I was lucky that it came in such a guise.

In Madrid the Royal Opera gave the best *Aïda* I had yet heard and, I believe, the first I had really enjoyed. That was a vivid performance and remains vivid in retrospect. Ofelia Nieto, young and slim and with sufficient voice, was the convincing Aïda, and Miguel Fleta, all fire and flame, was Radames. I was convinced after the Nile scene that I had at last heard the new Caruso. Fleta sang all over the world after that but never so well in my opinion as he did in Madrid.

Madrid also introduced me to flamenco singing and dancing, into which I plunged with all the *engouement* I had felt in Chicago and New York for opera. There were theatres all over Madrid in which folk singing and dancing, not all *flamenco* by any means but from every province of Spain, went on for half the night. They did not open until eleven o'clock and were not in possession of a full audience until midnight, so their main offerings were made in the small hours. I counted any night lost in which I had not seen and heard a few of the dancers and singers who seemed to form such a large part of the population of Spain.

It was London, however, which gave me the heftiest leg-up, the thrice-blessed lift. I was stationed there just at the time (1924) when the Royal Opera at Covent Garden reopened for a season, the first since the war. What I most needed to hear was something in a different realm from most of the operas known to me up to then—

something "new" in the sense of proportion or value, something in which the balance of forces would come closer to what (since my orchestral discoveries) I rather obscurely thought they ought to be.

The Royal Opera had been in abeyance during the war. Sir Thomas Beecham had had two seasons of his own there afterwards (from 1919) but the actual Royal Opera, under that name, came back into existence in 1924. The principal Conductor was Bruno Walter with Karl Alwin in second place. The company which re-opened the house was German—how it was chosen, assembled and organized, I do not know, but it seemed to be made up of everything that was best in Germany and Austria. At a later period it might have been possible to suspect some governmental intervention—some effort, that is, to put the best foot forward for an eminently German art. No such thing existed in 1924 in any country, because the era of the "public relations officer" had not yet arrived and the Goebbels technique, from which we still suffer, had not been invented. The Royal Opera season of 1924, historic in many ways, was a natural accident in that a demand existed for which there was a supply readily available.

Why it was available is another matter and one not likely to be settled by speculation. Defeat in war, economic prostration, a runaway inflation of currency wiping out all the savings of ordinary people (even though astute gamblers may have made fortunes)—these would not be the conditions under which, normally, one might expect a renewal of talent and energy in the theatre. Yet such a renewal had taken place in Berlin and throughout Germany. More than the seasonal crop of new directors, designers, actors, singers and conductors appeared during those years, and opera got its full share of new ideas and talents. The Royal Opera was not able to bring to London all the new stage settings in which the ideas of the 1920's were striving for expression. For Wagner's works it used its existing décors; but this was a small matter compared to the great joy given by the performances. Bruno Walter was himself one of the primary elements in arousing London (and me) to a pitch of enthusiasm seldom experienced. He conducted many of the works, as many as he could, and was in a general way responsible for all of them. He was (and has remained) one of the best conductors in the world, with a natural warmth and sympathy for every emotion and yet no tendency toward vulgar excess or facile effects. With his history—eleven years as general director of the opera in Vienna, nine in Munich—it was not surprising that he knew the managerial tasks, the nonmusical difficulties, as well as he did the scores he conducted. Walter, as an artist, was by no means postwar; he had been in important positions all through the present century; but he had the taste to appreciate the new artists and to welcome them to the fold.

The result was a season which nobody concerned could ever forget —neither participants nor audience. Walter gave us *Tristan* and the *Ring*, the essentials of a German season, with *Der Rosenkavalier* and (for the first time outside of Germany) the revised *Ariadne auf Naxos*. The artists who made their London debuts in these performances were to count for a great deal in the opera houses of Europe and America during the coming years. They included Lotte Lehmann, Frida Leider, Maria Olczewska, Elisabeth Schumann, Richard Mayr, Lauritz Melchior, Friedrich Schorr, Maria Ivogün, Delia Reinhardt and a considerable number of others from the leading theatres of central Europe. Except Richard Mayr, whose debut (as Hagen and at Bayreuth) had taken place in 1902, none of them had won recognition before 1914 and even Mayr was new to London. Some (Leider, for example) had been on the stage only a short time, but the general level, as the names alone indicate, was such as is practically never attained in an opera house. I heard all of them in central Europe afterwards, but never all together: such an assembly was not possible under ordinary conditions. At present it would not be possible under any conditions, because so many artists of the highest category do not exist in German repertoire.

The revival of *Der Rosenkavalier* took place on May 23, 1924, and I discovered both a masterpiece and a mastersinger. The work itself exercised its full enchantment on me, certainly; it was a good twenty years before I could see any weakness in it, and perhaps more before I realized that it was, when all is said, a masterpiece of the second rather than of the first quality. However, on that night it was all beauty, and Lotte Lehmann sang—for the first time—the part of the Marschallin. With her there was Elisabeth Schumann as Sophie, Delia Reinhardt as Octavian and Richard Mayr as Baron Ochs. The same cast, with Maria Olczewska instead of Reinhardt (an improvement in tone), afterwards made the famous Vienna recording, extensive though incomplete, which has remained one of the gramophone's permanent achievements.

Lehmann had known *Der Rosenkavalier* for perhaps a dozen years, having graduated through Sophie von Faninal to Octavian before she even thought of the Marschallin. It was at Walter's request that she studied the Marschallin for this London revival. Its gaiety and sadness were alike suited to her warm, lovely voice, and she had no trouble with it even though the time of preparation was short. The strong probability is that she knew it thoroughly already, without realizing that she did so. She was the kind of art-born and art-ridden artist who could never sing merely a part in an opera: she absorbed everything the whole work had to say before she gave forth her segment of it. Moreover, by singing with other Marschallins she had beyond a doubt learned (unconsciously, of course—singers cannot "learn" one part while singing another) everything they knew how to give. Whatever the contributing causes, her Marschallin was already, on May 23, 1924, a finished work of art, or so we thought —defined on the edges, integrated within, perfect as an example of the eighteenth-century spirit which the Hofmannsthal-Strauss work tried to convey, and perfect also as an example of the twentieth-century musical and dramatic style in which it was conveyed. She was beautiful to behold and the expressivity of her voice has never been surpassed in anything else. Under these circumstances it is not at all surprising that she awoke the next morning to find herself famous.

Ours was the continuing surprise, however, because her Marschallin grew more beautiful every year for a very long time, with greater subtleties and depths of feeling coming in as time made the part ever more poignantly her own. During the thirty years and more since her first Marschallin in London, nobody else has even distantly adumbrated the meaning she gave the part. It is doubtful if any performance of our own time (that is, since Garden and Chaliapin) has been so appreciated throughout the world. Here is what our sober-sided friend, Grove's *Dictionary*, has to say of it: "The lyric stage of the time knew no performance more admirably accomplished; it seemed to embody a civilization, the pride and elegance of old Vienna, its voluptuousness, chastened by good manners, its doomed beauty."

To me at twenty-four it was a revelation, and I do not know how
often I went back to it again. The first performance is the one of
which the impression is vivid, unmistakable. I used to go to Covent
Garden alone, with a frequency only less than that of my first seasons
in Chicago and New York, and sit wherever I could. This depended
upon what was left, what I could afford, and whether there were
any press seats unclaimed by higher priorities. (I was on an "American press" list there—not a high priority.) I sat in more or less every
part of the house at one time or another and grew to love it, with its
natural dignity of form and its fine acoustical properties, as much as
any opera house I ever knew. Strangers, especially from the continent of Europe, were often heard to wonder why Covent Garden
was built on the edge of the vegetable market, near the Bow Street
Police Station, and generally speaking, in a quarter which was prevented only by some monumental architecture from being a slum.
(Covent Garden, Drury Lane and the Lyceum all were there before
the vegetable market came, of course.) I not only didn't object to the
combination of the opera and the vegetables, but actively enjoyed it,
as I do today, and relish a whiff of the true Covent Garden odor as I
go in or out. The big square occupied by the market will no doubt
someday be clear again and although it may be very fine—it was
called the "piazza" in the eighteenth century and still is by many
people—it will take away some of the peculiarity which is Covent
Garden.

Frida Leider was another revelation. She possessed a formidable
voice, which had great expressive beauty in soft or low passages as
well as ringing power. Her musical and dramatic intelligence was
such that she could paint a picture of Isolde's conflicting emotions,
weakness, shame and rising anger (in the first act narrative) by vocal
means, and accompany this by a presence and action in perfect
consonance with the music. She was not a slight figure and yet her
plastic gift with the arms, plus (I think) a skillful utilization of
various head postures, combined with a variety of movement which
must have been thought out or studied—not all staticly pacing, by
any means, but some moves of tigerish swiftness when needed—made
her stage representation of the difficult Wagner heroines unique.

It was her intelligence (no other word seems to fit the case) which
fused all of Mme. Leider's gifts, aptitudes and acquired knowledge

into one expressive instrument, but it was her temperament which unleashed the whirlwind at Wagner's command. (Examples: *"Rache!"* in Act I of *Tristan;* the swearing of the oath at the end of Act II, *Götterdämmerung.*) There was a quietude, almost beatitude, in some of her singing in low passages, such as *"Ruhe, ruhe du Gott!"* in the finale of *Götterdämmerung,* the like of which may never be heard again. And she possessed for moments of extraordinary brilliance some reserve of tone which came out with a splendor not merely vocal, but of the highest emotional content, as if torn from her by a situation quite beyond her control. Such were her war cries in *Die Walküre* during all the earlier parts of her career. It was with that wild music, which as she did it was really wild, that she made her American debut one Sunday afternoon some years later in the Chicago Opera, when (by wondrous good fortune) I was again in the audience.

This takes me far beyond anything that could have occurred to the twenty-four-year-old American who heard Leider for the first time at Covent Garden in 1924. It is still probably necessary to state the case plainly, regardless of chronology, because there exists a whole generation of operagoers for whom all Isoldes and Brünnhildes have been summed up in the astounding vocal phenomenon of Kirsten Flagstad. By and large, this superb singer, with one of the greatest voices ever known, was temperamentally unsuited to the representation of Wagner's heroines. The beauty of her voice carried all before it, but the music drama best suited to her aesthetic gift was one of her final studies, Gluck's *Alceste,* while in earlier years it was *Tannhäuser.*

This is not to suggest that Leider was an ideal Isolde. There is no such animal. There never will be one until some beautiful girl comes along with a mature voice of enormous range and power, coupled with the temperaments of a tigress and a dove. With this there must also be impeccable musicianship and style, a full musical memory, great talent for movement on the stage, an emotional range which few mature women have ever attained and an overwhelming sense of the relentless power of human destiny. If all this were ever put together in one woman, there would be an ideal Isolde.

No; Leider was only the best, but to be the best of such a distinguished company is in itself a mark of quality.

Das Rheingold, Siegfried and *Götterdämmerung* were all new to me in 1924. It would be quite impossible to say that they meant very much. I think the whole of the Ring at that time was a tremendous wash of sound in which I swam more or less the way a spaniel puppy does when you throw him into the water. I knew what I was hearing well enough—that is, the words and something about the music—for I used to be fairly conscientious in my preparation for hearing any new work. But I was not "ready" for Wagner in some way, and here too "the readiness is all." I could appreciate performances, and did, without in any really fundamental way yielding to the whole work or absorbing its multiple significance.

4

My employment came to an end in 1925 and I returned to New York for a brief stay followed by a journey into the Rif mountains of north Morocco to see Abdel-Krim (my second). That and a book took up the rest of the year, and it was not until 1926 that I was living in Paris again. By then I had more or less given up hope of hearing any satisfactory music, aside from individual recitals, in Paris. It was then that the Comique arranged a series of special performances of *Pelléas et Mélisande* in memory of Claude Debussy.

I believe there were six of them. (Mary Garden does not remember any more than I do how many, but thinks it might have been six.) My recollection is that I went to them all, but it is quite possible that I missed one or two. The cast was almost exactly that of the original performances prepared by Debussy himself. One exception was Pelléas, originally sung by Jean Périer, now dead; Roger Bourdin assumed the role. The others besides Garden were Dufranne as Golaud and Vieuille as Arkel, Mme. Bérat singing the Queen and André Messager conducting.

How can I expect anybody who was not there to believe me when I say that Garden's Mélisande in 1926, that is, twenty-four years after its first performance, was still an incomparable creation? It is a violation of common sense to say that any woman of her age could play the part of the strange little princess from far away, lost in the forest of the world. Such, however, was the case. She not only played it, but gave it a shimmer of meaning not to be discerned in the library, where too often Maeterlinck's work is (as he once told me himself) *"imbécile."* The character was composed from start to finish by some light not of this world. Garden herself calls it *"irréel,"* and that is true enough, too, but it was also real with the sometimes frightening reality which transcends the real. As was the case with Chaliapin's Boris and Lehmann's Marschallin, this impersonation (if such it was) carried such power of truth that no other Mélisande could do more than sing the notes and walk through the action afterwards. It is within the province of such sovereign interpretations as this not only to illumine an entire masterpiece but to withdraw it, so to speak, from circulation—to make it inaccessible thereafter. We go to *Boris, Pelléas* and *Der Rosenkavalier* because we like their music (I have been to all three in the past year), not because we expect anything comparable to Chaliapin, Garden and Lehmann. The mystery seems to be primarily one in the composition itself. Each of these works is composed around one character of an irresistible emotional dominion over the spectator, and yet opera singers who can exercise such a dominion are the rarest in the theatre. Therefore, when one is found, by any miracle, the creator and the creation are one, and it may even seem that the work itself was composed to suit the peculiar talent, the special personality, of the artist thus born to express it.

As we know, Mussorgsky, Debussy and Strauss did not compose their masterpieces with any such singer in mind, and since in each case the highest part of the creation was (must have been) unconscious, probably none of them realized the rarity of the gifts for which they called. Debussy worked for twelve years on *Pelléas* and, since he was not a theatregoer, he had never seen or heard of Mary Garden until after the work had been accepted for production at the Comique. It was then that he saw, by chance, a photograph in Carré's office and said with assurance: *"Voilà ma Mélisande."* The months of daily work—at first alone with Debussy at the piano, then with the other characters, then with orchestra—may have formed the style, which they unquestionably did: the style was new and had to be made *ab ovo.* But before the style could be brought into existence, there had to be the personality suited to Mélisande and the voice capable of her strange utterance.

To a considerable extent the strangeness was not only in Garden's voice, otherworldly though it was in this part. It came also from her accent in French, which, although wonderfully clear and comprehensible, was never that of a Frenchwoman. The little wanderer from afar should not, of course, pronounce her words in any accent which has the associations of every day. That is, she should not speak like the lady at the cash desk outside or like the *ouvreuse* who shows you to your seat; she must not have the cutglass elegance of the Comédie Française or the gutturals of the boulevard; she comes from *"loin d'ici"* and she must sound like it. No Frenchwoman I ever heard attempt it has been able to do more than intone her words in this part: with the accent of Paris it is quite impossible to suggest what Mélisande is.

Garden's movements were, even in the absence of movement, essential to the creation and had nothing whatever to do with the semaphore style of "grand opera." She hardly moved her hands and arms for long stretches of the action: her head was usually bowed in submission, but when it moved it had something to contribute to the composition. Her body seemed completely merged into the flow of the music drama, almost as if it had been part of the orchestra. The voice had the pallor of the tomb at times; it was difficult to understand how such misty rose-gray and blue-gray notes could spin out from a human throat. It was *irréel*, indeed, and the intention of the composer must in this case have been fulfilled as hardly ever before in the history of music.

There was one thing at the Grand Opéra which did engage attention and even respect at this time, the first production there of *Le Chevalier à la Rose*. Gutheil-Schöder had come from Vienna to advise on style; Philippe Gaubert conducted an augmented orchestra; the Opéra put its best performers into the parts; the décor and dresses were expensive; there had been many rehearsals. The result, although curiously thin and cold, had its own coherence and value. *Il Cavaliere della Rosa,* which I saw at the Scala in Milan a little later, was far warmer and more spirited, but neither one was, to my mind, *Der Rosenkavalier.* I went to the *"première"* at the Opéra, was delighted within reasonable limits, and arose the next morning to read a monstrous outburst of abuse from the French critics. They called the work itself *"Schlag,"* found nothing in it to praise and devoted an immense amount of space to saying that the waltzes were an anachronism—such was the general line. Along with this was a complaint that so much time and money should have been spent on a German opera while French works of value went unheard. What works? Echo.

Music criticism in Paris was even worse than elsewhere in the 1920's because, along with all the customary vices of the trade (arising mostly, I have always thought, from power—the sense of power, the abuse of power, the frightful bossiness of petty people), it had a poisonous dose of nationalism in all its members. Nationalism in any art, especially in music, is a form of locomotor ataxia. The critics of Paris, unworthy successors to Berlioz and Debussy, were incapable of judging work on its own terms, because this wholly extraneous criterion intruded upon them every time.

After a long journey in 1927—actually around the world; I suppose that may be called long—I was in Berlin a good deal, off and on, during the last part of that year and parts of the next two. It was a very good time to be in Berlin, actually, as Bruno Walter had the opera at Charlottenburg and had made of it one of the most interesting in existence. The Wagner works could be heard in Berlin better than anywhere else and I heard them; they were creeping up on me. Leider's Isolde was better even than in London, and the Philharmonic in Berlin was quite conceivably the best then to be heard anywhere. Also in Berlin—at the Charlottenburg house—I heard and saw a stunning production of *Le Prophète* with Sigrid Onegin, a richly gifted contralto, as Fidès and Lauritz Melchior as John of Leyden. In some parts of the work, particularly in the Coronation Scene, I was able to see what Meyerbeer must have represented in theatrical effectiveness to his own age, but it aroused little beyond a historic interest in me and I have never gone to hear another work by this composer.

Rome, at some point toward the end of the 1920's, provided the first *Carmen* I ever saw which was frankly performed for its value as vocal music. That is, of course, one perfectly comprehensible way of performing any opera, although as a rule both the composer and the audience would disagree. In this case the great contralto Gabriella Besanzoni, who had a voice like very rich black brass, could not possibly have made her way through all the writhing, leaping, dancing, prancing movements which are involved in the enactment of the part nowadays. She was content to wear the costumes, to move very little, to act with her face occasionally and to present the essence of the drama with the voice. When Carmen herself is thus portrayed, as I saw her again later in Berlin, all others on the stage have to fall into a kindred style or the work is ruined.

My principal preoccupations even at this time, of course, took me far from the opera house. Such journeys as that to Persia (1926), China (1927) and Palestine (1929) were not only far afield geographically but were undertaken because of interests which superseded any concern with art or literature. At a time when I could have named you a perfect cast of *Carmen*, with reasons for each choice—when I was a college freshman, for example—I barely knew that the Russian Revolution had just taken place. Journalism as a way of living (that is, both means of livelihood and habit of life, including the necessary interests as well) had changed all that. I could be absent many months at a time from the music-making of great cities, and although I missed it, truly enough, the deprivation did not afflict me unduly. It is worth observing, just the same, that I lost no time getting to a concert hall or an opera house on each of my numerous returns to Paris, Berlin or any of the other cities of the West. On coming back to Paris from Russia in 1927, as a case in point, one of my first acts was to go and hear Stravinsky conduct *Le Sacre du Printemps* at the Salle Pleyel (then new). Perhaps there was some connection.

The notable performances of the time, the high lights, the glittering crests of many waves, stick in the memory without connection. I must have visited Chicago two or three times between 1927 and 1930, for there are strong recollections of several distinct high lights there. Leider's debut in the 1928-29 season I have already mentioned, and on a subsequent visit there was the first really fine *Don Giovanni* of my experience. In the *Don Giovanni* were Leider as Donna Anna and Tito Schipa (the best I ever heard) as Don Ottavio, with Vanni-Marcoux in the title part. He was one of the most skillful and accomplished of stage artists, with rather less sensuosity of voice and rather more style than we usually get in the part.

Alexander Kipnis, whom I heard often afterwards in Europe and America, was new to me then: he also sang a beautiful Arkel in *Pelléas et Mélisande* with Vanni-Marcoux as a memorable Golaud.

This performance in Chicago was the last I was ever to hear from Mary Garden. She was at the terminus, but her Mélisande retained its unearthly beauty and its ageless, timeless irreality to the end.

In New York there was no such interest either in repertoire or in artists, but Puccini and Verdi were in their usual full glory and Wagner had been for some years restored to the list with German artists and in the original language. Schorr was in New York now but most of the best German artists were yet to come. In default of Leider—who did not make her Metropolitan debut until 1933—the Isolde and Brünnhilde were entrusted to several singers of lesser caliber, Mme. Larsen-Todsen from Stockholm and Mme. Kappel from Munich among them. It did seem a little strange that Gatti-Casazza should have been so slow to get the best singers available for Wagner, but such was the case. Under these circumstances, although I heard a good deal at the Metropolitan, coming and going, it is not surprising that the routine Italian works seemed the best. They had the benefit of Tullio Serafin's work as conductor and of numerous remarkable singers. Gigli and Lauri-Volpi were among the tenors, Jeritza and Scotti were still flourishing in *Tosca,* Elisabeth Rethberg sang a good many Italian works as well as her native German; and all was worth hearing for an opera fanatic, even though the best that could be said of it was that it kept a good average. Far from average, however, was Rosa Ponselle, whose performance in *Norma* from 1927 onwards was probably the best thing the Metropolitan had to offer for several years. Hers was a wonderfully smooth voice by now, smooth as very thick silky velvet all the way from the top to the bottom, no breaks and no alterations of quality either by reason of breathing or extreme notes at either end. She had in her throat a more evenly integrated homogeneous voice than any other that easily comes to mind and it was also of ravishing beauty as sheer sound. The demerit of her performances, or at least the aspect of them that may be said to have kept her from true greatness, was an absence of dramatic urgency. All the desperate situations and horrendous tragedies to which the heroines of Italian opera are subjected could not wring from her anything less (or more) than wonderfully beautiful singing. She never imperiled her vocal chords by a cry of desperation. The absence of urgency in her operatic emotion, by the way, was never felt in New York so far as I know, except by me, and it is no doubt heresy to mention it. I might not have felt the lack myself if I had not been initiated to this kind of singing (the *Norma* and *Il Trovatore* kind) by Rosa Raisa. One thing nobody ever accused Raisa of lacking was dramatic urgency.

These were the exhibitions, here and there and the next place, which constituted my experience of opera toward the end of the 1920's and the beginning of the 1930's. There were others of less note, and there were probably some of more note in Rome (where I went steadily to opera in 1930) which have now faded from recollection. There was one very astonishing exhibition in one of those years, I forget which, by Fyodr Chaliapin. He put on a show with some Russian colleagues—perhaps a benefit?—in which he sang music we could not normally hear him sing in any country. It was in a London theatre with a London orchestra conducted by Albert Coates, who was himself almost a Russian. The first part was the inn scene from *Boris* with Chaliapin singing the part of the drunken monk, Varlaam. How he rolled about and enjoyed himself! He also hurled some superb bass tones at us in the Kazansky song, just to prove that he could still do it. This was followed by Rimsky-Korsakoff's one-act opera, *Mozart and Salieri,* a musical pastiche for the most part, in which Chaliapin as Salieri had a welcome opportunity to characterize the sinister old villain who was devoured with jealousy of the young genius. This view of Salieri's character is apparently just as false as the legend that he poisoned Mozart. No matter: it gave Chaliapin a field day and his audience a memorable evening in the theatre. Actually I remember his Varlaam with sharp clarity, his Salieri somewhat less, while I have forgotten his two Mephistopheles characterizations (Gounod and Boito) although I know I heard them both. In London, too, there was Lehmann's Marschallin to be seen every May or June, although not always with that first unapproachable cast. In Salzburg in the summer of 1930 I heard a different Marschallin—Mme. Viorica Ursuleac, which means Fioritza Ursuleatz if she spelled it phonetically—and by that alone the rarity of Lehmann's achievement could have been framed and lighted.

Coming back from Jerusalem in the autumn of 1929 I stopped for a week or two in Vienna and heard, among other things, *Così fan Tutte* and *Die Entführung aus dem Serail,* both for the first time. Clemens Krauss had just become general director of the Vienna

Opera that year, and *Così fan Tutte* was one of his new productions (I think his first). I loved it at first sight or sound. *Die Entführung* was almost equally a delight, and at some moments—with Schumann singing Blondchen—even more. I thought then that Mozart could never be played anywhere so well as in Vienna or Salzburg. It is a tenable opinion at any time, but his music yields itself so flexibly to treatment by any qualified group of singers and musicians that I am not so sure now. I have heard excellent Mozart in Italy, England, America and even in France; I have heard good amateur performances. Bernard Shaw once made a complicated journey by bus, underground and other means to the Isle of Dogs, in the Thames River at the thither extremity of the East End, to hear *Die Zauberflöte* performed by a cast of boys and girls from a social settlement under the direction of their clergyman; he told me it was excellent. So after all, Vienna and Salzburg can claim no real monopoly, although what they do is treasurable.

The catalogue of these performances of yesteryear may recall certain kinds of departed magic, but it is not for that reason that I adduce it. We all have some nostalgia for artists who can no longer be seen or heard, and yet—although no two genuine artists could be alike—I am robustly sure that there are just as good fish in the sea as ever came out of it. The precise combinations which went into Chaliapin's Boris, Garden's Mélisande, Lehmann's Marschallin, may never come together again—it would be in defiance of reason if they did—but something else there will be, we may be sure. I have not mentioned all these performances out of my own nostalgia or to evoke it in others, but merely to show the quantity and quality of experience which followed upon the simple gluttony of my early years as a listener: that is, in view of development and conclusion, if one may be reached, to tell the tale of how more or less every variety of dramatic music acceptable to the age was poured into my ears, year after year, to form some kind of corpus of musical thought for the rest of the journey.

5

In the years between 1927 and 1935 the principal center of musical excitement in New York was not the Metropolitan at all. It seldom is. It was the Philharmonic-Symphony Society of New York, with Toscanini conducting it.

He had appeared there as guest conductor in 1926 and then as a regular conductor in the next season, to remain with the orchestra until the end of the season of 1936. At first he shared the season in New York with Mengelberg and his own time between that orchestra and the Scala in Milan. In 1929 he severed his connection with the Scala altogether to devote himself to the Philharmonic throughout the season; Mengelberg then departed.

Of Toscanini there is nothing left to say in general; no conductor has been so thoroughly discussed in print. In particular I can still say that he came nearer perfection than any artist of whom I have acquaintance: to me, very often, he achieved perfection. He would of course deny this. It was characteristic of his extraordinary genius that he could never be quite satisfied, although (like any public performer above the grade of a trained flea) he knew to a certainty when he had achieved good results. Perfection was his aim, his goal, or at the very least the direction in which he had striven since the beginning of his musical life. He would be incapable of conceding that he ever attained it, but that effort itself ennobled a whole period of public performance in many countries. Wherever he went, whatever orchestra he conducted, the results were very nearly the same, allowing for some national differences (lovely woodwinds and pale strings in Paris, exquisite mellow strings and brass in Vienna and Berlin, a dryness that was transformed into clarity in London, etc., etc.). In New York he had a largely international orchestra of, perhaps, predominantly central European origin. It made little difference what his orchestra was so long as it could play the music: he did the rest, extracted all the rest out of them and thus gave back what they gave a thousandfold.

There were some awe-inspiring revelations from Toscanini in the late 1920's and early 1930's. They may not have been revelations to everybody who heard them, although I suspect they were. To me they were like the opening of the heavenly gates, or at least some golden gates into a region hitherto unknown. The Third and Seventh Symphonies of Beethoven and the First of Brahms were among these experiences—works known to me for at least ten years, that is, since my first acquaintance with such music, but now heard as if anew in their *himmelstürmendes* entirety.

It became the custom for the musical journalism of the day in New York, as in Vienna and London, to attribute at least part of Toscanini's "secret," that is, the secret of his power, to the fact that he played all music exactly as it was written. This, of course, is no explanation at all. It is possible at any moment to find a number of conductors who do the same thing; Germany abounds in them; but fidelity to the score does not give them the same electromagnetic command over a hundred and ten musicians and also, I dare to say it, over a great part of the audience. To say that fidelity to the composition explains Toscanini is like saying that good materials make good cooking. It is partly true but it leaves out the most important element, which is genius. I lived through the whole latter end of the Toscanini epic, for nearly thirty years (to 1955), right to that final rehearsal in Carnegie Hall when he broke down in fury (in the *Tannhäuser Bacchanale*) and went home. In all that time I never heard him get out of any orchestra less than an *augmentation* of their natural skills and a *better* tone than they normally possessed. He got from each orchestra not only its best, but that something extra which, nine times out of ten, it did not even know it was giving. The "secret," therefore, was not Toscanini's. No doubt he would have said that he studied hard, was faithful to the precise markings in every score, and rehearsed thoroughly when he rehearsed. He also had a memory. The something extra, the inexplicable something which I have called electromagnetic, was not for him or anybody else to explain but it was there. Any musician who ever played under his baton will tell you the same.

If these first years of Toscanini concerts opened the golden gates, as I think they did, there were a few other phenomena of the day which at least kept them from being clanged shut again. These were works performed as a rule (in New York anyhow) either during Holy Week or at Easter. They included the B Minor Mass in a church on Fifth Avenue (St. Thomas'?—I am not sure), not a perfect performance at all but a good one and my first; they included *The Messiah* at Carnegie Hall; and best and rarest, the *St. John Passion* as given by the Society of Friends of Music every year in the

Town Hall. Of these annual events I am sure I was lucky enough to hear the *St. John Passion* three times, through the hazard of being in New York in three successive springs. Elisabeth Rethberg, singing like an angel, Friedrich Schorr and Mme. Matzenauer in full voice and authority, Artur Bodanzky conducting as he never did elsewhere, gave these rites of spring everything to make them beautiful and memorable. Nowadays when all music can be heard at will, by the use of the gramophone, it is difficult for a new generation even to think how avidly we absorbed such rarely given masterpieces only twenty-odd years ago, and how much one such performance meant. Now I can play the *St. John Passion* to myself whenever I please, if I happen to be at home, but it is not quite the same thing.

A certain maturity may have been quite insensibly coming over my musical taste for some years past, making some works and some kinds of works more generally interesting than others, more productive of the reward we all seek. I do not think there was any volition in the matter, scarcely even any consciousness, merely a natural progression. There came a time when I seldom or never went near repertoire performances of opera any more. I never forgot them; I can go to them again now, when I am in the mood; great stretches of their words and music are solidly embedded in my memory and will never be dislodged. I often wish they could be, for sometimes one single phrase will arise in my tune-beset head and afflict me sleeping and waking, even though it may come from an opera I have not heard for fifteen years. It was toward the end of the 1920's that I ceased, not abruptly, but gradually and insensibly, to be the undiscriminating fanatic for all opera that I had been since my freshman days.

This coincided with the years of my first Toscanini concerts, the years of Beethoven and the *St. John Passion*. After all, time itself carries out some of these operations on the human consciousness. Moreover, all the life experience which had been crowded into these years, outside of music, must have had a decisive effect on the cortical convolutions or whatever it is that makes us think. China and Russia had given me a shaking-up; in Moscow I had endured a very great bereavement at the end of 1927. There had been black hours and days and weeks. I could no longer bring to the concert hall or the opera house the ingenuous eagerness of my earliest youth or derive youth's sensuous delight from every honeyed sound. Some other demand had crept in; I shall make an attempt to see what it was, in due course; but whatever it was, it brought music into a much more direct relation to the life of the mind with all its frustrations and occasional victories. *Tosca* and *Faust* had remarkably little to say to the questioning mind or the incomplete heart wherein the *St. John Passion* had evoked an echo. That is probably why opera of the repertoire ceased to exist for me during so many years—*Butterfly, Manon, La Bohème* and all the rest of them—until another age could take them back into affection without asking too much of them. The universality of music surpasses all understanding, and I know that the pleasures it can give in their own modes to the Chinese and Hindus are forever beyond me. Within that which is accessible to me, the Western musical art forms of about three hundred years, my way turned at about this time toward music which, either explicitly (as in Beethoven and Wagner) or implicitly (as in Mozart) concerned itself with man's fatal dialogue, that which goes on either with himself or with some higher and larger entity to which he feels himself attached in a manner beyond his own comprehension. It may be in the Mozart A Minor Quintet in a few phrases or the Seventh Symphony in a mighty storm, but it is there. I was turning toward that music not in any practical sense, not as we try a remedy or inspect a horse, but because the unknown permutations of my own life elements had brought me to this place at a time neither given nor appointed, but simply evolved. We "dichotomize the Kosmos," says William James, each in a different place, and as the place changes in time, so must its content, what it takes in and what it leaves out. "I" may *seem* to be a constant but "me" is not. So it goes on, the pure and the empirical ego in uneasy harness, moving through time as if magnetized in the direction of that force to which music (like the trees, the river and the stars) owes its being. The force itself may be nameless and forever unknown, but by its effect we at least can tell that it has light to shed upon what concerns us most, the splendor and misery of the human soul.

4 : An Imperfect Wagnerite

There was a story told in the days when Wagner was still a subject of great argument, and it seems to me that the person quoted was a celebrated French artist or man of letters: it was a favorite dictum of my father-in-law, Sir Johnston Forbes-Robertson, whose early years were spent in the midst of the late-Wagnerian epoch. It seems that a heated dispute over Wagner's work was in progress when the aforesaid man of letters quelled all disorder by remarking: *"Ah, Wagner? Il a de jolis moments, vous savez, mais de bien mauvais quarts d'heures."*

Most of us have made our first acquaintance with the music dramas of Wagner in precisely that spirit: "pretty moments" to enjoy, "bad quarter-hours" to deplore. And for many the "bad quarter-hours" have been half or whole hours. It was absolutely inseparable from Wagner's theoretical basis that the "endless song" of his orchestra, forever weaving and reweaving the same strands of sound, should seem at first almost infinitely repetitious and therefore unendurable. Only when the extraordinary variety of the repetitions—apparently incessant changes on the same themes—can penetrate through the flood of tone that assails our ears, and only when our inner listening

apparatus distinguishes the dramatic structure of the music enough
to perceive it as a new kind of tragedy, are we able to date the beginnings of Wagnerism in our own consciousness.

It was certainly not very early with me. The little I heard of the
master's work up to 1924 was not likely to bring about such a
result. Bruno Walter's *Tristan und Isolde* at Covent Garden in 1924
with Frida Leider was the first true experience, even in the simplest aural sense, of that music for me. It left a glow of excitement
which covered a good many other and lesser *Tristan* performances
later on, but it was not the opening of a new form of musical experience, but rather the culmination of an old one. *Tristan,* in a word,
was "opera." It was opera on a height unknown to me before, but I
do not believe it seemed for a very long time to be anything else. It
had its *"jolis moments"* and its *"mauvais quarts d'heures,"* the latter
a form of patient waiting for the former. Of course I did not hear it
all. I probably heard a good deal less than half of it and most of that
merely on the surface of the composition, never all the way down
through the orchestra. I doubt very much if I can hear all of it at once
even now, although surely more (far more) than I once did.

In my own mind I do not question the fact that an increasing
familiarity with the symphony orchestra and even a growing awareness of musical resource in all its parts—a pushing-out of the general frontier of music—had much to do with the growth of Wagnerism. I was hearing a great deal of music in the years which led into
Wagner, and much of it was of an anti-Wagnerian cast, historically
speaking—Brahms, for example. The first symphony recording I
ever possessed, complete, was the Brahms Third on an innumerable
collection of disks which had to be changed one by one, since the
machine on which I played them was small and antiquated. However, I also had an Eichendorff score of the work, and in the studio
flat where I lived in 1929 the Brahms Third and the reduced score
were worked to the point of extinction. I still think this symphony is
probably the most familiar of all to me because of those months
when it was the only one at hand, the daily nutriment. Later on
when I had the entire symphonic repertoire to choose from, with a
minimum of effort—long-playing records automatically changed—I
doubt if any one of them, even the Beethoven Seventh, was required to go through such constant repetition, or (by means of the

score) such detailed scrutiny. My respect for the orchestra of Brahms, so restrained and powerful, was well founded then and never shaken thereafter by the vicissitudes of taste, although I did doubt the "originality" of that master as a creator. ("Originality" seems more necessary to us at some times than at others, but it can hardly take the place of every other gift, as we all know by now.)

What I am saying here, that an increase in my knowledge of the orchestra and of all music led me into Wagnerism, is of course contrary to the case made by Nietzsche and, following him, large numbers of other anti-Wagnerites. They maintained (and still do) that the Wagnerian enthusiasm is, at its most characteristic, felt by the nonmusical, and is first and foremost an emotional state resulting from a kind of theatrical hypnosis. In *Der Fall Wagner* (*The Case of Wagner*), Nietzsche says: "Just look at these youthlets—all benumbed, pale, breathless! They are Wagnerites: they know nothing about music—and yet Wagner gets the mastery of them."

This may indeed be true. I am quite willing even now to concede that I know nothing about music in the sense that Nietzsche did. I should be incapable of composing the simplest fugal exercise. All I do say is that in the process of my own musical pilgrimage the turn to Wagner came after I began to know the orchestra (and all other music) more thoroughly than before, to hear it more acutely and at the same time more comprehensively than before. In the humble sphere of the listener (and where would any composer be without us?) Wagner did with me (and does with many others) correspond to, result from and also partially bring about a stage of maturity. I do not say absolute or final maturity, because I am not acquainted with any meaning for the phrase, but when I survey the field, I have no doubt that it can be called maturity with respect to what preceded and even to what follows, if anything does follow.

London and Berlin began the process; the Metropolitan in New York carried it on to the requisite stage of absorption in which I might have been, as I certainly for some years thought I was, a "Wagnerite." I use the expression not in the extreme sense of those devotees who surrounded Wagner in his last years. They accepted his doctrine in full—that is, the idea that Western culture and the soul of mankind could be and would be regenerated through art, the combination of all the arts in the "music of the future." No: such

ideas as that were always too German for me. But I did become a
Wagnerite in the more ordinary Anglo-Saxon sense of finding in the
Wagner music dramas a greater extension of consciousness, enhancement of being, than in any other works of music or the theatre.
It reached the point, too, at which it virtually excluded all other
works (*Pelléas, Boris* and *Der Rosenkavalier* excepted), so that I actually for some years heard and saw practically nothing but the later
works of Wagner.

Familiarity increased the pace of this absorption—increase of appetite that grows by what it feeds on—but there were other conducive circumstances.

The actual performances greatly increased in beauty, emotional
tension and musico-dramatic values of every kind after Frida Leider
came to the Metropolitan (1933). With Leider, Olczewska, Melchior,
Schorr, and a succession of good basso singers, it was possible to put
Wagner on the stage more acceptably than ever before, even though
the conductor, Artur Bodanzky, was not actually one of the most inspired. This great increase of Wagnerian excitement—not confined
to me by any means: the New York public seemed to feel it in the
same degree—came just when I was, in time and experience, ready
for it. I had heard all these works often by then, although not so
well presented, and they were already beginning to crowd out other
works from my own attention.

There were some purely "literary" reasons for it, too. That should
be added in haste because all who oppose Wagner's work and ideas
say, with an air of truth, that the Wagner enthusiasm is "literary"
even more than musical. Whether this is so or not can hardly be determined until some psychologist comes along with enough serious
knowledge of poetry and music to make a proper analysis. The ideas
of Wagner himself and of many who wrote about him have certainly
invaded a great part of Western literature and art. It would not have
been possible to grow up in this century without running into them:
and certainly no voracious reader, such as I, could live long nowadays without getting, willy-nilly, an exposure to Wagnerian concepts.
Modern novels are full of them: the "stream of consciousness" itself, William James' most fruitful notion in psychology, became
sheer Wagnerism when it was translated into terms of creative aesthetic. And as for books *about* Wagner and his works—there is no end

of them, and I had no doubt read a large number during the 1920's and early 1930's.

Even so, the literary experience which most directly led into Wagner was, I think, *A la Recherche du Temps Perdu*. This is not merely because Proust was a Wagnerite. He explicitly was, of course, and made his testament to that effect more than once. (He said, for example, that *Tristan und Isolde* was *"la plus prodigieuse attente de félicité qui ait jamais rempli l'âme humaine."*) His opinions, however, are nowhere near so powerful as his extraordinary work, which is in itself composed in "endless melody" and that unceasing variation upon themes or motives which was Wagner's own system. The subject matter and the instrument are very different, but aesthetically speaking the method is the same. It so happens that I spent a very long time just about then (1930? 1931?) reading Marcel Proust's novel from beginning to end. It superseded the world of every day for many, many months, so that to put it down was to subject my consciousness to a sudden and almost painful readjustment into its actual environment. I had read sections of the work before—*Le Côté de Guermantes* was presented to me on my twentieth birthday by somebody in Chicago who did not realize that it should have been preceded by *Swann:* I read *Guermantes* first, went back to *Swann,* and then dabbled at the others through the years. At the end of the 1920's I read it all through from the beginning to that wonderful end, the matchless final volume which I had never read before. Even though central portions of the book (especially in *Albertine disparue*) were left unfinished and contain great chunks of prose about one character repeated verbatim about another later on—even though there were shocks of an almost indefensible kind, such as the final demolition of Saint-Loup's character after volumes of construction lavished upon it so as to make it solidly believed— and even though there was a strong odor of the sickroom over great stretches of the work in the middle, it seems to me today, as it did in 1930, a masterpiece of the primary order. Nothing by any contemporary writer had its validity of creation and nothing since then has approached it.

This masterpiece, possessing its reader as few ever do, is so akin to the essence of Wagner's composition that the progression from one to the other—given a strong musical bias to begin with—is as natural as the passage of time. I can imagine a person not given to music reading Proust and stopping at that, or a person not given to literature absorbing Wagner's music dramas and stopping at that. What I cannot imagine is any kind of person who, being commanded by a love of both literature and music, could survive one of these experiences without being, and as it were insensibly, drawn into the other.

To my mind there can be no doubt that Proust knew it—that he deliberately composed in this system of "endless melody" and interwoven leading motives (*Leitmotive*). He even says so. But beyond his deliberate intention there is also the unconscious power in his own mind, pervading it throughout, of all the related ideas which he had absorbed from various sources, amalgamated, developed, modified and extended until they were in fact conterminous with his mind and hardly to be distinguished from it. These ideas—the ceaseless flux of experience, the simultaneity of past, present and future in the consciousness, the associations and choices and decisions and turning points in the flow—were natural to him, no doubt, but they also came from *L'Evolution créatrice* of his cousin, Henri Bergson, and from other works, as well as innumerable conversations with that luminous animator. Through Bergson it goes back, then, to William James, whose *Principles of Psychology* (1890) presented for the first time the reasoned theory of consciousness as a continuity, and of states of consciousness as being both "transitive" and "substantive." In this work, which Bergson accepted with joy as grist to his own mill, the chapter called "The Stream of Consciousness" had a most fructifying influence on all modern psychology and thought in general, with consequences in literature (particularly novels and poetry) which James could not even have imagined. Proust was one of the progeny, by a sequence of strange alliances in his immediate ancestry: the aesthetic of Wagner, the ideas of Bergson and William James, not so different in essence after all, were the highly important elements in the full orchestra which Proust conducted through *A la Recherche du Temps Perdu*.

2

The Wagner to which I increasingly yielded from about 1930 was, of course, the later Wagner—namely, *Tristan und Isolde, Die Meis-*

tersinger and *Der Ring des Nibelungen*. You can find earlier proof of Wagner's way in *Lohengrin* and *Tannhäuser,* even in *Der Fliegende Holländer,* for that matter; but if he had stopped with *Lohengrin* he would never have exercised the dominion he did over successive generations in Western culture. His own original and distinctive methods, technically speaking, his power of emotional evocation and his theatrical hypnosis (if we rate it no higher than that) all grew together into the *Ring, Tristan* and the *Meistersinger,* by a really surprising simultaneity of all parts at once. (Let us leave *Parsifal* aside for the moment: it is a special case.)

The world of gods and heroes into which this late Wagner takes us is as remote as anything can be from our ordinary lives. All the passions are there, greed, jealousy and hatred, as well as love and compassion, but they are pushed up into a dimension altogether larger than life and not so much abstracted from as magnified out of what we all experience. This gigantism of the whole is what repels many from Wagner: "It is easier to be Titanic," says Nietzsche, "than to be beautiful." And precisely the gigantism, the overscale drawing and the inflation of content which inevitably accompanies it, did eventually check my Wagnerian raptures and reduce to moderation the wild surrender of my first full Wagner years. In 1931, and on until at least about 1937, there did not appear to me to be any element of exaggeration, overemphasis or rhetoric, any false glory or vulgar strut, anywhere at all in the great works I loved. I was well aware of the opinions of others, but I did not share them and I thought they came very largely from a dislike of greatness. It is still my fixed opinion that many of those whose notion of music is governed by ancient instruments and seventeenth-century form are afraid of greatness, and in some cases I know it to be true. In the years when I was new to Wagner's greatness, I was also completely impervious to all those faults (in the works—not in the man—I always knew the man to be faulty) which afterwards so clearly appeared.

In the first place the outsized or oversized subjects of the music dramas made every emotion more powerful than it could have been in lesser situations or with lesser effigies. If the boy and girl in Benjamin Britten's *Turn of the Screw* had to sing over a fully developed Wagnerian orchestral crisis (to invent an extreme example) they would not only *not* be heard: they would also become ridiculous. The tempest would be too much for its own landscape. In the kind of wild opulence of emotion Wagner's genius threw out, only such grandiose personages and situations as he invented were at all appropriate. The "Titanic" was necessary because Wagner's peculiar genius was itself Titanic and rejoiced in its own enormous power. Therefore it never seemed at all strange to me that we moved into a world on a superlative or superhuman scale, where no one being was recognizable and no feeling was less than overwhelming. All of this seemed demanded by the nature of the creation. For this composer to have taken lesser themes, such as Verdi's in *La Traviata,* or Debussy's in *Pelléas,* would have been a strange perversion of his gift and would have produced a result difficult even to imagine.

Music and drama were overpoweringly effective in part through sheer dimension, but also by the beauty of development toward successive crises. I learned in time that an attack upon the nervous system was, must have been, integral to Wagner's scheme of things. I learned it from others—though at first, and for a long time, I thought the peculiar suffering to which I refer was mine alone. This is Nietzsche's "illness" which he considers to be the state produced by Wagner's music—the "physiological objection"—and of course in this, too, he was right.

The Wagner stage was at its best in those days when Bruno Walter had the Städtische Opernhaus in Charlottenburg and all the other houses (Covent Garden, the Metropolitan, the Vienna Opera, Chicago and even sometimes the Grand Opéra de Paris) borrowed his artists, his ideas and often his own services. Berlin was experimenting in the direction of simplicity—lights often taking the place of elaborate scenery—but in New York we still had the same sets for all the Wagner works: the sets which served every year from 1914 to 1948. They were old-fashioned, vintage Kautsky, but never bothered me much: I was able to see what I was supposed to see, whatever tattered daubs were placed on the stage. And from 1933 onwards we had at the Metropolitan for a few seasons (too few) the enriching and enlivening presence of Mme. Frida Leider.

I was not at Leider's Metropolitan debut for the excellent reason that I could not get in. She and Olczewska made their bows together as Isolde and Brangäne. By this time the trumpet tones at the top of

Leider's voice had more or less gone, so that certain extreme notes (such as the two C's in the second act of *Tristan*) were more sketched or indicated than really sung. There was nevertheless a wealth of meaning in everything this artist did in the two parts, Isolde and Brünnhilde, which were peculiarly her own. I had seen and admired what she did with other things (Donna Anna and the Marschallin, for example), which were not really her own, but Isolde and Brünnhilde were hers and there are no moderate ways of expressing how deeply she could move us in them, how absolute was her sway over our emotion during the high moments. I have been so shaken by her Isolde, again and again, that I could no longer stand up, and had to sit on the floor of the house in that area at the back where the standees go. Some of those *Tristan* performances left me very uncertain of my own surroundings—so dazed that it was physically difficult to get out of the crowd and into the cold, wet street where reality slowly returned. This physiological effect of Wagner is extremely well known and has often been described and analyzed, but it worked on me for a long time before I realized that it was a phenomenon of general and usual occurrence. A routine performance could never do it to me, but in the Leider-Melchior days no performance was ever simply routine. I think it is the historic fact, which other singers and conductors who worked with her can attest, that Leider was quite incapable of a routine performance. She could give a bad performance sometimes when things went wrong but never an ordinary one, because the mysteries of the human personality had endowed her with a temperament suited to the tempestuous music of *Tristan* and the *Ring*. With such gifts she was good or bad, she was often great, but she was never mediocre.

I went to the afternoon cycle of the *Ring* in those years—the annual subscription series of six Wagner works, uncut, including the four of the *Ring*. I was therefore present on an occasion which is remembered in the Metropolitan's history when Leider's voice failed to emerge from her throat during her scene with Wotan in the last act of *Die Walküre*. I was sitting in the middle of the sixth row, so close that every detail was impressed on my retina as well as my ears. I have never had such an instantaneous and overwhelming horror in my experience in the theatre. If she had not very quickly regained the power to sing, I believe I would have been sick there and then, helplessly. (These are Nietzsche's "physiological objections" to Wagner—we shall get to them again.)

She was on her knees before Wotan (Friedrich Schorr) with her noble head humbly bent and her left hand at her throat. She wore a flowing white dress and a red cloak over it—traditional; but I am telling it exactly as I see and hear it even now, more than twenty years later. She had reached the point where she had to sing the phrase *"War es so schmählich?"* She sang the first two words and notes—that is, *"War es"*—after which a strange, very small sound came out of her throat and no note followed. That weird small sound is quite impossible to describe and if I had not been sitting so close I could not have heard it; I suppose most of the three thousand people there present did not. The click (if it was a click) seemed like the electrocution, the murder, of the great voice. A sound then came from the wings on the word *"schmählich"* and continued the development for five notes more.

(We all learned afterwards that Dorothee Manski from the Berlin Opera, who was one of the Walküre and had been standing in the wings anxiously watching Leider, had thus saved the day by singing her notes.)

Leider kept her head down and I saw her shake it in a kind of fury. I have never had any opportunity to ask her about this but I imagine her sensations during those few seconds must have been as acute and tumultuous as any singer has ever felt. She had been singing the whole performance over a bad cold, so bad that she could not even speak. Now the voice itself, the very sense of her existence, refused its divine grace and there she was, on her knees, with the ruin of a great career in plain view before her. Such a concentrated ordeal seldom befalls an artist.

I felt, or imagined I felt, the struggle of her will to conquer her body. Then she threw back her really grand head and looked out beyond all the three thousand of us to some utter truth beyond us, opened her mouth with confidence, it seemed to me, and by some power (I could see her throat quivering) the voice was given again.

From then on to the end of the act Leider sang with everything an artist has to give, although the sacrifice of her voice must have been tragic. My friend Janet Fairbank, who was there, spoke as we went out to Heinrich Schlusnus, the fine lyric baritone of the Berlin

Opera (then singing in the Chicago Company), who had been backstage to kiss Leider's hand before the last act. Schlusnus, weeping
without restraint, said that even before the act began Leider had
been unable to utter a word in the spoken voice—even to an old
friend and colleague like himself. My own sense of awe and terror,
not from what Schlusnus told us but from what I had myself seen
and felt, lasted for many hours. (I can only compare it with the terror which overwhelmed me at Toscanini's last rehearsal twenty-one
years later.)

The week passed without any news of Leider's voice except that
she had suffered a bronchial attack of some kind and was under
treatment. The Metropolitan was extremely reluctant to make any
statement for two quite obvious reasons: first, the remaining Wagner performances might have depleted audiences if it were known
that Leider could not sing; second, it was not at all to the credit of
the Metropolitan that they had obliged this unique artist to risk an
irreplaceable voice by singing when she could not even speak.

We went to the *Siegfried* performance on the following Friday
afternoon in the hope that Leider had recovered, but were greeted
by announcements that Mme. Dorothee Manski would sing.

Manski was an invaluable soprano who knew everything in the
German repertoire and had sung everything at one time or another.
She had shown her mettle by singing the notes for Leider the week
before. She usually sang small or smallish parts, Gutrune being
about the biggest assignment she ever had, but Bodanzky could be
sure that she would deliver Wagner's music. And I must say she really
did. She was rather beautiful lying there on the couch of the long
sleep—a thin, blonde lady quite unlike the great Brünnhildes in
physique—and when she woke up she sang with spirit, intelligence
and meaning. Her voice, however, did not suit her to such very great
music, and it was an extraordinary demonstration (which is why it
has remained in my memory so distinctly) of how all the brains and
training in the world cannot take the place of a voice. Voice, too, of
a kind, Mme. Manski had. She proved it at the end of the opera by
singing the high C—a pure, clear note exactly on C and exactly on
the very middle of C, not a fraction above or below. It was the only
time I have ever heard that high C in an opera house with one exception: this time, and the exception also, were unmusical or anti-

musical experiences. Mme. Manski's high C was precise but had the effect of a surgical knife, a strange and clinical severance of the Wagnerian web. The other (the exception) was Mme. Anny Konetzni of the Vienna Opera, whose high C was an appalling scream. I never have heard the final high note of the *Siegfried* from anybody else, although it is reliably stated that Mme. Flagstad sang it during her first or second season in New York when I was not there. In all the *Siegfrieds* I heard her sing she took it an octave down—as did Leider and, of course, Traubel.

So, then, we went to the following week's offering in some trepidation: Mme. Manski was announced to sing the *Götterdämmerung* Brünnhilde, although I doubt very much if she could have survived the attempt. At all events her immolation was not required. When the curtain rose upon those lascivious (and incestuous) rocks, and the measures came for the emergence of Siegfried and Brünnhilde, it was Leider who came forth—Leider pouring forth tone of such warmth and expressiveness as one had seldom heard even from her.

She sang that whole *Götterdämmerung* on an ecstatic height even though, as I afterwards heard, she was not altogether recovered from her bronchial disturbance. It was one of the most thrilling performances I have seen or hope to see. The swearing of the oath on the sword reduced me to a single electric current, something near to dissolution into electricity, pure electricity; and the immolation turned the rest of the world to nothing. Such were the powers exerted by Wagner's music when Leider, Melchior and Schorr and Hofmann—all at their best—sang Brünnhilde, Siegfried, Gunter and Hagen.

I have told the story of Leider's loss and recovery of her voice at some length because it illustrates at so many points the characteristic Wagner experience—the "physiological objections" and the rest. It is worth recording, anyhow, because of its influence upon the subsequent career of an artist unequaled in our time. Leider was never restored to full vocal power after that. She never ceased to be the finest Isolde, the most sincere and moving Wagnerian soprano of the age, but the extremes were always a little beyond her physical means after the ordeal of the 1933 spring at the Metropolitan. She had two more seasons of unrivaled control over the

great opera houses as Isolde and Brünnhilde, and during that time—
perhaps in uneasiness about the future, for Hitler had come to
power just then and Mme. Leider was married to a Jewish physician
—she sang in all of them. Whereupon there came down the Nordic
avalanche, the vocal phenomenon of Kirsten Flagstad. By that time
Leider no longer cared to sing in New York, London or Paris. (She
was offered contracts simultaneously with Flagstad but refused
them.)

Certainly I, for one, could never have encompassed the meaning
of Wagner's later and greater work if it had not been for Leider. I
could never have learned their meanings from Flagstad; she did not
know them herself. I am not capable of learning theatre meaning
from the printed page; I have not been able to do it even with
Shakespeare. Theatre work must be absorbed in the theatre, and to
my mind Wagner's work is the most distinctly theatre work of any in
existence excepting Shakespeare alone.

3

Die Meistersinger stands in a separate place from the other mature
work of Wagner in that it makes no such assault as they do upon
the emotions. It is a mystery how the same phase of creative activity
could have produced both *Tristan* and *Die Meistersinger,* one all
flame and the other all good humor and humane acceptance. Everybody knows the facts of the case, but nobody can explain them. He
stopped working on the *Ring* right in the middle—that is, after
the first act of *Siegfried*—and for twelve solid years, so far as can be
known, he never put down another word or note upon that subject.
The state of his mind during those twelve years we are entitled to
imagine, but there is no record of it. Out of the twelve years his
product was *Tristan und Isolde* and *Die Meistersinger.*

I have already said enough to indicate that *Tristan und Isolde*
is for me one of the supreme aesthetic experiences of a lifetime. It
goes into the same category (for me—I speak only for myself) as
Michelangelo's work in the Sistine Chapel, Bach's in the *St. John
Passion* and the *B Minor Mass,* Mozart's in *Don Giovanni* and
Shakespeare's in *Macbeth.* These are the highest values life has to

offer in that mystery called art, the work of man which most approaches the work of God.

Now, if this is so, how about *Die Meistersinger?*

The surest thing there is about the shifting of taste and opinion on Wagner is that *Die Meistersinger* survives it all. I have known a great many persons of intellect and musicianship who can no longer endure to listen to any Wagner work except *Die Meistersinger*. I have also known persons of no intellect and no musicianship who say precisely the same thing. In effect, the mature Wagner seems to have provided in *Die Meistersinger* his one reliable insurance against neglect.

And if Wagner ever had needed insurance against neglect, this kind of work would have provided it.

Contemplating those two statements, is it possible to doubt that this was precisely his calculation? That is, if the two statements are true: if we observe the effect and also observe that the cause was wonderfully adjusted to the external result, it must occur to any of us that the wily old fox was playing a certainty. Whatever his tragic works might encounter in future, his "German comedy" could provide the anchor to windward.

This is not to deny the spontaneity or naturalness of Wagner's inspiration: it merely proves him to be a man of the theatre through and through. There seems to be a law in the theatre which compels such an effort at variation—as we see in Verdi's lifelong search for a subject of lyric comedy, ending at last in *Falstaff*.

Die Meistersinger's separateness from all the rest, its robust good humor and its inventiveness have kept it out of what we may call the "Wagner quarrel." True, Nietzsche made a case against it: it was "anarchical" in its attack upon all canons of taste or tradition in composition. Not many people nowadays could take that objection very seriously. Most audiences in our time refuse to bother their heads over the meaning of Beckmesser: the work is a lyric comedy and is so received by many who could not sit through the *Ring*. But I have my own reservations, just the same, and have had them all along. I think it is an elephantine comedy, overwritten both in length and depth, and seems to me a fine example of the way in which a great genius can impose its peculiarities upon material unsuited to it. Wagner's sense of humor, abundant in his letters, was not really a sense of comedy; it was verbal rather than intrinsic. The music of the apprentices in the *Meistersinger* shows the quality: delightful indeed, but humorous and verbal (orchestrally verbal) rather than comic. The one comic creation is Beckmesser, and here the opportunities for argument are many and tedious. All I want to say is that Beckmesser is seldom funny and never sad—two elements essential to comic creation—and if I have missed his meaning it is not for lack of attention on almost innumerable occasions.

What a different notion we should have of Wagner if *Die Meistersinger* were the only work of his known to us! It would be, I think, a false notion—it would contain none of the most determined character, essential and intrinsic, in modern music. It would have all the harmonic innovations and all the opulence of scoring (too opulent for the subject, I might dare to say). It would not contain the sense which Wagner intended to give his own life and work, or anyhow very little of it. For this and a variety of other reasons, I deem it the one, among all these mature works, which it would be least painful to lose; that is, if it were to disappear Wagner would still be almost intact. If the *Ring* disappeared there would be no Wagner.

4

When Wagner takes over a human organism and turns it into a Wagnerite, an event which occurs as frequently today as it did yesterday, the agent of the metamorphosis is some one work in which the urgency and supremacy of the master's genius makes itself deeply felt. It can happen after years of acquaintance with this work: one performance of *Tristan und Isolde,* thoroughly heard and felt, will do it. We know in the case of King Ludwig II of Bavaria (who was less than eighteen at the time) that the work which gave him a lifelong passion for Wagner was *Lohengrin.* There are cases known to me in which the revelatory experience came with *Die Meistersinger.* But to most Wagnerites of the present century the shock of awakening to Wagner has come with *Der Ring des Nibelungen,* which has every Wagner characteristic in music, including some which appear nowhere else, and which has the further power of being, so far as its meaning goes, almost literally all things to all men.

When we say this of a work of art we often speak only of what is common to every creation. Last week I was in the house of a lady whose pictures include a Renoir, a walk through shrubbery. I remarked that I had looked at it a long time before I had seen "the girl." My hostess declared gravely that there was no girl. Actually it is branches and greenery, but so disposed that from a certain angle the beholder may well see a girl dancing. My hostess admitted that many had seen it, but contended that nevertheless it was not there and that Renoir did not put it there.

Who can tell what Renoir put there? Many have seen the dancing girl: others may have seen it as a cloud or a fern, but there is something in the greenery besides trees or shrubs. Moreover, the same kind of thing is to be found with a great many paintings, and no man can be altogether sure of what another man sees or indeed of what the painter put into his work.

There is a sense in which this variability and suggestive power may inhere in all music, poetry and painting: beyond doubt the symphonies of Beethoven, after the first two, have it in a very great degree and we can never be wholly sure that we are hearing exactly what our neighbor hears. But the *Ring* is the most extreme example we can find of this range and variability in meaning, because here the highly suggestive music is at the service of an allegory which lends itself to interpretation with the ease of the Sphinx and the plausibility of "Mona Lisa." The man sitting next to you in the opera house is no doubt not only hearing things which differ considerably from those you hear, but is fitting them into a view of the world in which every symbol is distinct from what your own mind has taken it to be.

Is this, then, the reason why the *Ring* exercises such power over generation after generation? Is this why it turns them into Wagnerites, at least for a time?

I think it is largely so. First of all this is great, compelling music, and absorption into its tremendous flood is only natural, especially in youth. But what delivers us (even if only for a time) over to the wizard of Bayreuth is the conviction that all this means something of the most vital consequence to ourselves, to all mankind and to human history on this earth. Once this conviction has taken control, we are Wagnerites: we may not be able to formulate our own meaning for the allegory but whatever it might be, we feel sure, contains the truth of man's life on this planet.

And that, of course, is exactly that Wagner intended us to feel. I do not believe he knew himself what the work meant. After all, his genius was at least as intuitive and unconscious as any other, even though he had such a passion for explaining himself afterwards in print. It is surely significant that he never explicitly authorized the identification by name of the leading motives of the work: even though most of them had been labeled before his death, they were not so labeled by him. And if he had been aware of a comprehensive and intelligible interpretation of the *Ring* allegory, either while he was working on it or after it was finished, would he not have said so? He loved to write pamphlets, essays, polemical outbursts and every kind of contribution to the press, as well as many long personal letters. If he had fully known himself what the *Ring* poems meant—which is to say, what the music also meant, since they are so united—he would undoubtedly have written something to put it all on an authentic foundation before his death.

He did not. Whatever partial explanation he occasionally gives— as in his references to Schopenhauer—he is misleading and does not carry belief. Schopenhauer may have had something to do with *Götterdämmerung,* possibly, but what can he have contributed to the buoyant assertions of the earlier *Ring?* That "pessimistic old counterfeiter," as Nietzsche called him, could never have engendered the young Siegfried. The fact of the matter seems to be that Wagner got very annoyed at the constant request for "explanations" of the *Ring;* sometimes he answered such requests, although only in part; at other times he burst forth angrily as in this letter to Roeckel: "It is wrong of you to challenge me to explain it in words: you must feel that something is being enacted that is not to be expressed in mere words."

Here he is telling the truth: he *did not know how* to explain in "mere words" what the *Ring* meant. Furthermore, it is altogether probable that he *did not know what it meant.*

This is not to say that the *Ring* is without meaning. It has indeed so many meanings that none of us will ever get to the end of it. All I say is that its creator did not know to the full what his half-intuitive genius had done.

And certainly I do not, although I have listened to the work in the theatre many times more often than Wagner ever did. As a matter of fact, I was familiar with a good many versions of the meaning of the *Ring* before I had heard it all the way through, and of course time only adds to this kind of burden: the last war (thanks to Hitler) gave us another. We are laden with interpretations. The honest truth is that I know many such and accept none. Like its own author, I think "mere words" cannot tell.

The earliest known to me—and still the most refreshing—is that of Bernard Shaw in *The Perfect Wagnerite*. Shaw's socialist view of the saga was written in 1898 and revised on subsequent occasions, the last time in 1923: it presents a perfectly logical Marxian fable in which the domination of the world is at stake between social and economic forces. Siegfried is an anarchist identified with Bakunin, the mentor of Wagner's revolutionary days (whom Shaw, of course, calls Bakoonin). The struggle for the gold, the instrument of world domination, is followed out through all the action of *Das Rheingold, Die Walküre* and the first two acts of *Siegfried,* falling with uncanny precision into Shaw's own world-structure, with capitalism at bay before the revolution. Every character thus plays a part in the drama of modern man (Church and State speak through Wotan, etc.) so that if Shaw is on his own showing the perfect Wagnerite, Wagner himself becomes the perfect Shavian.

When I was soaking in Wagner as a sponge soaks in the sea, missing no chance to hear any part of the *Ring* if I could help it, Shaw's version of the work seemed downright funny. It came a cropper, of course, just where so much Wagnerism does, between Act II and Act III of *Siegfried.* In that strange interval when twelve whole years passed without a note being added to the *Ring,* what happened to Wagner's view of the allegory? Indeed, what happened to Wagner's whole view of life, of man and his destiny here below?

Shaw, of course, leaps up with a ready explanation. The young revolutionary had beheld the failure of all his dreams, had lost faith in them, had accepted the Kaiser and Bismarck as the German reality, had himself seen the "administrative childishness and romantic conceit of the heroes of the revolutionary generation." The whole difference between the Wagner of 1848, the ardent ideologue of Dresden, and the Wagner of the 1870's, a plutocrat and potentate in his own right, is exhibited by the change from Act II to Act III of *Siegfried*. From that point onward the allegory of social revolution is abandoned. The last scene (Act III, Scene II) of *Siegfried* and the whole of *Götterdämmerung* are "opera and nothing but opera," says Shaw: the inspired music drama of man's fate is ended.

Now, funny as all this seemed twenty years or more ago—made funnier by Shaw's distinctive gift in that direction, with such embellishments as putting the Nibelungen capitalists in top hats—it holds together better than almost any other theory today as an explanation of what Wagner was really doing, not of what he *thought* he was doing. It makes the whole allegory of world domination a product of Wagner's youthful revolutionary enthusiasm (he was thirty-five in 1848) and since this was the period when the poem as a whole was conceived and mostly written, it has a psychological validity which time has not shaken. *The Perfect Wagnerite* was by no means a joke: it was Shaw's application of a Marxian analysis and holds good, very seriously and soberly, up to the point where Wagner himself abandoned it.

But Marx is not the only doctor of our modern world. (How very simple it would be if he were!) Our doctors are Marx, Freud and Einstein, and between them they seem to cover everything as systematically as did the scholastics of the Middle Ages. We have no reliable record of what Professor Einstein thought of Wagner, although we can be sure he thought something and probably had a theory to fit even the troublesome ending of the *Ring*, that *Götterdämmerung* which leaves the created world, as Shaw says, with "everybody dead except three mermaids." Freud and his disciples have applied their own interpretative apparatus, which, given a few principal sexual symbols, is not at all difficult. Wagner's work as a whole, but in particular the *Ring,* has presented psychoanalysts with a rich case study, sometimes so rich that it seems (like the Greek tragedies) to have been evolved expressly for the exemplification of the Freudian system. It took a larger dramatization, that of life itself on the most colossal scale, to make us all aware that the *Ring* allegory had the power, as it had the sources, of myth, magic and religion.

Adolf Hitler had not been taken very seriously in the 1920's and his Wagnerian dream (like Shaw's Marxian treatment) aroused more laughter than disquiet among non-Germans. The "beer hall *Putsch*" in Munich in 1922, coming in my most fledgling days as a cub reporter in Europe, had been greeted with a good deal of ribald laughter by my older and wiser colleagues: it was followed by the prison term during which Hitler wrote *Mein Kampf*. I cannot remember hearing Hitler seriously mentioned as a danger to the German Republic by anybody before 1931, even in Berlin, and the terrible swiftness with which he thereafter rose to power was so surprising to most of us that we had no time for alarm. Hitler was actually in power (from January 30, 1933) and well into the nightmare of his dictatorship before most of us in other countries realized what had happened.

This nightmare was not only unconsciously, but also consciously and explicitly, Wagnerian. Hitler as Siegfried was another of those concepts which non-Germans took very lightly indeed—and many was the joke we got out of it—before we realized the depth of its awfulness in actual historical enactment. In another year or so, when Germany was flooded with post cards showing Hitler as Siegfried with the sword, we began to have some inkling of the grisly significance of the dream. If followed all the way through to the present, this deliberate appropriation of the *Ring* allegory is not to be contemplated without disquiet even in the circumstances which today have changed the world.

The debuts of Leider and Olczewska in *Tristan* at the Metropolitan (January 16, 1933) began the new reign of Wagner in that house, the rejuvenation of the *Ring* there and along with it the period of my own most complete absorption in it. Certainly I, for one, was far more absorbed in Wagner than in anything that took place in Germany at this time or for another three years. And yet just two weeks after that *Tristan,* Hitler took power in Germany and began, with the least possible delay, the creation of the Third Reich. We who were most concerned with Wotan, Siegfried and Brünnhilde in that very period were most unaware that an attempt was in progress to make their drama gruesomely real, involving us all in its uncoiling.

The National Socialist version of the *Ring,* as developed by allusion and suggestion during the 1930's—fortified by those postal cards which never failed to make a comic effect on non-Germans—was, in brief, as follows: the hero Siegfried, reforging the shattered sword of his fathers (the 1918 defeat) wins through every obstacle, overcomes the dragons of international finance and Jewry, seizes the instruments of world dominion and awakens Brünnhilde, Germany, to a new day. (*"Deutschland, erwache!"*) In her fascinating little book on war myths, Marie Bonaparte, Dr. Freud's pupil, friend and translator into French, gives a somewhat more extended account of the Nazi allegory, but this is its main line. As can be seen, it goes up to the end of *Siegfried:* from then on the allegory became too true even for the Nazis. The treacherous "stab in the back" from Hagen (World Jewry? International finance?) kills the hero Siegfried, whose immolation is accompanied by that of Brünnhilde (*"Ich bin dein Weib!"*). If the myth is carried out as Marie Bonaparte interprets it, that is, to the very end, it must have left something in the collective unconscious of Germany which will require generations and perhaps centuries to eradicate.

No other such transference of myth to enacted history has occurred during the times of which record exists. Homer dominated the mind of classical Greece certainly, but there is no case we know in which a literal attempt to transfer his myths to fact took place. Alcibiades may have been stirred by the thought of Achilles, but there is no suggestion that he ever believed himself to be that warrior, much less that anybody else so thought. Alexander of Macedon outdid the mythopoeic imagination in his own life but he always knew it was his own life.

There are elements in the German consciousness, its predilection for metaphysical speculation, first of all, which makes it relatively easy for it to slip from dream to reality and back again. This is not merely among the philosophers with their cloudy abstractions: they, after all, are only the professionally licensed scribes for thought which, as any German will tell you, flourishes with unique profusion and intensity in German minds. It is not strange that so many world systems, metaphysically speaking, have originated in Germany. An addiction to theory comes early there, and the desire to create the world seems to be just as powerful among intellectual workers as the desire to understand it, even though the two often supply hostile motives and irreconcilable results.

Wagner was certainly no exception, but rather a prime example of the world-creating metaphysical preoccupation. Hegel and Schopenhauer and right on down the line, the nineteenth century in Germany showed a similar welding of real materials into a structure of idea or ideal. There must have been, even in all the hard-headed engineers and industrious laborers who made the material Germany of modern times, the same innate thirst for the clouds: why else were they such easy prey for myth and legend? If the German were only, as Nietzsche says, an obedient man with long legs, he would never have given so much trouble to the rest of the world or have come so near to enslaving it. His long legs and his obedience are at the service of a higher power arising from the ancient forest and simultaneously from the single German mind, taking the form of myth very often and once consecrated—once specifically in the German *daimon*—almost beyond human capacity to overcome. Long after the fall of Tunis and the expulsion of the Germans from Africa (1943), our prisoners of war on their way to internment in America refused to believe the facts. Why? Because these facts contradicted the most sacred myth they possessed, that of their Siegfried (Führer) with the invincible sword.

Wagner is in no way "responsible for" Hitler, of course: to state it in any such form (as has been done in my hearing) is to make nonsense out of a significant historical phenomenon. No: Wagner and Hitler both were creations of, and extrusions from, that same German subconscious which made the interrogation of every German prisoner of war a fascinating psychological study. Hitler found his mythology all ready-made in Wagner, which was convenient, but he could have gone farther back and discovered the same symbols. His devotion to Wagner, his annual visits to Bayreuth, his approval of the *Ring* symbolism in Nazi party work, all have seemed to me, on closer inspection, a little spurious—part of an attempt, that is, to perpetuate his demonic power over the minds of the German people. He once went so far as to contemplate marriage with Siegfried Wagner's widow, it is reliably said, and desisted only when he perceived that such reinforcement of his mythic status was no longer necessary. Friedelind Wagner, Siegfried's daughter, knew him from the time she was five years old until she escaped (with the aid of Toscanini) on the outbreak of war; he used to stay at the Villa Wahnfried every summer; but she has told me that she never discerned in him any sign of *musical* knowledge or appreciation. It seems likely that he was drawn into his Wagnerian impersonation, culminating in his Wagnerian death, by the myth alone—that which was so profoundly congenial to him that he could live it out even though it cost half a world. It was unquestionably made far more pervasive and irresistible by the music, which he did certainly absorb in quantity: however, he listened not as a listener, but from the first as a participant.

Now, whether or no the man was clinically insane, it is beyond any doubt that his identification of himself and his whole collective force with the Nordic myths passed normal limits. What are we to think, then, of the many millions who accepted it with such enthusiasm that they were willing and even eager to live or die for it? Were they also insane? Normal they must have been for their time and place, since their conduct was the norm—it was the sane who were "abnormal" in Nazi Germany—but hardly anybody outside of central Europe could think of their course as being natural.

It was animated by the demonic power of myth, and the center of this myth, before, during and after its enactment, was the Nordic saga of the *Ring*. After hearing a good many prisoners of war under questioning, and after talking to a good many of them myself as an air force officer, I came to the conclusion in 1944 that the Christian religion had left scarcely any traces in these young German minds—however devout they might be ritualistically—but that the compelling force, the nerve center of their acts and beliefs, was the pagan saga of their remotest ancestors: Siegfried with his sword bestriding the world.

Ten years earlier hardly a trace of this strange enlargement of the *Ring* allegory came my way. I gave myself up to it, very nearly, in the fashion of the "Wagnerites," that is, to music, poem and myth all at once. It was tremendously exciting to feel that in this masterpiece there was contained, somehow, the clue to the universal riddle. I think I was held off from full surrender even in 1933-1935 by a lurking sense of the mingled absurdity and horror of these hero tales from the northern forests. They carried all before them at their strongest, but too often they exacted more than any theatre, any singer, settings, lights or production could give: in attempting to do too much—to make a world in an opera house—they threw the beholder back on the real world with a sense almost of relief, of awakening from a bad dream.

For, little by little, the music began to seem overexpressive, overextended, overdramatized, and the outsize heroic characters took on the attitudes of melodrama and rhetoric. This had nothing directly to do, so far as I know, with the growth of the Nazi movement in its myth or in its fact; I do not think I became fully aware of all those dangers until 1935 or even 1936, and in any case I never at any moment attributed them to the Wagnerian epic of which they made such use. No: the Wagnerism of a few years wore itself out naturally —and in part because other musical interests grew steadily after 1935—while the awareness of the Nazi nightmare was coming on from another direction. What I believe firmly, however, is that it would have been quite impossible to understand either Hitler's own obsessions in 1938 and 1939, or the blind, ecstatic devotion which the German people gave them, if I had not spent at least a few years under the Wagnerian spell. The "physiological objections" of Nietzsche to Wagner wore off, in my case, after a while, but I saw them with my own eyes wreaking their effect on grown men and women —Germans—when Hitler spoke to them. The women who fainted and the men who wept were all perfect Wagnerites.

5

The debut of Mme. Kirsten Flagstad at the Metropolitan Opera House on Saturday afternoon, February 2, 1935, was the beginning of a period during which Wagner's mature works had their most incessant hearing in New York, London and even Paris. Leider had restored the excitement of the great days, but in this season she had decided that she did not wish to undertake the journey to America. In the search for a substitute, Gatti-Casazza and Bodanzky gave an audition at St. Moritz, during the summer of 1934, to the Norwegian soprano who was destined to make *Tristan* and *Götterdämmerung* the most popular of all operas for a few years.

Flagstad was forty-five and considering retirement when this opportunity came to her. She had been successful in her native Oslo, chiefly in Italian works (*Tosca* and *Aïda* were among her best). She had lately taken to studying Wagner and had just sung, although without much acclaim, both Gutrune and Sieglinde at Bayreuth. She did not know the other and greater Wagner parts which, in Leider's absence, she might be called upon to sing. When Gatti and Bodanzky—without enthusiasm—decided to try her in New York at a modest fee, they sent her to Prague for a period of intensive coaching with Georg Szell. It was not until her first rehearsal in *Die Walküre* in New York that Bodanzky realized—probably because of the acoustics of the house—how very much more than an ordinary soprano was here.

The story will always remain one of the classic tales of the opera world. Her debut was in *Die Walküre* as Sieglinde: she knew this part and had sung it at Bayreuth. The matchless beauty of her voice startled New York that afternoon. Four days later she sang Isolde, for the first time on any stage, in a house filled to its full capacity. From then on for six years the house was crowded every time she sang, for her regal beauty and her unique voice provided the Wagner parts with a majesty they had never possessed before. She sang two of the Brünnhildes and Kundry in that first season, also for the first time on any stage; *Tosca* and *Aïda* never claimed her again. In the following season (1936) she did the same thing in London with an equally extraordinary success, which was repeated in Paris. Only Berlin and Vienna, in the following year, refused to be carried away by her superb natural endowments; they found her lacking in Wagnerism, to put it in a word.

And in retrospect many would now agree that they were right: many (of whom I was one) felt it at the time. This regal lady had the greatest voice any of us had ever heard—greatest in volume, range, security, beauty of tone, everything a voice can have, and all of one piece, never a break in it, all rolling out with no evidence of effort or strain even in the most difficult passages. The only defect to be found in her remarkable performances was that they did not express what Wagner wrote. The immense audiences which gathered to hear her from 1935 to 1941 did not care a fig what Wagner had written: they wanted to hear this golden flood of tone over the massive orchestra. It is beyond question that they never got from Flagstad any reason for the "physiological objections" of Nietzsche. The physiological effect of Flagstad was a thrill—a powerful one to be sure—caused by her wondrous singing. She never frightened, alarmed or repelled; she was not in the very slightest degree demonic; she enraptured her audiences, and what did it matter about Wagner?

The curiosity aroused by accounts of Flagstad's triumphs in New York made her London debut a great occasion, which her own superb gifts turned to more serious account. We were living in Ireland at that time and since my wife was incarcerated in a Dublin nursing home for another week or so, I made a flying trip over to London alone to hear Flagstad's Isolde.

It was a rare evening in the opera house. Fritz Reiner was conducting (he also conducted her last New York Isolde sixteen years later). Flagstad was beautiful to behold, especially in the first act, and the radiance of her incomparable voice was quite dazzling to one who had never heard it or anything like it before. And yet even on that night, startled as I was at the sheer wonder of all this, I missed a great many meanings that should have been in the part. When I thought it over afterwards (even between the acts) and could hear that voice echoing in my ears, I realized that the meanings were not there because the singer had not put them there.

Isolde's first act is an intricate web of such meanings, suggestions, implications. The rest of the part is simple lyricism by comparison. I do not intend to load down the page with examples; one will do. Isolde in her grief and rage is telling Brangäne what she *imagines* Tristan might say to King Mark on offering to him the captive Irish princess. It is a quotation—it is so marked in the text—and comes from the turmoil of Isolde's mixed emotions, certainly with all the bitterness she can put into it. The words are: *"Es war ein Schatz, mein Herr und Ohm . . ."*

That night after the first act was over this was one of the many passages that echoed in my ears and I perceived that Mme. Flagstad had sung it beautifully indeed, but like a folksong—like *"Heiden-röslein."* The savage mockery, the false sweetness, the snarl: of this nothing was left. It could have been "The Last Rose of Summer."

When I remarked upon this and similar passages to my companions that evening, I was told that Mme. Flagstad had not yet sung Isolde very often, which I knew to be true then (1936). I heard her sing it a large number of times afterwards, right up to the last

(American) performances in 1952, sixteen years later, and she never did seem to me to know what Isolde intended at this precise point. Even sixteen years later it was still a folksong.

Well, of course, Mme. Flagstad had only one voice and even though it was the greatest in the world, you need more than one voice for Isolde. What else does all that first act mean? The voice of the rapturous duets or the ecstatic love-death will not do for many passages in the first act. But quite aside from the gorgeous monotony of an unvaryingly beautiful voice—a voice which could not be twisted or bent to ugliness of feeling—it is also questionable whether Mme. Flagstad herself felt, in her innermost being, that wild range of fury and despair, the love-hate and bitterness, which tortured Isolde before the philter solved and dissolved it all.

Sibelius told a friend of mine once that he thought Flagstad was best in the Brünnhilde of *Götterdämmerung* because it was nearest her Norse-goddess temperament. (I do not know where or how Sibelius ever heard it, but this is what I was reliably told.) In spite of his opinion, even in *Götterdämmerung* there were always, for me, passages in Act II and in the Immolation Scene where Flagstad lacked the expressive variety demanded by the score. It was all absolutely wondrous singing and it will be long before we hear its like again: but even so, there are a good many passages in the late Wagner works where wondrous singing does not express and cannot express the intention plainly set down.

And this, as a concatenation of ironies, seems to me worthy of remark. The Western world or its main capitals, London, Paris and New York, had a great Wagnerian flare-up on the very brink of Hitler's Wagnerian war. They had it chiefly because of the vocal and personal beauty of Mme. Flagstad and the great suitability of her voice to Wagner's orchestra. (It was not the same in the Queen's Hall with a piano!) It so happened, however, that Mme. Flagstad had made her career chiefly in Puccini and Verdi (an excellent schooling) and came to Wagner late, almost as an afterthought. She does not seem to have worried very much about the meaning of what she was doing in that extraordinary season (1935) when she learned and sang Isolde, Kundry and the Brünnhildes all for the first time. Her Kundry is said to have been learned in three weeks, just before she sang it. These things which other artists work upon for years before they exhibit them to the public (if they ever do) were regarded by Mme. Flagstad, in her preternatural placidity and perfect confidence, as being ordinary business. She probably did not realize for some years that what she had done, with such miraculous suddenness, had never been done before.

So, all things considered, it is perhaps not so strange that she failed to give her Isolde and Brünnhilde everything that Wagner wanted; indeed, she may not have been conscious of what he wanted aside from the broad lines. It seems downright impossible that any woman could seize the meaning of Kundry in three weeks, although the words and notes (it is short enough) would give no difficulty. It all happened too quickly; there was no time to take it in; Mme. Flagstad's natural calm did not permit instinctive comprehension of these tortured heroines, and the great public—the largest Wagner ever had in the West—did not care anyhow. I see her now in her dressing room at the Metropolitan as I saw her once between the first and second acts of *Tristan:* calm and majestic, smiling kindly, braiding her hair with a vocal score of the opera open on the table before her, an Isolde who had never suffered humiliation of spirit or the wish to die. She had been knitting and put the work down beside the *Tristan* score while she talked to us. After we left I imagine she resumed her knitting until she was called to the stage for, of all things, Act II of *Tristan.* No more tranquil approach to unbridled passion has come under my observation.

The West, then—if it could experience one of its most intense Wagnerian periods under such placid wings—obviously cared little about Wagner's meanings. In every audience at any period there is a strong element of listening for sound alone. This evidently dominated, at least in New York and London, during the years of Mme. Flagstad's reign. Yet those were the years in which the later Wagner operas were most often given: in which Wagner became, for the only time I can remember, popular enough to interest the ticket speculators, and to be repeated to crowded houses many times. It was success—success at last, solidly grounded on incomprehension.

Aside from the enormous pleasure I derived from Mme. Flagstad's singing, the most interesting result of her six years' reign to me, privately, was that she caused the "physiological objections" of Nietzsche to disappear. So far as I can tell from what he wrote, Nietzsche never lost them except by the simple but drastic expedient of refusing to listen to Wagner any more. *Carmen,* which he installed in the place of all Wagner's work, apparently had no physiological effect, which I find strange. But Wagner gave him a sore throat. "I can no longer breathe with ease when this music begins to have its effect on me," he says in *The Case of Wagner.* He becomes hoarse without knowing it (and how often it has happened to me, too!). In order to listen to Wagner he has to administer to himself Gérandel's pastilles, whatever they were. In a word, Wagner "makes me ill."

The physiological attack made by Wagner was perfectly deliberate—he knew he was beating on the nervous system of his hearer and knew exactly how to do it—but although it is greater in quantity and more intense in quality, I doubt if it is a different phenomenon from the nervous excitement which any remarkable performance is likely to engender. Some listeners (Nietzsche, for example) are more under the tyranny of the nerves, and therefore more liable to physiological symptoms, than others. That is about all it amounts to—it does not make Wagner a criminal (as Max Nordau would have us believe) for deliberately attacking us in this way: he only does what a great deal of modern music tries to do with less result.

But in my own case these physiological symptoms began to disappear from the time Mme. Flagstad took over our opera houses. Perhaps it was time for them to go. I was already well on my way out of the deeper shades of Wagnerism by the time Mme. Flagstad dawned upon us. What she did was to substitute admiration, astonishment, wonder and at times a kind of musical joy for all those dark terrors which used to beset me. There is nothing wrong with any of this; musical joy, in fact, is a high element in our response to Mozart and Beethoven. But in objective fact it does substitute a thrill—a great thrill—for some quite different symptoms. The horror we once felt in the ending of Act II of *Götterdämmerung* becomes a thrill of joy and wonder. Is this what the work means, intends, or ultimately signifies in humanity's pilgrimage?

I think not. I believe that the de-Wagnerization of Wagner, its sublimation (if the word can be borrowed for the purpose) under the Flagstad regime had little or nothing to do with the Wagnerian dream either as it existed in the mind of its creator or as it was re-born in the minds of perfect Wagnerites from the young Nie-tzsche to the ageing Hitler (him who wanted war "before he got too old for it"). But it served my own turn excellently well: for just as I was emerging (thanks to Vienna and Milan and more personal influences) from the dark forest of the myth, along came a new ver-sion of the music which made it live as music alone and dispelled the sense—which had been lurking for years—that this grandiose composite contained, somehow and somewhere, the clue to our com-mon fate. From then on it was possible to listen to these works not as apocalyptic revelation but as compositions of genius for voice and orchestra.

The point is one which not many Germans reach: they tend to be Wagnerites, as Nietzsche was from *The Birth of Tragedy* onward for twenty years, until they become anti-Wagnerites (as he became in *The Case of Wagner*). They cannot take it or leave it as others can, because it is too much a part of their own consciousness, individual and collective. The robust make their own allegory upon its ele-ments, as Bernard Shaw did, and it can be wonderfully valid, too, whether Wagner had ever thought of it or not. That, after all, is irrelevant. Nine years before *The Perfect Wagnerite*, Shaw had per-formed the same operation on the works of Ibsen. In his preface to *The Quintessence of Ibsenism,* he says he has shown "that the ex-istence of a discoverable and perfectly definite thesis in a poet's work by no means depends on the completeness of his own intellectual consciousness of it."

One imaginary interview which I wish I might have seen and heard in reality is that which Shaw once suggested, in conversation, between himself and Hitler. He had asked me to lunch in Whitehall Court on June 18, 1940, a day which turned out to be the beginning of "the fall of France." We had all heard broadcasts on that morning announcing that Marshal Pétain had asked the Germans for an armistice. *"Il faut cesser le feu,"* he said.

Shaw talked a great deal on that subject and at one point re-marked: "The one person really qualified to deal with Hitler or negotiate with him in any way is myself."

As was expected, I asked why.

"Because he and I are the only men on either side who have read Wagner's *Art and Revolution.*"

This may have been, for all I know, the literal truth: many of Shaw's sallies derived their sharpness from being only that and nothing more. But however firmly Shaw and Hitler based their view of the world conflict on the Nibelungen Saga, I feel humanly sure that their exegetical processes had already carried them far apart, and all the *Art and Revolution* in existence could not have bridged the gap between the anti-vivisectionist and the patron saint of the crematorium.

Wagner, considered as a disease, was over for me by the time I was thirty-six or so, lingering in remnants here and there for some years. To many the disease is incurable except by surgery, and there is some sense in Nietzsche's remark that the old wizard was "bad for young men and fatal to women." Nietzsche's own famous diatribe begins like this: "I place this point of view first and foremost: Wagner's art is diseased. The problems he sets on the stage are all concerned with hysteria; the convulsiveness of his emotions, his overexcited sensitiveness, his taste which demands ever sharper condimentation," and so on to the conclusion which Nietzsche puts in French, as if it were a quotation, to make it stand out from the page: "*Wagner est une névrose.*"

That, too, may be a simple truth. Much of the obsessiveness which Wagner in life and art appeared to demand, or at least to obtain, has a neurotic contour. A surprising number of his devoted and intimate followers in life became insane or committed suicide or both. (Poor King Ludwig II of Bavaria, the quintessential idolater, was only the most conspicuous.) Nietzsche in his own insanity, wavering between the identities of God the Father and King Victor Emmanuel II of Italy, seems to have purged his Wagnerism at the cost of his reason. These casualties have not affected the eagerness with which successive generations have plunged into the neurosis when their time comes for it. We go through the dark forest and come out on the other side (like Dante to *riveder le stelle*) only by leaving a great deal of cumbersome baggage behind. Myth and philosophy, the doom of the race in the world-struggle, the urgency of *immediate* destiny—all this has to fall away itself or wear away by time, until, in the end, we emerge with nothing to show for the journey but a leaf or a branch or a flower, a trace of the passage perilous. This leaf or branch or flower is, of course, the music and not even all of that— but enough, enough.

5 : The Church and the Theatre

That our Western theatre originated in the medieval church is a commonplace of history books. Latin liturgy in general, the sacred drama of the Mass in particular, gave the signal to inventive imaginations: the masques and mysteries of the Middle Ages were in fact performed in the church, and retained traces of their birth for long thereafter. It is to be expected that even at the present moment the Latin Mass, when it is treated by a great composer, suggests to us a form (the earliest and purest, but a recognizable form) of what we call opera. The Beethoven Mass in C Major, not particularly "operatic" in style, made just this impression on me last Christmas Day in the chapel of the Hofburg, in Vienna: in all its beauty, great and high, it has a kinship to the kind of music which, expressing a dramatic evolution or telling a dramatic story, belongs—or so we say —in the theatre. In its "Benedictus" it provides a glowing example of that exact musico-dramatic contrast, as of sunshine after a tempest, which we so highly value in compositions for the theatre—it leads us to reflect that the Mass is indeed a drama, and that any composer with mind, heart and imagination to illumine his talent must necessarily treat it in a dramatic manner—in short, as opera.

Milan is the only one of the great music capitals which makes a simple geographical demonstration of the link between church and theatre. It is, of course, an opera capital. I should say it was probably the primary opera capital, unless that special palm be given to Vienna: the two of them run it fairly even in concentration on their great opera houses. Somehow or other in Milan it so happened that the church and the theatre grew up near each other, and were linked during the nineteenth century by a great cruciform Galleria of shops, cafés and other worldly enterprises, brightly lighted under strong glass roofs so that in the most inclement weather the Milanese can stroll up and down there dry-shod, with an evening's entertainment at one end of the gallery and eternal salvation at the other. This suits the requirements of the Milanese, and we remember that in the eighteenth century when the theatre once burned down, the Empress Maria Theresa, in far-off Vienna, urged her son Ferdinand, viceroy of Milan and Lombardy, to get it rebuilt as soon as possible: she knew that the opera house was not a luxury but a necessity to her Milanese subjects.

The theatre is, of course, the Scala—Teatro alla Scala, theatre-at-the-stairs, although the stairs disappeared so long ago that it is not sure just what they were. And the church is the Duomo, the Cathedral of Milan, the monument of North Italian Gothic, a little squat to our eyes nowadays, but elaborate and intact today as it was when the Scala was built. Between these two very living monuments the life of Milan flows back and forth, reciprocally renewed and enhanced thereby, as if the church fed the theatre and the theatre the church, through the garish umbilicus of the Galleria. If the theatre burns, or is damaged, or even partly destroyed, as it was during the bombings from the air in 1943, it must be repaired again as soon as possible and in exactly the same form as before; the same is true of the Cathedral. The great city of the Italians cannot live without either of them, no matter how many banks and factories, department stores, insurance companies, barbers' shops and coffee machines may gather round the center which they together constitute.

The theatre was born (1778) because of the total destruction of its predecessor, the Teatro Ducale, by a fire at carnival time. It has survived other damage since, worst of all the great Allied bombing on the night of August 16, 1943, which virtually gutted the central part of the theatre and all of its backstage studios, rehearsal rooms, storerooms and dressing rooms. By fortune alone the lovely façade was not injured, its shape remained, its stage was more or less intact behind the iron curtain, and the general outline or essential form of the Scala was left for the effort of the first peaceful years to restore—and improve—into the house we see today.

When a popular opera is being performed, the Piazza della Scala is a sight like no other to be seen on earth. It is a busy square, of course, in which tramways which reach out into every corner of the great city have their center, and the air is never quiet here; but on the days of particularly favored performances there is a different aspect. This comes not only from the good-natured and noisy crowd, hundreds growing into thousands, which surrounds the theatre itself, but from all the others who come to gape, to make fun, to shout jokes, to admire and catechize. The men who sell the libretto of the opera, at the tops of their voices (and what voices!), do not restrict themselves to the waiting enthusiasts near the theatre. They go into every side street around the theatre and into the Galleria itself, almost as far as the Cathedral, shouting, "Libretto!" They operate on the theory that on a day like this everybody in the entire neighborhood is either going to the Scala, wishes he could go to the Scala, or may be quite likely to buy a libretto and with it imagine that he is going to the Scala. The box office opens at two in the afternoon on a Sunday for the performance at three: since hardly any seats are for sale before, the public in general must therefore wait in line, and it begins to do so at about ten in the morning. Four or five hours later this great crowd, languidly eyed from time to time by a pair of uninterested *carabinieri,* has become boisterous, singing songs, shouting shouts. So many hours of patient waiting come in the end to wear down their vociferous Italian throats, and they make noises merely for the sake of making noises—happily, contentedly, but not in the least musically: just noises.

This kind of scene occurs in particular when a popular favorite sings an opera beloved of the whole people. It has just occurred, a few days ago, when Maria Meneghini Callas, known in Milan as La Callas, sang *La Traviata* on a Sunday afternoon. La Callas is a phenomenon of this present day, not in the very least to be compared to any celebrated prima donna of the past: she obviously learned her stage techniques from the films and her public (which means the great public of Italy and of the world) is far more steeped in film techniques than in the opera of the past. For one evening at the Scala (the most expensive theatre on earth) an Italian has twenty or thirty evenings in a cinema theatre. Consequently his view of the opera is inevitably and irrevocably conditioned by his view of films. By the time he has patiently saved enough out of two months' income to buy one seat in a gallery of the Scala, he has already seen thirty or more films treating approximately the same subjects of love, jealousy and death. He therefore expects not only singing, as his grandparents did, but all sorts of very broad effects depending upon vivacity of movement, loosened hair, shoes kicked off, disheveled dress, incessant movement and posterlike attitudes, with a general treatment of the whole stage (the stage of the Scala) as if it were an enlarged screen for indiscriminate stampeding. This he obtains from La Callas and the host of her imitators, who by now include all the young singers of Italy if they are slim enough and active enough.

Along with this man, who expects the opera to be a sort of glorified film, there is the older one who wants it to be opera even now, but seldom gets a chance to find it so. Singing is not what it used to be; but La Callas can also sing, when she puts her mind to it. So there is a sort of cross section of every public Italy has to offer to opera, which means a cross section of all Italy. (Among the Italians I have known in my life, only Benedetto Croce, in his seventies, confessed that he did not like opera—for the rest, I think the *liking* is universal although in a good many cases, particularly with intellectuals, the *habit* has been abandoned.)

The crowds in front of the Scala are almost entirely men. It has seemed to me, not only just now but twenty years and more ago, and ever since, that the entrance of women to the theatre must be a highly contrived affair. The men get the tickets for the women as well, of course, but as in some cases only one ticket will be given to each person, it must mean also a sacrifice, a substitution. You will see an audience in the theatre which is half women, or almost half, although there is no way known to modern history whereby tickets to the Scala may be obtained without those long, exhausting waits in the public square.

And the good cheer, the infinite high spirits, of those crowds!

They have been there, many of them, since nine or ten in the morning; on special occasions they even start standing there before dawn; they have good, sturdy Italian legs and good, strong Italian cynicism to hold them up. They just do get a little tired after the first several hours, and start jeering at the taxicab that pauses, the lady who picks her way fastidiously through the puddles, the tram that is overcrowded or the schoolboy who runs to catch it and misses. Any little incident in the Piazza della Scala will provoke a roar of enjoyment from these patient devotees and grandsons of Papa Verdi. Nobody could blame them: have they not given their entire day (not to speak of a week's income) to the sustained effort of getting into this almost hermetically closed theatre, the glory of Italy? And you can depend upon it that once they enter the magic portals they are not going to be reticent about it: they will speak aloud when they choose— *"Bene, bene,"* they will say when La Callas chooses to sing a long, soft phrase on one single breath—and they applaud at will, even for a single note in the very middle of an aria. They will say, "Look, look," when La Callas pulls her hair out or suddenly falls down or otherwise emulates her cinematographical mentors, and they say it in wonder, true wonder, as if they can hardly believe their eyes and are not sure that others see what they see. They have struggled hard to get into this theatre and they propose to enjoy themselves to the utmost without inhibitions; if they had their own way they would even demand repetitions of their favorite bits and pieces, but the bitter modernity of the century has taught them that this is no longer possible—has not been possible since the arrival of Toscanini long, long years ago, before the century was born, before most of this crowd was born.

For the crowd is predominantly young. It is made up of the kind of young men who in a period when I knew the Scala moderately well (in the early 1930's) would have been Fascists, in black shirts. That was the thing to be in those days; it paid well and you could yell even louder, and it meant nothing much; it was a fashion. The one thing which is not a fashion is the opera itself. It is permanent. It has come to Milan to stay. As a matter of fact, it was in every true respect actually born here, is native and inexpugnable.

Dr. Johnson's definition of opera as an "exotic and irrational entertainment" may have been literally true of the London in which he lived (not of the London of today). It certainly was never true of Milan. The one place on this earth where we may be quite sure that opera is not exotic, but rootedly native as well as endemic, is Milan. It has been borne in upon me in just these past weeks that the only place I know of in the world where the chambermaid hums or sings opera as she works the vacuum cleaner is Milan; the only place known to me where a respectable middle-aged businessman walking down the street after lunch will sing opera quite loudly and without disturbing his neighbors is Milan; the only city, town, province or area in which a television program of opera (as was the case with *Madama Butterfly* only a week ago) will be simultaneously on every television set to be discovered in a mile's walk—that is, every house, bar, shop or establishment of any sort which contains the requisite machinery—is Milan.

In Vienna it is true that chambermaids sing while they work the vacuum cleaner or the carpet sweeper, but what they sing is old Viennese waltzes; I have remarked it for thirty years and I have remarked it again just lately in the Sacher Hotel in Vienna, to which, as all know, the opera house is practically an annex. They sing waltzes. I never heard anybody humming anything in Vienna (absent-mindedly, that is, in nature) which was not a waltz. It is in their unconscious just as the opera is in the unconscious of Italy but above all of Milan.

The Milanese owe this first to the general Italian tradition, which regards the lyrical form of drama (especially tragedy) as higher and more concentrated than the spoken form. It comes from the Renaissance as much as from the church, since the Greeks created it (Aeschylus, Sophocles and Euripides wrote opera librettos, not tragedies). But the Italian tradition, creating opera in the seventeenth century, collided with the German genius and there resulted some sort of bifurcation, after Mozart, in which Milan really came into its own as the home of a specific Italian form. In our own times, which I take to be roughly two hundred years, the Italian lyric theatre has found its heart to be in Milan, from which the blood of the forever-new is pumped to every part of Italy and the whole world.

There is something in this which is not quite like any other phenomenon in the same category. We go to Stratford to hear and see the works of Shakespeare, and when they are especially illumined (as they were in 1955 by the genius of Laurence Olivier) they are worth the longest journey; but Stratford remains, in its essential character, a museum. Nothing new, no fresh work, no creation for the future, may be expected from Stratford. It is even more marmoreal and anesthetized than Salzburg, in which the sovereign ghost of Mozart does sometimes permit totally new and strange works to see the light of day. The "festival" towns are all in the moral region of a reward for virtue ("You be a good girl and maybe you might get a meringue glacé for supper"), as the conscious rectitude of their patrons incessantly declares. But Milan is just an ordinary big town, an ordinary city—the most ordinary, in the sense of being the most composite, bustling, commercial and preoccupied, in all Italy. Most of the persons who subscribe so heavily to the annual seasons at the Scala, and thus keep the general public out of the theatre, are merchants, bankers and other kinds of businessmen who, with their wives, children and visiting clients, abetted by the occasional second cousin from the further reaches of northern Italy, actually enjoy this form of entertainment and prefer it to any other. They are not "fans" in the American sense. They would never dream of standing all day and all night in line to get a ticket of admission for the *abattoir* in the back of the house. They only go when their subscription comes around—every other week, say—and they go in perfect comfort, in excellent seats on the ground floor or else in boxes which are practically footstools to their own sitting rooms at home. They would never dream of going at other times, times when they would be obliged to scramble (as the rest of us do) for tickets. They are quite safe: nothing that is produced in the theatre, under the system at present, can possibly escape them: every production reaches them sooner or later. If there are five representations of any given production, there will be four for the subscribers and one for the general public. That is the rule, and if there is deviation from it (as there has been this winter) it is the public which suffers, not the subscribers. The four subscription performances are always given— they are guaranteed—and if the fifth, that for the general public, must be omitted, it is the public's loss.

Now, every opera house on earth has subscribers, and in some capitals they had immense power in the past. (Forgetting the Metropolitan, which actually belonged to its boxholders until 1940, we may recall the Paris Grand Opéra as it was in the mid-nineteenth century.) The difference in Milan is that these subscribers have a lively sense of what they are seeing and hearing. They are in some way housebroken in a way that no other subscribers to opera are in my experience. True, their behavior would startle most of the old ladies at the Metropolitan and at Covent Garden. They shout when they are excited; they have certain expectations and express either satisfaction or disappointment as a result; they do not mind interrupting any part of any performance if their feelings carry them away. At times they talk aloud in a manner which makes their less experienced guests (such foreigners as I) actually cringe with embarrassment for them and for the music. It should be said plainly, for once, that it is not the "galleries," those ready scapegoats for all guilt, who make most of the noise at the Scala. The really agonizing noises come from one's nearest neighbors in the boxes and on the ground floor, who never stop expressing their views: the noises of the galleries, when I have been up there, were far more spontaneous and natural, simple cries of delight or disgust and not so much opinion, far easier to accept as the natural response of a natural people.

Yet this noisy audience does actually know extremely well what it has come to see and hear, and it does listen. It would be totally impossible for any Milanese boxholder to ask you to a performance at the opéra without knowing what the opera was. This has happened to me more than once in New York: "Come to dinner and the opera on Monday the 25th." Inquiry: "What opera?" Answer: "Oh, I don't know, but it's my last Monday." In Milan such a conversation could never occur: if I told it in Milan just as I have told it on this page I might even be accused of inventing it. The New York subscriber (or boxholder) may not know three weeks in advance what the opera will be, but by a simple telephone call it is possible to discover what it is *likely* to be. The same is true in Milan, but in Milan this little extra trouble would be taken because the little extra interest is there.

Little? It is more than a little. Milan pays heavily for its opera and always has done so. For some centuries the aristocracy alone carried the load. It was the Milanese aristocracy which built the Scala; all they got from the Austrian Empire was the actual land on which the theatre stands and a modicum of relief from taxes upon it. The

Empress Maria Theresa was thoughtful and kind, but not to the extent of dipping into her own purse for the enterprise. The Teatro Ducale, which was the Scala's predecessor until the great fire of 1776, was in effect the property of the Milanese aristocracy, who used it as such. They had meals, drinks, card-playing and regular receptions in the back part of their boxes, which were their personal property (a part of their houses) and could be shut off from the rest of the theatre at will by a system of doors or shutters. The gambling in the Ridotto, behind the boxes, was famous: many men went to the opera to gamble and never looked at the stage at all. These habits carried over into the Scala itself, and up to about 1860 the aristocracy still owned a good many of the boxes and used them in the old way. These boxes were individually decorated and furnished (some of them beautifully) and were actually regarded as sitting rooms of the noble ladies and gentlemen who owned them. In the middle of the nineteenth century the impoverishment of the aristocracy set in, and the boxes passed in increasing number to prosperous members of the bourgeoisie. The official history of the Scala, which is sold in the theatre museum, says that there were more bourgeois than aristocrats among the boxholders from 1860 onward, and the tendency, of course, accelerated. Today the aristocracy, practically speaking, has vanished, and the bankers, merchants and professional men hold the boxes, control the policies of the house, and, of course (through the complicated machinery of the Ente Autonomo, an artistic and administrative unit) take their full share of responsibility.

The thing was planted naturally—because of a desire that existed for it—and it just grew. It was probably a century or so before the Milanese themselves, even those princes, dukes and counts who valued the Scala most highly and themselves created it, began to realize that it was a source of pride, an institution to shed renown upon the city, the province, the nation. In one form or another the whole process of musico-dramatic representation had been going on for so long in Milan that it had become a condition of life—and, by the eighteenth century, a necessity of life. Two years before the discovery of America, at the time when Gian Galeazzo Sforza married Isabella of Aragon, there was a festival opera, or spectacle with music, performed in honor of the occasion in the courtyard of the Sforza castle. It was called *Paradiso,* and seems to have enjoyed a great success. Its ideas and outline (or scenario) were by Leonardo da Vinci, who also painted the scenery and directed the stage action. The words were by the court poet Bellincioni. Leonardo took an active part in producing other musico-dramatic spectacles during his years at the Sforza court, and may thus have played a decisive part (although we know nothing much about it) in the evolution toward what became, a century and a half or more onward, the form we call opera.

Well, those are old things, and not many Milanese give much attention to them. The Milanese regard opera as the most living of institutions, perhaps because it is the only one (aside from the church) which has been forever renewed in their long, turbulent story. No matter how proud they may be, municipally or institutionally or historically, of the Scala, they never hesitate to shout their disapproval when they think it deserved—today or any other day. In those Italian romances of George Meredith which seem to me so false and overwritten (although once greatly admired), I find one thing to be true, the central vividiness and pervasive importance of the opera house in the life of the people. Stendhal conveyed repeatedly his own sense of the fact, but, as was his way, made it personal— the Scala was the center of the world to *him,* he seemed to be saying, and rewarded the longest journey, bound up the deepest wound: he expressed more penetratingly, and more personally, a fact he found all about him in his life in Milan. As it was in the ferment of the Napoleonic days or the great upthrust of the Risorgimento, even so to the present moment the Scala is the heart-house of Milan and Italy. Sometimes I have wondered what a good Milanese, a true Milanese, would do if he had to choose—that is, if he had to sacrifice one or the other, the Church or the Theatre, the Duomo or the Scala, out of his life for good and all. How could he choose when they are intertwined in his consciousness as they are linked in the physical existence of his abiding place? "Or the golden bowl be broken . . ."!

2

After the Wagnerian saturation which I have described, it was in my own life a kind of sunrise to live in Italy for a while, to go to the Scala and hear quite different kinds of music. In 1934 and 1935, in particular, this happiness befell me and had its result, although not all at once. I had been to Milan before, but never when the Scala was in season; my opera-going in Italy had been chiefly in Rome. Now, living on Lago Maggiore, it was no trick at all to go down to Milan for a performance and back even the same day if necessary. It seems to me downright funny now to remember how Philistine my first responses were to the works which I have since learned to respect so deeply. Italian opera was no novelty; I had heard it from childhood; but Wagner had marched his conquering legions over all that and perhaps I had even partly forgotten what I once had loved. Wagner, as innumerable others can testify, obliterates everything else for a while. Certainly if you have swallowed that particular pill which induces the belief that *Tristan und Isolde* and *Der Ring des Nibelungen* are the only things worth attention in a theatre, you cannot, at first, appreciate the joys of *La Traviata*. Such was my case, and it was, unless I am grossly mistaken, precisely *La Traviata* which was my initiation to the Scala. (Either that or *La Forza del Destino*). The singers in *La Traviata* were Gina Cigna, Tito Schipa and a baritone of lesser renown or older vintage. Schipa was well known to me from New York and Chicago, but I tended to regard him as a "Mozart singer"—we used such labels more often then than now—and perhaps I thought he was doing a little careful, patriotic slumming in Milan, acquiring merit on the home ground, so to speak, by appearances in *La Traviata*. Beniamino Gigli, the other reigning Italian tenor of the time, was in *La Forza del Destino*, but I am sorry to say that this singer, in spite of great vocal beauty, always seemed more than a little comic to me. Both Schipa and Gigli were very short men, but Schipa had a native dignity, a way of moving and holding himself straight, which made one forget it; Gigli bounced about the stage like a rubber ball. *La Traviata* and *La Forza del Destino,* my first experiences in the Scala, seemed to me old-fashioned in the highest degree, full of antiquated effects and operatic nonsense, emphasized by the simplicity of Verdi's orchestra at that stage of development and his way of reducing it to a mere accompaniment, in simple chords of tum-te-tum, to the line of vocal melody. I remember laughing quite helplessly at Gigli's great scene with the baritone (*"La gloria dell' esercito!"*) in which the little man's florid pomposity and ridiculous appearance were the fine flower of operatic parody, no matter what luscious noises he made. I also remember laughing at Preziosilla's aria and its chorus, which seemed to me then sheer organ-grinder stuff, and has not vastly changed to my ears even now.

La Traviata was not so funny. In spite of my conviction that these works were mere guitar music, there never was a time when some passages in *La Traviata* did not overwhelm me by pathos and a certain kind of poignant lyricism which even Verdi never wrote again. I suppose it contains a young man's sadness, perhaps, or some other quality of the universal which conquers any local or temporary prejudice. But although *La Traviata* is irresistible, on the whole—and I shall go to my grave regarding it as one of the finest of all operas, a true masterpiece—it does also contain some of those bits and pieces in which Verdi wrote like other theatre composers of his time, perhaps in haste, perhaps in fatigue, for he worked too hard and too much, perhaps, most of all, because he was actually just forty years old and had half (the greater half) of his productivity still ahead of him. He was of his time and had not yet found out that he could ignore it. So there come things like the drinking song in the first act, which even today I think is absurd, and the tenor's very conventional aria (*"Dei miei bollenti spiriti"*) in the beginning of the second, with the baritone's good old organ-grinder piece, *"Di Provenza il mar il suol,"* at the end. Such music I can hear today and put in its place as resulting from the weaker moments of a very great genius. After all, between the tenor's banalities and the baritone's banalities in Act II there are inserted pages upon pages of the most exquisite and sensitive conversation piece one could find in all nineteenth-century music, the long scene between Violetta Valery and Giorgio Germont. This may be a series of "duets" as they were called in the conventions of that day, but the music bears the same relation to ordinary "duets" as *As You Like It* does to a Broadway musical comedy.

And yet—and yet—I also laughed at some moments in the *Traviata,* the ones I have indicated. Twenty years later I think of this as a deplorable aberration and wonder how it came about. Wagner, of course, is the immediate answer, but I should have had more sense: ah, how often we have to say this . . . ! Considering the case, I think one of the by-products of the Wagnerian obsession must be, for others as well as for me, a disregard for common chords, an almost moral condemnation. When you come to think it over, Wagner made some stupendous effects out of common chords—the prelude to the *Rheingold* is nothing whatsoever but the chord of C major, and what could be commoner? I might have composed it myself!—but his instrumental wizardry, his way of weaving and interweaving the instruments of the orchestra around the simple triads, makes the whole thing a magical invention for the listening ear. We completely forget that it is nothing but *do-mi-sol-do*. The Verdi of 1853 had not yet "complicated the modeling" (as some painters say) enough to disguise simple harmony; that was to come; and when he lapsed into guitar music he did it as frankly as a street musician. Yet, even in guitar music, there are differences: and can any honest person with ears deny that the opening of the most characteristic *Traviata* tune (*"Amami Alfredo!"* is its usual identification), as it originally comes in the prelude to Act I, is wonderfully true, human and beautiful? It is done with such deliberation, such an opening of the curtains and bowing, that one feels Verdi himself saying, "Well, this is the way we do it, and whether you like it or not, gentlemen, this is how we shall now do it." "Plunk," he says slowly, and then, equally slowly, "Tum-tum." And the strings then sing.

During the entire Fascist period Italy seemed to me like a pot with a lid on it. Fascism was the lid. It never did become a deeply national phenomenon like the Nazi mania, for it was, in fact, not a mania at all, but a mode or fashion, a way of doing things, an acceptance without faith. The pot took the lid. The Nazi crime was deep and may not be uprooted from the German consciousness for generations because it permeated every part of German life. Fascism was far more superficial, contingential, circumstantial, and in some ways to many Italians more convenient. Think no more, simply live: that was what Fascism said to the Italians, and they were generally content to let that be the rule of their existence, up to the time when it became hideously inconvenient. Then they all at once discovered that they never had been Fascists at all—that it was a mere fiction, a fantastication by the ruling gang, Mussolini's camarilla—and you can travel from one end of Italy to the other at this very moment without discovering any person who frankly says that he was a Fascist and believed in it. I could have told them that long ago and can prove it by books published during the 1930's: they never were Fascists at all, and I never met a true Fascist, a true believer in Mussolini's nonsense, in all the years of that regime, although I knew many members of the Fascist party and some of them quite well. Fascism was always a fiction: Nazism was the reality.

And since it was a fiction, it had no real effect upon the more permanent reality of Italy, in which opera must be counted. The Fascist regime never did anything serious to the Scala. It did attempt to make the Rome Opera more important—this was part of the general notion of *Romanità,* a pipe dream of the uneducated Mussolini— and for some years the productions of the Scala, totally or partially, fed Rome too. Toward the end of the Fascist dictatorship the Ente Autonomo was brought under Fascist domination. Mussolini was empowered to appoint its president and determine its policies, but in actual fact I cannot see that Fascism did anything to the opera house. It may have been inconvenient for some sopranos and tenors to travel back and forth between Milan and Rome, as they were obliged to do. Their lives are spent in travel most of the time anyhow, so it cannot have made much difference to them. Toward the end of the twenty years of the Fascist nightmare one restriction upon opera singers came to have a certain importance: they were not allowed to leave the country, because Mussolini knew that he intended war and he did not want to have the chief operatic artists out of Italy at a time when they would be most important in keeping the people submissive. Thus a considerable number of good artists, such as Maria Caniglia, a dramatic soprano of unique integrity, and Mafalda Favero, a lovely lyric soprano who afterwards died under the bombs, were forbidden to fill their contracts at the Metropolitan in New York and in other theatres outside of Italy. America's loss was Italy's gain, for these and other excellent singers helped to maintain the sense of permanence and sanity during the war years when to most intelligent Italians the entire world seemed to have gone to perdition.

However, Mussolini never interfered with the repertoire or productions in the Scala or any other opera house so far as I know. He was not, fortunately, very fond of opera, although he occasionally went to the Costanzi (which he called the Royal Opera and is now simply the Opera of Rome). He seems to have known little of music, and even his knowledge of literature and history was never more than a semiliterate smattering. Unlike Hitler, who changed the repertoire of all the opera houses every time he made a change in foreign politics, Mussolini does not seem to have connected the soul-life (of which opera is a part) with that of the external configurations; in that, as in so many other respects, he was a mere clown, and a very coarse one, compared to his German emulator, disciple and master. J. V. Stalin, who kept a sterner hand on the opera house than either of them, seems to have been actuated more by motives of Soviet puritanism (the "Soviet morality") than by political ideas in his various acts of dictatorship toward the Moscow Opera, but it can be seen that in their varying degrees all three of these self-imposed or charismatic masters of their peoples, wishing to see unified (*gleichgeschaltet*) that which can in its essence never be anything but various, counted the opera as an element of control. Mussolini made vain gestures, Hitler switched and changed, Stalin supported or expunged, but all of them recognized to the limits of their intellectual powers that opera had a deep effect upon that which they were attempting to subject, the consciousness of the people. It is a happy thing for mankind that in each instance opera won out: dictators cannot win over composers who are dead. Beethoven always wins.

It was during the Fascist period that I knew both the Scala and the Costanzi best before the war. I cannot remember ever having met or heard of a singer who was a convinced Fascist—but then, as I said before, no Italian was ever a Fascist: they only pretended (that is, ninety percent of them) to be. The war was not even over when I went, in the uniform of the United States, to speak to a very exalted gathering of ladies in Rome. With the permission of the Allied High Command, I told them about the cultural damage which the war had brought to Europe. (I was far more impressed by it then than I am now—now I think it was minimal.) A considerable number of these ladies had been known to me, either by name or in person, before the war. There were, as Leporello's catalogue has it, princesses and peasants, countesses and baronesses, all the various elements which go into the making of Roman "society" (i.e., aristocracy, prosperous bourgeoisie, intellectuals, of whatever origin). Many of them came to speak to me afterwards. I shall never forget the deft phrasing in which every single one of them said to me, in one way or in another, whether in Italian, English or French, that they had suffered under the late tyranny and had bitterly deplored the ruin which they felt it must bring to the cultural heritage of our beloved Europe. Well—okay, kid—I personally knew that almost every one of those ladies had worn Fascist insignia, most of them had been outspoken Fascists for almost twenty years, had worked for Fascist "causes," had been decorated by Mussolini. . . . I hope that I received their successive protests with the gravity which manners and morals demand from the representative of a great Republic in the hour of victory. Inside myself I felt a little bit sick.

I remembered the dead and dying in Spain seven years earlier, and the glittering Italian airplanes that came over us to maim and destroy and, above all, to intimidate. The primary characteristic of Fascism was *prepotenza,* the cruel demonstration of power over the powerless. (It was never of the slightest good against power.) These ladies in Rome had all embroidered banners and blessed them and sent them to the invading Italian legion in Spain, and to the Italian air forces which did their best to frighten the world into slavery. If Mussolini had been enabled to annex Spain in one way or another, as was his intention, calling it a "Fascist cognate" or something of that sort, these same ladies would have rejoiced exceedingly and made merry.

Well, that was Italy under Fascism—a pretense. It was succeeded within twenty-four hours after our entrance into Rome by the precise opposite, a pretense that there had been no pretense, that all had been the result of tyranny and impotence. A certain Roman princess, well known to most of my readers, a lady of anything but Roman origin, is said to have given a dinner party to Field Marshal Von Kesselring on the night before we occupied Rome, and a dinner party to Lieutenant-General Mark Clark on the night after we occupied Rome. This is Fascism.

The Scala and its repertoire lived through these years as an almost prototypical example of the eternity of aesthetic value. I know of no other in the world which did it so thoroughly. In Germany and Austria, in Russia and the United States or even in England, there was no such continuity of purpose or adherence to enduring things. One of the silliest incidents I know about in the realm of "psychological warfare" was the disappearance of *Madama Butterfly* from the repertoire of opera in the United States during the war, because it showed an American boy doing wrong to a Japanese girl. I have myself heard this opera performed to an audience consisting exclusively of American soldiers in Italy, at the royal theatre in the palace at Caserta, and heard it cheered to the echo—even at the end, when the bereft orphan is shown waving the Star Spangled Banner. (This detail is often regarded as too poignant to endure even in peacetime in the United States.) Our G.I.'s, thank God, were not "psychological" warriors.

The Scala survived Fascism chiefly by ignoring it. The productions went right straight on, without interruption or change, until the very night when the Allied bombs effectively destroyed the theatre. And thereafter the Scala company simply carried on in other places, a variety of places, including the Teatro Lirico in Milan but also a sports stadium and various refuges, until it became possible to rebuild and proceed anew, after peace had come and it was discovered that nobody was a Fascist and nobody ever had been a Fascist and nobody even knew anybody who had ever been a Fascist. Next to the discovery of America, and at the distance of four and a half centuries still not unrelated thereto, this is probably the most profitable discovery any Italian ever made.

3

There is no desire on my own part to lighten the shadows which lie across Mussolini's woeful part in Italian history. Many suffered and died, more were starved and dwindled into half-life. Anybody who wishes to know what an Italian of mind, heart and conscience endured during those years should read *Schiavitù*, by Sem Benelli, the narrative of what this dramatic poet, the author of *L'Amore dei Tre Re* and *La Cena delle Beffe,* survived to tell of the age of the reborn empire, *Romanità* and *Mare Nostrum*. Mussolini, in his half-literate way, seems to have had a shrewd respect for culture, although he did not know quite what it was. He was genuinely afraid to imprison or silence Benedetto Croce, whose work he was unable to read with any comprehension; he was acutely embarrassed by the Fascist imbecilities which drove Toscanini out, and I was personally assured that he did everything possible (I was in Rome at that time) to assuage the Maestro's wrath and induce him to remain in Italy; he always treated Gabriele d'Annunzio with the most lavish respect, endowing even his senile vices with the support and approval of the Fascist state; he was Jupiter in a golden shower to Luigi Pirandello, that placid, half-mad creature who understood Fascism just as little as Mussolini understood talent. These persons in their various ways represented aspects of the eternal, and Mussolini, who was a shrewd mountebank, knew in the marrow of his bones that they all outranked him before the bar of history. There were, of course, vulgar reasons as well—Toscanini because of world opinion, D'Annunzio because he was (as person, not poet) a fellow scoundrel, Pirandello because (without knowing it) he spun a web useful for cannier spiders to catch flies in. The one of the four who had no popular support in the outside world, no moral complicity or intellectual servitude, nothing, in fact, to protect him, was Benedetto Croce. I have always thought that Croce represented the tribute of vice to virtue: Fascism did not dare to touch him because Fascism itself realized that Croce was half in heaven. During the years when I lived in Naples and knew Croce as well as any much younger man (and foreigner) could know him, these reflections dwelt much in my mind, for there never was anybody who spoke more frankly than Croce about the ignominious gangster regime. He spoke and wrote incessantly and was allowed to do so. Mussolini used to say, "Nobody reads what he writes, let him alone." Or (as I have also heard): "Croce is unreadable, nobody can understand what he means, let him go on, he would be more trouble dead than alive." It is true that Croce's audience was never large and never will be. Neither is Dante's.

Sem Benelli, a writer for the theatre, concerned most of all with getting his plays put upon the stage and unfolded before living spectators, had a very different experience: Mussolini tried to cajole and flatter him into submission and did not altogether fail for a while. Later on, when Benelli continued to write plays in praise of human freedom or concerned with struggles against tyranny at various historical periods, with analogies which every Italian could appreciate, the fury of the Fascist gangs drove him out of the theatre and—in effect—did what the "peoples' democracies" of eastern Europe do today: took his ration card away. The most successful of all Italian playwrights could not earn a living. But even in this case it was not the *Italian state* which openly and decisively suppressed him; the Italian state (through its censorship organization) licensed his plays and allowed them to be performed; it was the Fascist gangs which rioted in the theatres and forced the plays to be withdrawn. It is a case which shows in full the hypocrisy and cowardice of Fascism, to which, now that it is all over and no choice is valid, one might even declare that Nazism was preferable: at least in Hitler's state you knew you were condemned to death or slavery, without equivocation, whereas in Mussolini's state you never knew what corrupt fancy might strike you down or which subterfuge would exsanguinate your life's resistance. Hitler would have murdered Croce without a qualm, made lamp shades out of Luigi Pirandello and employed Gabriele d'Annunzio to scrub floors in prisons for the criminally insane. Such creatures as Mascagni and Marconi could have attended to the toilets, as they did for Mussolini. But it just so happens that Hitler was a true monster—it takes rare genius to be such a true monster—whereas Mussolini was only a false monster, a hypocrite in the head and a coward in the heart, gnashing his rubber teeth at paper tigers and foaming soapsuds.

I may be permitted a personal confession here: I was afraid of Hitler. I never entered his dominions without fear of torture and death or (at the very least) some kind of police frame-up. This was perfectly reasonable fear, as can be historically proved by the fact that the Nazi regime issued a special decree on January 9, 1940, making it a crime for any citizen of the Third Reich to read, print, carry, buy, sell, publish or otherwise deal with anything written by me on any subject. The decree was retroactive and it was special, individual (that is, it applied only to Vincent Sheean, officially declared an enemy of the Third Reich). Such decrees were usually issued against whole blocks of names at a time, and I dare say all of my friends and colleagues were equally taboo to the Nazi state, but my pride, such as it is, clings to the plain fact that the decree of January 9, 1940 was for me alone.

Nothing like that ever happened in Italy, where I went quite freely throughout the whole period of the Fascist deviation, speaking my mind without diffidence. I never was afraid of Mussolini. My contempt for him was absolute and could not have been mitigated by any amount of force or violence. Of this I made no secret and there have been many times in Rome, Naples and Milan when—usually after the opera, over supper—I have only ceased to declare it out of consideration for my Italian friends. They, living in a police state, had to keep up their fears or go away, and it was not very easy to go away after about 1935. They were not Fascists, although some of them wore Fascist insignia (I repeat: there never were any Fascists and even Mussolini was not a Fascist because there was no such thing as a Fascist). They were simply Italians, living in Italy.

This seems rather a long way around the opera house but it is necessary to say these things in order to make it clear how opera could flourish in relative freedom under Fascism, and how a foreign anti-Fascist (a very notorious anti-Fascist, for in the 1930's I never ceased writing and speaking against the twin dictatorships of Italy and Germany) could happily go to Italy, and even live there for long periods, taking delight in Italian food, wine, talk and smiles, growing year after year more addicted to Italian music and literature. I never set foot inside Nazi Germany without an infinitude of precaution and without being paid extremely heavy fees in advance by magazine editors; I used to notify all embassies and consulates, the Army and the Navy and the Coast Guard; every time I went there I thought I was walking straight into death, and I never met an American official who did not implore me to leave at once lest trouble ensue. Such dark uncertainties and premonitions did not becloud a single day in Italy, and if occasionally there were some evidences of police surveillance, this did not trouble me (it never does); it was a condition of life in that time and place, and most people of my acquaintance had grown thoroughly accustomed to it.

The Rome Opera was in some respects even more resplendent than the Scala during the Fascist era, since Mussolini's general effort tended toward the aggrandizement of Rome. The leading singers and conductors were the same in both houses, and aside from the fact that the Costanzi showed some signs of special favoritism from the Fascist hierarchy—visible in black-shirted clumps in many boxes every night —and probably received financial aid in proportion, the two houses were not so very different. The Scala retained more independence, right up to the final phase—that was about all the difference came to. A great deal of money was spent on the Costanzi, after it was rechristened the Royal Opera, and there was plenty of fresh paint and gilt about all through the period, but both for the beauty of the hall and the perfection of the acoustics I always preferred the Scala, even apart from the undeniable psychological influence of its insinuating and pervasive prestige. There was some special added excitement in the Scala even *before* the curtain went up: this might be one way of saying it, and the same can be said today.

The San Carlo in Naples was another haunt of the Italian years. My honeymoon was spent near Salerno, and the Pompeian *autostrada,* substantially empty since there were so few motorcars, led straight to Naples and the Opera. The San Carlo is one of the prettiest of all theatres, of course, but nothing like so much money had been spent on it in recent times as upon the Scala and the Costanzi. Funds for elaborate productions and profuse rehearsals were never available there, and as a result the performances sometimes (even with emi-nent principals singing the chief parts) had a much more provincial quality. We enjoyed them, just the same—and how thoroughly we enjoyed them, sometimes in ways the composer had never intended, was due to their very provinciality. Tenors let their high notes run away with them almost every night, sopranos got so excited they could hardly sing, baritones bellowed like the Minoan bull at high festival. Insufficient rehearsal, and therewith insufficient authority in the conductor's beat, accounted for some of the goings-on, but the au-dience accounted for the rest. It was one of the noisiest of Italian audiences and it would stop the performance utterly if it did not have its own way. Favored pieces (usually the worst ones) were there-fore repeated whenever the audience showed its determination, which was frequently. Such an air as *"La donna è mobile,"* for example, is lyrically and dramatically right, suited to the character and situation, when performed as Verdi wrote it, but the way they liked it in Naples—with prolonged high notes, a cadenza and other ornaments including a piercing *acuto* at the end—it was difficult to endure even the first time. I remember Lauri-Volpi, whose voice was in any case much too big for that house, singing the thing three times over. It was enough to give one a gloomy view of tenors forever after.

In all this opera-going, off and on, in Milan and Rome and Naples, there was growing up inside of my own musical consciousness, such as it was and what there was of it, a new attitude toward most of the Italian works and, centrally, a quite new frame of mind and general sensitivity toward the work of Giuseppe Verdi. The more I came to know his work, even the most familiar parts of it, the more it took on depth and meaning. After a few years it was no longer possible for me to laugh even at the pages (too frequent in many of the works) where the composer lapsed into "guitar music." It was dawning on me that even his guitar was a good guitar, which, after all, makes an enormous difference. The "Verdi revival," as I believe it is called, was already going full tilt in Germany, Austria and England, with all sorts of exhumations taking place: it had even begun in the late 1920's. Such early works as *Luisa Miller* and *Macbeth* (neither of which I ever saw) were received with enthusiasm all over central Europe in the 1930's. In Italy, where Verdi had been taken for granted for a long time, the revival took the form of more careful productions (more musical, better studied and with better scenery and staging) of the tried and true. Not so much of the early Verdi was dug up during these years at the Scala or the Costanzi, and none at all at the San Carlo. On balance, however, Italy had less to revive (or "exhume," as the Italians say). In Italy some works which Europe at large had almost forgotten, such as *La Forza del Destino, Simon Boccanegra, Don Carlo* and *Un Ballo in Maschera,* now being received with the delight of discovery in Berlin and Vienna, had never really been out of sight or out of mind for long. They returned every few seasons to the Scala's list, as they have done since they were written. The whole of Verdi's immense work cannot remain in the regular repertoire there or anywhere else, naturally, but it goes through a cyclical process in which, from time to time, even the less popular operas can get a hearing. Italy had less of a "Verdi revival" than the rest of Europe, therefore, simply because there was no necessity for it—the bulk of the old master's work had never been forgotten in his native land.

The gist of it for me, just the same (and for probably millions like me—the whole musical public of the 1930's), was some kind of renewed interest in Verdi, a reëxamination of the known and a wondering introduction to the unknown. A good many of the most familiar examples, such as *Il Trovatore,* took on new life during those years when care enough was lavished upon them to bring it forth. The outsize grandeurs of Wagner were not promptly succeeded by a concern with the human passions and sincerities of Verdi—nothing is quite so simple as all that—but without in any way excluding each other, the Italian works, relying on vocal line and color in a way so perfectly suited to the Italian genius, grew upon my own consciousness as strongly as the German works, in their totally different way, had done in the preceding years. There was peaceful coexistence, but I think the cure of Wagner as "neurosis," if we accept that word for the Wagner obsession, came in good part from Verdi and the Italian opera as reborn in the 1930's—as well as from Mozart and Beethoven, Salzburg and Vienna.

This could have happened anywhere. As I have said, Germany and Austria took the lead in the revival of interest in Verdi, and it certainly would have been easier to hear the relatively unknown early pieces in Berlin than in Milan. Some of the great German conductors —Bruno Walter among them, from the 1920's onward, and Fritz Busch in the 1930's—had displayed an apostolic zeal in bringing these forgotten works to light. But, to return to the thesis which underlies all I have to say of Milan and Italy in music, the central European efforts were redolent of the conservatory, if not of the museum, whereas the Italian offerings had the unmistakable accent of truth and nature: *La Traviata* in the Scala was at home as the plum blossom is at home on the plum tree. Nothing "exotic and irrational" here: this is the free growth from seed to flower and fruit. If ever any phenomenon belonged to its own environment, grew almost without thought or arrangement out of the surrounding conditions and adhered (almost vegetably, almost as an effect of climate) to its own landscape, it was Italian opera of the nineteenth and twentieth centuries.

4

What, I wonder, makes this naturalness and inevitability? There must be many answers containing parts of the truth. The one I venture to put forward as providing conviction for me is that suggested by the title of this section—the connection between the church and the theatre. The church seems a far less gloomy institution in Italy than elsewhere in Europe, closer to the life of the ordinary village, more bound up with ordinary things. It would be hard to find an Italian family which had not some member in either the clergy or the monastic orders, which as a result seem familiar from childhood to Italians—not set apart as in other lands. It would never do to say that Italians were more religious than other peoples (they too obviously are not) but there is a ready-made cousinage in their relationship with the church, and perhaps even the primacy of Rome in the presence of a vast churchly court there helps to make it all an Italian family matter. To pursue the argument might lead us very far from the subject, but in brief it seems to me that the Latin Mass as performed in most Italian churches—not Gregorian chant, of course, but everything since then—is the earliest musical experience of all Italians and is essentially a lyrico-dramatic, or operatic, experience. It leads into opera smoothly, unconsciously, and perhaps even the element of language (church Latin as pronounced in Italy is very close to Italian) has a great deal to do with its growth. In one of the greatest of all compositions for the church, the *Manzoni Requiem* of Giuseppe Verdi, as adverse critics have always said with great eagerness, an "operatic" pulse is felt throughout; it is an "operatic" composition. In being precisely this it is also most Italian, for it expresses that intimate and fundamental connection between church and theatre (Mass and opera) which is the special character of Italy in music. From birth to death this is, I think, the Italian musical experience.

Life in Italy affords examples almost without number of the kind of efflorescence I have called "natural" and "inevitable," seeming to take place without much thought or excessive effort. Some thought, some effort, there must always be (as there is even in the plants, in a blind way). But all the forces, favorable and unfavorable, which surround a musical life in England and the United States—whether it is the life of a composer, singer or instrumentalist—exist in Italy only in much mitigated forms. Nothing really impedes the progress of a talent in Italy and nothing forces it unduly, except in very unusual cases. The normal state of affairs takes talent for granted, expects it to unfold, to work itself out, and is on the whole favorable to it, but without expecting too much too early and without ever forcing it to race along too fast. There always has been plenty of musical talent of all varieties in Italy, that is, since the seventeenth century, and as no shock of surprise is experienced at its rarity, no temptation exists to magnify, exploit or overwork it; but since opportunities are many in a country with many opera houses and concert halls, neither is there any special effort to keep it down or close the doors to youth and novelty. In so far as anything in the realm of art can be said to exist in a state of nature, I believe music, and in particular opera, exists in that state here.

That, probably, was the gist of my discoveries in Italy in the 1930's, the point of them, leading on to great pleasures in the evolution of a wider taste. By the time I knew the Scala well I also had friends among the singers, instrumentalists and even some composers of my own and other countries. I was able to see how an environment could determine or deflect a musical development and the fate of a talent. Some of the reflections of 1934 and 1935 merge into those of today and yesterday, for there has been no great change in the general state of affairs since I first knew Milan, and the contrasts then made vivid in my own mind have only been confirmed by later observation.

Take, then, a singer—any singer—growing up in America, or for that matter in England, and compare or contrast the case of a singer with similar gifts evolving in or near Milan, somewhere in northern Italy with access to Milan as the musical center. I say singer because the case of the instrumentalist would not be profoundly different, and the psychological climate has its effect even on composers, with all their private woes and secret battles: all, in the end, depend upon us, the public, and it is we who differ most from one country to another. ("All sopranos are alike, whatever country they come from," says a singer friend of mine. "All tenors are the same—they constitute a nationality of their own.") *We* are that part of a society (national or regional) which goes to listen to music, but we, as musical public, have the characteristics of the society to which we are native, and, along with such things as economic condition, level of culture, degree of commercial exploitation and other elements, we make up the "environment" into which every new talent has to expand for recognition and fulfilment.

Well, if I had been born of the tenor nationality, for instance, I should certainly have chosen to be born in Milan. There are a dozen obvious reasons: the language, the prevalence of opera and concert, the ease with which good teachers can be found at fair fees, the social consideration attached to singing, the widespread understanding of a singer's effort and result, sharp discrimination between good and bad, eagerness to hear new voices—all those things which go into the "naturalness" of the phenomenon. I am of a mind to choose one example of this natural development, a basso not a tenor, who seems almost created to prove the point: Cesare Siepi. There are no doubt a good many other contemporary examples but Siepi's career has been so smooth, untroubled, unimpeded and unforced that it has given him a wide international public in one short decade. Granted, he is extremely gifted—a handsome young man with one of the finest bass voices of the century, a stage presence seldom seen in opera, an innate skill in performance quite aside from vocalism. To take such a child of good fortune may seem to be stacking the cards, but I shall try to show that similarly gifted artists produced in our own environment—I intend to name Lawrence Tibbett and several other American singers who have been my friends—do not find it quite so easy.

Siepi was born in Milan in 1923 of a family long established there; his father's people some three centuries back were from Pesaro, but there is record of his mother's family in Milan back as far as the Sforza period. More or less everybody in the Siepi family, so far as Cesare knows, liked music and listened to it a good deal, but there were no musicians or singers among them; they were good, respectable Milanese citizens like most of those who make up the public at the Scala. Cesare was earmarked for the teaching profession, by some parental decision, and did his first more or less serious singing when he was a student at a school which trained teachers for the elementary classes (what in America is usually called a "normal" school). This process did not go far: he never taught, and just before he became a professional singer, during the period of intensive preparation, he was actually working in a bank.

His childhood was filled with tunes. He sang everything that his acquisitive ear picked up from films or records or in the street—bits of opera, popular music, folk songs, anything and everything. The voice was tenor, not soprano, and it may be that all this singing in childhood tended to "cover" it still more, to give it the harder finish. He was a mimic by nature and had a memory which, without much effort, collected even the words of tunes and hoarded them after a single hearing. (If his memory failed him on words he made them up.) He recalls that in all those solemn discussions which parents and other elders usually have about a child's future he kept his silence but was always sure of one thing: that he would be in some way or other a public performer, whether it was a clown in the circus or something less dazzling. His childhood was not at all "musical" and he hardly discriminated between the various kinds of tunes and words that ran through his head and out on the stream of his voice.

Then came the tremendous event of every boy's life. At thirteen, with great suddenness, he became a deep basso. Little indeed is known about the human voice, but it seems to be usual (or more usual) for boy-tenors to become man-tenors and for boy-sopranos to become basses or baritones. Cesare's voice became such a deep bass that it had for some time no higher notes at all, although the deeper tones at the bottom of the scale were there from the beginning. At thirteen he was very big—"a monster," he says—almost as tall as his present six feet and much heavier. He was in demand for school athletics, swimming and track coming first, with singing as a poor second choice for quite a while. What won him, gradually but decisively, to a paramount interest in singing was the work he did for about three years in the Coro di Madrigalisti della Città di Milano. There he was one of the five basses, rehearsing and performing works by Palestrina, Monteverdi, Orlando di Lasso; learning vocal polyphony, learning above all to subdue his own heavy voice to the choir— learning, as he says, "not to yell"; he regards it as the finest training he could imagine for any soloist, and he went through it from his fourteenth to his seventeenth year.

By this time the quality of his voice had attracted attention; he sang for a recognized or established baritone (the father of a school friend) and was sent to a teacher, Chiesa, the only one he has ever had. Here, with two lessons a week, he unfolded rapidly, and at eighteen he won first prize in the national contest for young voices (Concorso Nazionale per le Voci Giovani, at Novara, 1941). His bravery was at least equal to his skill, for he sang *"Il lacerato spirito"* from *Simon Boccanegra*, along with the big air from *Salvator Rosa* (Gomez).

From then on there was not much doubt of where the young man was headed. When the "Fascist Republic" took over Milan (that is, in reality, the Nazis—after Badoglio and the King had joined the Allies in 1943), Siepi got out to Italian Switzerland, where he continued to study until the war was over and he could return. (From Lugano to Milan is no journey at all.) His first experience on the opera stage was in small parts in small theatres—Pavia, Piacenza and other cities—but his development was extremely rapid: at twenty-three he sang the title role in a revival of *Nabucco* at the Fenice in Venice, Tullio Serafin conducting. He had leading basso parts during that summer in Trieste and made his debut at the Scala on the opening night of the season (December 26, 1946), as *Nabucco* with Serafin. (*Nabucco*'s popularity just after the war was due partly, anyhow, to its great patriotic chorus, one of Verdi's earliest national successes, which exalts freedom.)

Thus Siepi at twenty-three was in a position at the Scala which it would take an American of equal talent much longer to achieve, there or anywhere else. At twenty-seven he became the leading Italian basso at the Metropolitan in New York; he sang in Bruno Walter's memorable performances of the Verdi *Requiem* there in 1951. He was not much over thirty when he sang his *Don Giovanni* at Salzburg, with Furtwängler. Today, at thirty-three, having appeared in all the Italian cities, the two Americas and a good part of Europe, and having recorded much of his repertoire for the chief gramophone companies, he has as great an international public as any other basso and probably commands the highest fees in that category both for opera and concert. It seems to be a career which has taken place without any real opposition or difficulty beyond those inherent to all life; it has been so natural as to seem easy, although of course it does involve a great deal of hard work. And, disregarding the material success, it must also be said that Siepi's mature art at its finest, as in *Simon Boccanegra*, has no equal to my knowledge anywhere at the present time: it has the inward origin which seems the mark of the best, a blessing to the singer and the song.

The question as it comes naturally is this: what would have happened to this youth, handsome and highly gifted, if he had been an American? The hypothetical question could only bring hypothetical answers, wide differences of opinion and no proof. During Mr. Roosevelt's presidential press conferences he was subjected to such questions at times and replied that they were "too iffy" for a straight answer. To make both question and answer less iffy, to put them on the plane of fact, we can only think of what actually did happen to a number of Americans comparable to Siepi in natural endowment and talent.

Lawrence Tibbett was probably the most successful American male singer in opera during my time: he had twenty-five seasons at the Metropolitan, all but the earliest ones in baritone parts of first importance. He made films (or at least one), was in constant demand for concert and recital, drew full tribute from the radio, and lived in that unremitting hubbub which seems to be inseparable from fame and fortune in the United States, at least for native Americans. (The hubbub is itself inimical to the artist's work, and I have constantly observed that European artists in America succeed in insulating themselves from it far better than our own do.) Larry, we called him: a brilliant baritone voice, strong and true, a very fine stage presence—tall, like Siepi, and with a figure that never deteriorated—gifted for impersonation, for character, for stage action. Nobody could possibly say that Larry Tibbett was unappreciated or that his career did not bring rich rewards, in their own way, in an American way. The last part of his operatic career was harassed by physical bad luck (throat trouble), but during the 1930's, at the very least, after the initial stages were over and before the first touch of vocal misfortune, he occupied a position such as no American baritone had achieved before. His training and studies were all made in America and his European appearances (in London, Stockholm, Vienna and some other cities, mostly as Scarpia) occurred after he was already famous throughout the world.

Tibbett had every advantage and it cannot be said that in contrasting his development with Siepi's there is any trickery of false weights and measures. Both had talent, luck and success. The point I wish to make is that while Siepi's growth seems to have been as natural as that of a cabbage or an apple tree, Tibbett's was a battle from the start and never ceased to be a struggle against a number of enormous obstacles which, in the case of Siepi, did not exist. I know something of Tibbett's struggle because he used to tell me about it; so did other American singers who went through similar processes; it is by no means unique but is, on the contrary, an example.

The first necessity for the kind of voice Tibbett had, a dramatic voice suited to the opera theatre, is somewhere to sing—a stage, an audience. Opportunities for stage experience in small parts in small cities, a precious boon to every young Italian, hardly exist in America. Tibbett started his stage life at the Metropolitan and was given, in his first season, the very grateful part of Ford in *Falstaff* (January 2, 1925). The resonance and beauty of his youthful baritone carried that audience away, and after his "jealousy" monologue there arose a demand for him, by name, which stopped the performance for about fifteen minutes and attracted great attention from the newspapers. He had been unknown until that night but was never unknown again. Without enough stage experience or enough repertoire stored up in his memory he had to embark upon the career of a leading baritone, learning as he went along.

He had, of course, a good memory, plenty of voice and confidence: it was all quite possible to him, but the difficulties—the obstacles in a path which in another society would have been smooth—were incessant. First of these was language: every part was in Italian, French or German, none of which was really familiar. Tibbett pronounced his words so well in all languages that it was an astonishment to me to discover that he had learned the parts just as most other Americans do, by rote. An American singer with purely American training and experience has no chance to *speak* a foreign language: he is too busy learning to *sing* it. One night in Salzburg I sat next to Larry Tibbett at a supper party after the opera (it was Rose Pauly's first *Elektra*, I remember, first at the festival: somewhere along about 1935 or 1936). He asked me to order his food for him because he could not read the menu. I had myself heard him sing, eloquently and beautifully, the music of Wolfram von Eschenbach in *Tannhäuser*, and no native German could have given the words more meaning; now I found that he did not know the language at all. As I came to know more and more American singers I found that this was practically the universal rule: they learned word by word and note by note—the meanings of the words as well, naturally—and many of them were able to turn this kind of knowledge into a convincing rendition of a text on the stage. At the same time, hardly one of them could order a meal if hungry or ask for directions if lost in a foreign city.

This obstacle is tremendous. It increases the work of learning an operatic part by some unknown multiple, probably ten or fifteen times. Every sentence, indeed every word, has to be studied for its meaning, its pronunciation and accent, all those things like doubled consonants in Italian and *Umlaut* in German or nasals in French which are completely alien to the American tongue. An American singer cannot simply "Memorize the words" because he does not know the words to begin with: they are not *in* him, so the texts which he studies are all, to start with, unknown country. I can memorize a sonnet of Shakespeare without much trouble because all the words are already *in* me—it is only the magic of their arrangement which needs to be committed to memory. Suppose a Hottentot with only the most elementary acquaintance with English were to try to memorize the same sonnet . . . ! Something of this kind is what the American singer goes through for years, until practice—experience—makes the unnatural process quicker and easier. It can never become a natural process.

What does this do to the actual interpretation of a text? When I remember how superbly Tibbett sang *Simon Boccanegra,* with, so far as I could tell, every meaning there was in the part, it seems to me some kind of miracle, and my imagination boggles at the amount and kind of work required. It must be observed that many and many an American singer, less gifted or less serious than Tibbett, treats an opera text as so much gibberish for long passages at a time, usually between the high points or the show pieces which have been more thoroughly studied. Another incidental circumstance which I have often observed is that American singers with a little European experience tend to have a "favorite language," even when they do not know it very well: it is the language of the teacher or of the boarding house where the boy or girl lived in Milan or Paris or Berlin. This is a language in which they have at some time or other been obliged to order a meal, ask for directions, buy a pair of shoes or try to read a newspaper. It may even have been—not to be too prosaic about it—a language of love at some moment in youth. At any rate it means something a little more than just the words learned by rote to fit certain notes and stage actions. And it is very noticeable that such American singers are always at their best in the "favorite language" because it cannot fail to signify a little more, in the depths of the consciousness, than the mere vocalizing of alien sounds.

European singers have the same difficulty when they face a language totally unfamiliar to them—it is not an American disease—and many thousands in the New York public must remember such disasters as, for example, Maria Jeritza's French. But Europeans start to sing in their own languages and usually continue in them; if they learn a role in a foreign tongue, it is generally one they already know thoroughly in their own; very often at least one foreign language has been familiar since childhood. Such an artist as Mme. Hilde Gueden of the Vienna, Scala and Metropolitan companies, although she is something of an exception, can converse fluently and correctly in all the main languages current in the world of music (German, Italian, French and English). This must have come from childhood, from some period before the intensive training and study of an opera singer set in: for once the hard work of the career begins no singer really has time to make a proper study of language as such, language for life as distinct from language for repertoire.

Tibbett belonged to that generation of American singers which was blazing a new trail by staying at home. Earlier generations (those of Nordica, Eames and Farrar) depended upon Europe for at least the final stages of training and the early stages of experience, if not more: they all seem to have spoken foreign languages to some extent. Edward Johnson, as I remember, who was of Tibbett's generation but in an earlier wave, spoke excellent Italian and French both. Since then (and since Tibbett) there have been many American singers whose entire preparation took place, as his did, on the native heath, with a repertoire laboriously acquired in completely alien tongues. It will not suit the case to mention failures, of whom there have been examples almost without number; failure can always be attributed to something else, and to sheer lassitude in the struggle most often; but among brilliantly successful singers in full career it is possible to name Eleanor Steber, one of the loveliest sopranos in existence, and Blanche Thebom, one of the best contraltos in the Metropolitan company. How much their work has been increased by the language obstacle only they can know or guess.

After language, an element hostile to the unfolding of such talents in America is the paucity of stages available, the limited chance for a singer to acquire experience and repertoire. The Metropolitan is the only established company with a long season in the entire country. (Chicago is reviving again, but had decades of little or no opera.) The San Francisco and Los Angeles seasons are short and the company which gives them consists almost wholly of established artists. Opera is given in New Orleans sometimes, or at summer seasons in parks in various cities, or in sporadic productions (half amateur) here and there. Where, then, can a singer build up that stage experience and accumulate that repertoire which are necessary to a life in opera?

For Tibbett and for a very few others (Steber is one today) the Metropolitan Opera has supplied the answer by giving opportunities to progress through smaller to larger parts. This is the best that can happen: and it is rare. Usually the inexperienced American singer gets into small parts, stays there a while and vanishes; conversely, such a singer may be artificially magnified by some freak of publicity or sheer chance, may start, blind, at the very top, dwell there uncertainly for a season or two and then return to oblivion. In the 1930's there were a number of quite young girls—the pride of Omaha, the pearl of Kansas City, the nightingale of Tuscaloosa— who were catapulted into leading parts at the Metropolitan without any notion of what they were doing or how they got there. Some of them might have had talent, and as I heard few of them I cannot say, but no talent could survive such treatment.

Leaving them out, since such a brief flicker of success is only a variety of failure, and sticking to the criterion of a real talent really unfolding through the years, we come up against the fact that the best and the luckiest of the Americans are unable to acquire experience, in the Metropolitan alone, which equals the ordinary and natural experience of a young singer in Europe. Not long ago, at the Edinburg festival, Sena Jurinac of the Vienna Opera remarked to Howard Taubman, critic of the *New York Times,* that she had just celebrated her hundreth performance of Cherubino. Mme. Jurinac was at that moment (the summer before last) under thirty years of age. Mr. Taubman, in reporting this to his newspaper, rather sadly inquired how many years it would take an American singer to acquire the amount of experience which is represented by one hundred performances in *Le Nozze di Figaro.* The answer is X —an unknown number of years which would probably exceed the whole stage career of the singer.

Tibbett's roles were all new to him throughout his twenty-five years at the Metropolitan. That is, he never had a chance to acquire any experience in them before he exhibited them on that stage. His qualities made this possible, but they could not make it desirable. Once he had acquired the role and made his first appearance in it, how many times was he likely to sing it in one season? A maximum of five or six, usually, and whether it would be in the repertoire another season or not depended on the whims of the public, the management and the press. I do not have the figures, but I strongly doubt if any of the great Tibbett parts (Boccanegra, Scarpia, Rigoletto, Iago) got up to anything approaching a hundred repetitions during his whole career.

And Tibbett, mind you, was enormously favored. How many there are who have a harder time! John Charles Thomas, a baritone of rare lyrical quality, sang in concert in New York as early as 1920, but it took him another fourteen years to reach the stage of the Metropolitan. Under the American conditions, Dr. Johnson's dictum seems to be true. In spite of a colossal public—eighteen million persons are estimated to listen to the broadcasts of Metropolitan performances on Saturdays—and regardless of the fact that every seat in the theatre is generally sold both in New York and on tour, opera seems to be, anyhow for an American who wishes to take part in it, an "exotic and irrational entertainment."

If you are such an obstinate freak as to want to sing opera, and if your will power conquers all that strives to thwart it, you may, as Larry Tibbett did, achieve the aim. If so, a whole new set of impediments are piled up by the very rarity of your achievement. Competing managers, press agents and entrepreneurs of every kind bedevil your existence. There are great rewards in this: the amounts of money paid to reigning singers in the United States for subsidiary activities, such as radio, film, television, and the like, and even for regular concert tours of respectable music, are far greater than anywhere else. The opera itself may not be profitable to an American singer (seldom is), but the words "of the Metropolitan Opera Company" on a concert program or an advertising poster are golden. A singer who receives a fee of three hundred dollars for one performance in the opera, and has no more than eight or ten of them in a year, may collect $3,000 for each concert and have as many of them booked, a year or so in advance, as the human frame can endure.

The fee not long ago for a certain Sunday afternoon radio program in which many of our best-known singers frequently were heard was (Tibbett told me) $5,000. For this it was customary to sing one rather ambitious offering, an opera air perhaps, with something simpler (generally in English) during the second half of the hour. Two songs, in effect, for $5,000!

The temptation toward overwork, deterioration of the instrument itself, slack and lifeless repetition of the same program three or four times a week, must strike any eye. There are subtler temptations, those toward self-satisfaction and all the deadly sins, leading toward a cessation of the basic work (the exercises) upon which a voice depends. America, in effect, throws a fortune at you, but in so doing makes it difficult for you either to keep it or to continue to earn it. I am reminded of a prima donna of my acquaintance on the brink of her first long concert tour in the United States, who said: "Vot? I should sing my high C t'ree times a veek? On tour? Get out of a train and sing my high C? I do not." As it turned out, she did: the fees were as high as her C.

5

Audiences in Milan make their contribution, a very solid one, to the environment in which the composition and performance of opera become, like food, sleep and language, an element of life. Audiences anywhere and everywhere have a great deal to do with the efforts that are made in their behalf: you can prove that point quite easily by attending a rehearsal and a performance of the same work—any work; a play or a violin recital as much as an opera. The rehearsal may be better or worse, it may come out shorter or longer, funnier or sadder or louder or softer, but it is never the same thing as a performance. The added element, the audience, has an almost incomprehensible power over performers. Acoustically a full hall is very different from an empty one. The great opera houses of this world, so far as I can make out, are always full to overflowing, which is beneficent to all on the stage; these would be frightful caverns if they were, say, half empty. (At the beginning of the war I had to speak in the San Francisco Opera House on the night of an air raid, the first one, during which the population was asked by radio to stay at home: few indeed were the brave or the incredulous who ventured out, and who could forget the hollow vastness of that echoing cave?)

Aside from the physical or acoustical fact, the audience has some other power distinct even from its approval or disapproval as manifested in applause, cheers, silence or hissing. It has a co-consciousness, as it has been called, a form of communication between persons in groups, which is pervasive, collective, and can be felt early and late by those who work on the stage. Someday the phenomenon I mean, which approaches telepathy, will receive enough study to produce an explanation. So far it is a mystery but that it exists nobody connected with the theatre or any other kind of public appearance (even politics) would doubt. You can feel an audience listening or not listening; you know when it is holding its breath; you can almost touch and weigh its boredom when it is bored. Moments of excitement flash like some invisible current through the crowded hall, and their opposite, the dead spots in the performance, are felt like flattened air, exhausted air. The remarkable thing is that some cohesiveness in the audience, some collective personality, seems to appear before the performers on the stage have had a chance to do anything. They can feel very early that this is a "good" audience or a "bad" one, as they say, and it has a corresponding effect upon their own effort, however valiant. (It is true even for speakers.)

There have been terrible examples of audience cruelty in Italy, most of all at the Scala. The audience there can be hostile and intolerant beyond any other we know, sometimes making it difficult for new work (if it displeases) to be heard at all. The first night of *Madama Butterfly* (1904) was an extreme example, but even today manifestations of the same kind, the catcalls and the vegetables, are not at all unknown. In the Callas-Tebaldi rivalry of the past few years partisans of the two prima donnas have gone to every length except actual armed riot. In the season during which I write, the Atlantic Ocean separates the two sopranos, but their fanatical partisans are still here, and some of Mme. Tebaldi's worshippers actually threw vegetables at Mme. Callas on the first night of *La Traviata*. It takes a certain amount of bravery to pick up flowers which have been thrown on the stage when you cannot be sure whether they are roses or radishes.

But possibly this fanaticism is part of the larger liveliness, the robustious and superabundant vitality, which an audience at the Scala can claim as birthright. The extremes of attention and appreciation, the storms of approval, which delight any singer's heart and lead to constantly renewed effort, might not be possible if they were not counterbalanced by the frank, even brutal, excesses in the opposite sense. What it comes to, on the whole, is a lavish expressiveness on the part of the audience which is unknown in other great opera houses. At Covent Garden it is regarded as indecorous to interrupt any performance by even polite applause, even at the conclusion of an aria written solely to elicit it. Applause for Calaf's show piece in *Turandot* was gently deplored by the *Times* this past November as an interruption of the musical continuity. (Puccini would have been horrified if the piece had not been applauded.) In Milan applause can come not only at the end of a set aria, but at any given moment when the audience sees fit to bestow it. Boccanegra's single cry of *"Figlia!"* in Act I of that work is traditionally rewarded with applause (two notes) although the music makes no pause to allow for it. One single note may be applauded, and often is.

Fastidious persons who wish the music performed for themselves alone have never felt really at home at the Scala. This is so even today, with all the airs and graces of modernity, and it is also true at the Piccola Scala, the new theatre opened on December 26, 1955, for works of an intimate character. The Piccola Scala is so small that it is not suited to musical performances of any kind, according to my ears, and every remark made in it by a member of the tiny audience is as audible as anything sung on the tiny stage. Does this discourage our good Milanese? Not at all! On the night when I went to the Piccola Scala to hear *Così fan Tutte* conducted by Guido Cantelli with an excellent cast, having paid $15 for this exalted privilege, I had a full running criticism given by the ladies who sat at the left, at the right and just behind me. They were addressing their husbands, not me, but they might as well have done so from the little stagelet itself. The Milanese audience is used to the vastness of the big house, in which conversation, if not actually screamed, does not greatly disturb; that is, conversation is general enough, and discreet enough, to be no more destructive to the music than the roar of the subway is to the concerts in Carnegie Hall. Any transfer to the miniature thea-

ter of the Piccola Scala, to be true, to "catch on" after the novelty of
the first season has worn off, would not only require a whole new
race of singers trained to scale their voices down to chamber size, but
a whole new race of Milanese who would learn to whisper during
the music rather than to talk out loud. As it stands now, this theatre
is quite impossible for music of any description, and it is one of the
jokes of the century that it should have been attempted in Milan, of
all places. In Germany, where silent attention is the rule, it might
have been just possible, although even there the singers would have
had great difficulty adjusting to the tiny space. In Milan it is
reductio ad absurdum.

The big house, the Scala itself, exudes a warmth of psychological
temperature which makes the uninhibited behavior of its audiences
not only comprehensible but actually, when you get used to it, part
of the show. Like the going-out of the lights, a wonderful effect of
slow dimming which the Scala's structure (as of boxes from floor to
ceiling) turns into magic, the conduct of one's own neighbors and of
the audience as a whole takes on some kind of relationship to the
performance. The talk, which is abundant but not constant, is always
on the subject of this performance. That is one notable point. There
is a great deal of talk at the Metropolitan, too, although conducted in refined whispers for the most part, or during periods
(such as the Tristan prelude) when no singers are visible or audible; but at the Metropolitan I have hardly ever distinguished a remark made about the performance. It is usually something like
this: "Letty, did you remember to call up Virginia? Now I told you
you ought to do that first thing. Oh, really, you should have called
up Virginia." I have heard weird fragments, such as, once: "She
isn't really his daughter, you know. Perhaps I ought not to be telling
you this."

At the Scala every word one hears has to do with the performance
one is hoping to hear.

"Guardi, guardi!"

"Bene, bene!"

"L'hai sentito?"

"Ah, la bella vestita!"

This is the kind of small, running comment all over the house,
depending chiefly upon the assumption (we must suppose) that each

such person regards his, or usually her, companion as being blind and deaf. "Look—listen—did you hear?—what a pretty dress!—what a wonderful scene!" Those are the small elements of the chatter. The longer and more important elements can never be followed out to their conclusion if we wish to hear what is going on in the opera itself: they are prolonged sentences and discussions, but from the parts we cannot escape hearing, these, too, have to do with the performance. When Cesare Siepi sings Don Giovanni, there is one comment you will hear time without number from every woman whose voice drifts your way: *"Che belle gambe!"* (What beautiful legs!) It is the musico-dramatic summary, apparently, for that superb impersonation.

What goes on at the Scala seems to me to mean just one thing, above all: that those who go to that theatre are having a wonderful time. They are having an absolute *whale* of a time. Whether they love or hate what they see and hear, they do so whole-heartedly, with the happy abandon which makes even anger a release and a sort of joy. The great part of the audience does not often get to this theatre, where the seats at first performances range in price (with taxes) up to $20 each; even the subscribers only have one show every two weeks or so; it is not made up of special "opera lovers" of the sort who (in New York or London) go three and four times a week. It is not made up of anything special, merely of Milanese, all sorts of Milanese, and as the opera house is their own, more peculiarly their own than anything else in Milan except perhaps the Cathedral, these occasions are relished to the utmost.

Even the very first time I entered the Scala I realized that this was an audience out to enjoy itself. In spite of the fact that hostile demonstrations are one of the oldest traditions of the house, and can take place this season or next just as they did a hundred years ago, I have never seen one myself. I have seen almost every degree of pleasure and excitement manifested, and I have certainly (even lately) heard prolonged cheering of the kind hardly ever evoked any more in New York or London. The riotous hostility which, just fifty-two years ago, irrevocably damned *Madama Butterfly* and threw it out of the theatre, has not occurred for quite a long while, but if it ever does, I would not be at all averse to witnessing it: it might prove cruelty and intolerance and dozens of other things, but one thing it could never even adumbrate is indifference. So far as this aesthetic form is concerned (its breath of life being excitement) I believe indifference is the one mortal enemy.

There is illusion, however, in the idea cherished by many foreigners that the best Italian audience (which is this one) knows its operas by heart. The audience knows favorite lyrical sections (tunes) out of half a dozen Verdi operas, three of Puccini, one each of Rossini and Donizetti, one, perhaps, of Bellini. That is about the size of it. It comes to quite a collection of familiar tunes, and a knowledge of them is very widespread—people hum them, sing them, whistle them, all over the place and under all sorts of conditions. It forms a melodic background, so to speak, to Italian life. But even in the most familiar and beloved of all operas, such as *La Traviata,* the greater part of the work is a musico-dramatic texture. I might run through the text of *La Traviata*—I am doing it now— without finding more than a dozen such tunes, or portions of tunes, which are familiar to most Italians. This means familiar as tunes. Very few Italians would know the words, except in spots; very few would know just what the dramatic significance of the melody might be or where it comes in the work. In the first act there are only three: the Brindisi, the duet *"Un di felice, eterea"* (containing the most familiar melody of the opera, here fitting the words *"Di quell' amor,"* and in Act II fitting *"Amami Alfredo"*), and finally, the soprano's great war horse at the end of the act, fragments of which are dinned into the ears of any Italian from childhood. That makes three passages, and for good measure the jolly little jig that brings up the curtain might be added: I have never heard an Italian workman whistling it, but when or if I do I shall not be surprised. That is a lot: it is more than audiences elsewhere would know, even of *La Traviata.* But it certainly cannot be described as "knowing the opera by heart."

From less familiar operas the known tunes would be far fewer. I am speaking, naturally, of tunes an Italian simply absorbs without knowing much about them: tunes which are "in the air," as we say, and nowadays literally in the air, since radio and television use them incessantly. Millions who can never afford to set foot inside the Scala know these tunes, which are as much a part of the national patrimony as the Apennine hills. The Scala audience, having heard more operas more often, may know in a general way something more than the famous tunes: it will often know "what comes next," for instance, although even that is not universal. You have only to hear the gasp that goes over the house when a beloved melody comes gushing out—the gasp itself indicates surprise as well as delight.

However, aside from these melodic episodes treasured among all the people, there is another kind of familiarity which is more valuable for the reception, in particular, of works less often performed. It is this audience's knowledge of the swing of things—"how it goes" —essentially, in a word, what opera *is*. Very keen ears for the art of singing, a love of sound in itself, an appreciation for precision of tempo and for the orchestral body in more complicated works, and a breath-taking excitement over the dramatic intensities—these are the high characteristics of the Scala audience. They are far more valuable than knowing the old familiar tunes or knowing any opera "by heart" (an achievement really reserved for performers—I know several operas more or less "by heart" and could not get through five minutes of any of them without a mistake). These are the characteristics which make the Scala audience so receptive, generally, to new and to foreign works, simply, in sum, that they know what an opera is and know how to listen to it. Mozart, Wagner, Mussorgsky, Debussy, Stravinsky, Prokofieff—such composers, whose work is regularly performed at the Scala, would get scant hearing if everything depended upon the cherished melodies of Papa Verdi. Verdi himself, in his two final masterpieces, never produced a single tune which entered the folklore of his own country, melodious though both *Otello* and *Falstaff* are. *Aïda* was the last of his works to contribute the kind of tune the chambermaid hums while she uses the carpet sweeper, and even in *Aïda* these are very few.

What strange ideas it is possible to form of Italian opera, opera houses, audiences and general musical culture from a distance! Until I began to go to the Scala I had the general notion—not that I had given it much thought—that Italian operas were the staple fare in that house and that not much else would be offered. If this ever was true, and we may suppose it was so once, it is true no longer. In our time the foreign works will sometimes outnumber the Italian works in any given season, and they are always somewhere equal in number. Works which are either new for the whole world, new for

Italy, or new for Milan, take a prominent place in every year's effort; Benjamin Britten, William Walton, Gian Carlo Menotti, along with their continental contemporaries, all get a hearing at the Scala. The "exhumations" are as notable as the novelties: works which have not been heard for a century and more are brought forth so that Vivaldi, Alessandro Scarlatti and other early masters take their turn. The Scala has not one or two or three new productions a year, as the Metropolitan now (after decades) has achieved in the Bing regime: the new ones at the Scala, entirely new, scenery and costumes and stage direction from scratch, average about twenty-four or twenty-five in each season. It is such an impressive total (meaning probably eighty to a hundred stage pictures) that the layman's mind can hardly take in the full extent of the work involved.

The audience has created the Scala, of course. ("To be great poets there must be great audiences too.") That is one reason why I no longer have a vestige of sympathy for those self-appointed censors, arbiters of taste, highbrows of the high, middle and low divisions, who grudgingly admit the excellence of the house and its perennial company but declare themselves unable to acclimate themselves to the audience. Such persons are just what I was at the age of thirty-four when I first frequented the house: I had some hallucination to the effect that only thickly orchestrated music with terrible intrinsic difficulties for the human voice could give the dramatic and musical enhancement which (I thought) opera at its best demanded. Along with this there goes the notion that such music, and also all music, must be heard in religious silence. A good season or two at the Scala would dispel such phantasms from any healthy mind, because the fact is that the best theatre music, if it is true music sincerely performed, excites certain audiences beyond control. I still prefer silence, and always will—except when I feel irresistibly compelled to say something myself. (And, aside from good behavior or manners as imposed upon us, would this not be the same with anybody? Some of the best musicians I have ever known, such as Koussevitzky, have talked out loud almost continuously through performances which aroused their interest enough; another of my acquaintance, one of the greatest artists in the world, hums in his nose, perhaps unconsciously, and also beats time with his fingers.)

The Scala audience is at some remote degree related to those very fine artists, and they are numerous, who cannot keep still during any performance which profoundly disturbs or excites them. The Scala audience does not know the music but it feels the swing, the push, the thrust, the mounting aspiration, the thousand voices arising from the depths. In so feeling, it has perhaps no manners, but there are more important things than manners in an opera house, although not, perhaps, in life.

6

There used to be a small pensione in the Corso Vittorio Emmanuele in Milan, just behind the Cathedral, which was frequented by students of singing and operatic repertoire. They came from more or less every country, and two of them, a boy and a girl, had taken to visiting my lake on their doubtless unlawful occasions. The village where I lived was not at all inaccessible from Milan but not many explorers had found it out, and those who did, including the two students, could hardly long remain strangers to the only other foreigner there. In my first really familiar acquaintance with Milan and the Scala I used to stay in their eighth floor boarding house behind the Cathedral.

It does not exist now. The bombings in the war made away with it and the buildings just next: one big one would have done it. It is altogether likely that it was destroyed on the same night as the Scala (August 16, 1943) since that was the biggest load of destruction Milan ever absorbed.

The Pensione Agostini was a lively establishment, if only because of the noises it made. Signora Agostini (she had beautiful red hair of a most extracapillary color with a dramatic plume of white proceeding from the center of her brow to the north-northwest) permitted her boarders to keep pianos in their tiny bedrooms. No doubt she made up on the food for the privileges thus granted, and anyhow it was hardly possible for her to take any boarders who were not singers, musicians or stone-deaf. In a bedroom at the Pensione Agostini there was room for one single bed, very small, one chair and one piano with its stool. These pianos (and their stools) were rented by the month, tuned by the proprietor according to his own lights, and promptly removed if there was a day's delay in payment. They were not very large, but they were real pianos, not the miniature stringed instrument which America had evolved just about at that time.

My friends, and they may as well be called Rosina and Bill, had pianos of this kind and I suppose they must have worked sometimes, although when I was in Milan they seemed chiefly to be enjoying themselves. Rosina loved to sit at the piano for hour after hour and play German songs which she would sing in the smallest possible thread of voice so as not to "tire" herself on such forbidden pleasures. She was supposed to be singing exercises all this time, of course, every kind of vocalise, arpeggios and trills and runs—she was a coloratura—but she liked Schubert and Schumann and Brahms and nothing delighted her more than running through song after song, hour after hour. Since nothing delighted me more, either, than to listen to them, I spent a great many hours on that bed doing so. Bill, her friend, was a tenor, half-Italian and half-English, and was at this point supposed to be working on repertoire. Specifically it was Rodolfo in *La Bohème,* but the only thing I ever heard him sing was the opening phrases of the opera, about the rooftops of Paris. Maybe that was as far as he ever got. At all events, he, too, spent many hours in Rosina's bedroom while she sang Schubert and Schumann and Brahms. Sometimes I sang them too, in my voice as of an ungreased wagon wheel, but greatly to my own pleasure because each time I learned more about the songs.

Those were rather curious days, not to be repeated, not to be exaggerated either, but they had their value. The pinnacles of the Cathedral were straight in front of us, out the window. The Pensione Agostini was on the eighth floor, as I remember, at the highest point of the Cathedral. From all the other rooms in the boarding house, especially after about half past three or four in the afternoon, there came squawks and yells of every description. There was also a violinist in the house who sawed away at what seemed to be the same three or four notes for hours every day, week after week. I never spent more than about three days in the place, in which my own variety of work would have languished unutterably—I always went back to Lago Maggiore to work and only returned when I wanted to hear something at the Scala.

Rosina seemed to know every American singing pupil, and many others of the most disparate nationalities, whether they lived in the Pensione Agostini or not. With her and her Bill I met quite a few of them. It would be pleasing to think that some of those young folk had come to great rewards in the years afterwards, but I never heard of one who did. Rosina herself did give recitals in America, I believe, for a while. There was a thin, terribly serious boy called Giovanni—an Italo-American—who had the best voice in the boarding house. When he worked at repertoire with an accompanist, which he could not afford to do very often, there was no use competing with it: nobody else in the Pensione Agostini could attempt to practice because his voice ruled the air. He was working on *Rigoletto,* and some months later Rosina and Bill and I, with some other singing students who were his friends, went to Intra on Lago Maggiore to hear him sing it in the little theatre there. He was very good, but after a season or two in touring companies in America he, too, vanished from my ken.

The fact was that Milan at that time was filled with students whose purposes were either too serious or not serious enough. Giovanni worked too hard: I have an idea that his voice was worn out before it was ever exhibited in public. Rosina did not work nearly enough; Bill did not work at all. And there were many who had come to Milan out of sheer misconceptions of one sort or another, such as the notion that a few months in this home of Italian opera would—with or without work—make it possible to get lucrative engagements in America, England, Czechoslovakia or Norway. One of the strangest cases was that of a Negro boy I met in the Galleria with Rosina. We had an apéritif on the terrace of the Biffi café there one spring morning with him. He was studying *Otello:* not voice, not singing, simply the part of Otello, as straight repertoire. He was a very small boy and seemed very young. I looked at him in utter amazement. I asked him if he had ever heard the opera and he said he had not. I asked if he had those terrible high notes and all the brassy power which the part demands and he said he did not. He told me he was a light, lyric tenor not at all suited, so far as he could see, to the part of Otello, although since he had not heard it he could not properly judge. He had heard a few records from *Otello* and had his own doubts if he could ever make enough noise to be heard over that orchestra. I asked him why he was studying it. He said, with the quite unconscious pathos of the very young, "They tell me it is the only part a Negro tenor can ever sing."

They were, many of them, pathetic; some were even ridiculous. But I think the one that seemed to me most truly woeful was that poor little American Negro, whom I saw only once. I might have said to him that an Otello of his size, even if vocally competent, would find it hard to play the part in a great opera house. I might have said that all the teachers on the broad earth cannot make a heroic tenor out of a light lyric tenor—they are more different, in some ways, than tenor and soprano—and I might further have said that a good *tenorino* is always better than a bad pseudo-dramatic tenor. All that, indeed. But I was silenced by the simple statement, which, alas, I know to be a fact, that Otello is the only part open to a Negro tenor. He must sing that or not sing in the opera house at all.

They were a strange lot, those students, and there must be the same lot in Milan today: every year there must be the same rush of eager ignorance into a citadel which is all too ready to take their money and let them go. Only a few years later, I was myself, although vicariously, involved in this pathos of ignorant ambition. There was, in the village in England where my father-in-law's family lived, a tenor. His wife, a charming woman, was cooking for us that year, and doing it extremely well. It was some months before I learned that her husband was a high and very strong tenor who had received encouragement from numbers of part-time teachers in the country and in London, but had been unable to pay for the training requisite to a career. He was employed as an occasional agricultural laborer—in effect, as a ploughman. This seemed to me an outrage, one of the maleficent results of a haphazard social organization, if, that is, he really did have a voice. I set about arranging to hear a few songs from him one evening in the small drawing room of my father-in-law's house, where the piano was—I thought it would be about right for an amateur voice and we could save the trouble of moving the piano to the big room. Nobody was present except my wife, her parents, her sister and other members of that household.

I had naturally left the choice of the songs up to the tenor, whom we met for the first time that night. He was large and handsome, which is no handicap, and he seemed perfectly confident. I was a little dismayed to see that he had brought extremely ambitious music with him, and still more dismayed when the accompanist proved (from the very first note) incapable of playing what was written. However, the tenor sang.

It is of record before witnesses that he sang Rodolfo's narrative out of the first act of *Bohème* and the arioso of Canio from *I Pagliacci*. After that I was so stunned that I did not know what he sang, but I believe there might have been the last act lament from *Tosca* and perhaps something else, all of these things in Italian and all at the full strength of an absolutely stentorian voice. He had not the remotest notion of what he was singing. It was quite obvious from the way in which the words were pronounced that no one of them had any meaning to him. (That is, he might have been told what *amore* meant, or something of that sort, a few raisins in the pudding, but the text itself was total gibberish.) And yet the power of the voice was so tremendous that we were all nearly blown out of the room. I regretted bitterly that I had not taken the trouble to have the piano moved into the big room so that there could have been a fair opportunity to hear the quality as well as the power.

After that rather deafening experience my wife and I had a few days of reflection and discussion. I thought that it was unfair to raise the tenor's hopes, and that we should therefore do something. I did not believe in English singing or English teaching—the occasional exception, such as later occurred in the case of Kathleen Ferrier, could never convince me—and I thought if we were to do anything we should do it right: give him a year in Milan with the best available teacher for a tenor, pay for his entire maintenance and that of his wife, since I regarded it as a criminal interference in the lives of others to separate husband and wife. All this was a fairly big project, even though at the time I was not foolishly unconcerned about sums of money. I did not quite know what to do. My wife suggested that a few well-chosen friends might help us in making a sort of purse to sustain the couple for a year in Milan.

The war and all the stupendous events connected with it have erased a good deal of this from my memory, but what I recall is that George Arliss and his wife Flo, who were neighbors in our village, gave us twenty or thirty pounds, as did my wife's sister Blossom and her husband, Mr. F. G. Miles. Probably our friend Sidney Beer, the conductor, was also tapped for this high purpose, and I know that there may have been one or two others, as well as Lady Forbes-Robertson, my mother-in-law, always so kind and good. The bulk of the money had to come from me. I arranged through the banks to have it paid regularly in Milan and then had to find living quarters (not in the Pensione Agostini, which was full) and a teacher and all the rest of it for my loud, high tenor and his shy, charming wife.

The finding of the teacher was the worst part. I was determined that it must be the best in Milan, which in my view would be the best in the world—this boy had enough handicaps to surmount anyhow, since he came from a class without social or economic advantage in his own country and had received little education, and was in any case thirty years of age, which I knew to be too old. Only the best would do. And what a tremendous undertaking that turned out to be! I appealed to Toscanini, John McCormack, Chaliapin and I hardly know how many other great artists of my acquaintance. They did not have much to suggest because they none of them believed very much in teachers for a case where the groundwork had not been done. Chaliapin, in fact, told me that no teacher was any good whatsoever, that nobody could learn anything from a teacher but only from colleagues. By some complicated process of comparing notes I settled on the Maestro Cotone, already quite old, who had been a pupil of Edoardo Garbin, the original Fenton in *Falstaff*. Cotone received, as I remember, the accolade of Toscanini too, in some complication of the correspondence (through somebody else).

At all events the tenor and his wife went to Milan and spent a year there and had all the lessons Maestro Cotone thought he could take. I had quite a few letters from the wife, charming letters too—none from the tenor. I had regular reports from Maestro Cotone's secretary. I have a pretty shrewd idea that my ploughman-tenor did not work and that his native intelligence was not sufficient to put him into command of even a rudimentary knowledge of the Italian language in that entire year. His wife learned Italian; she would have learned everything else for him too if she could have done so, but there are things a human being must learn for himself.

At the end of the year, and it was also the outbreak of the war, the Maestro Cotone wrote to me that it was of no use for me to spend my money any more on this tenor. He said that the young man showed no real progress at all. The Maestro had written to me, at the beginning of the year, to say that the voice was strong, high, loud (which I knew) and might be brought into some kind of musical compass with work, although much work would be required. If it could be contained, disciplined, it was the kind of voice which might be good in opera. Now, at the end of the year, he said that there was no possibility of doing anything with this voice because its owner seemed utterly incapable of learning either his words or his music correctly in anything, even in the simplest song. He could *not* learn to sing Italian correctly and he could *not* learn to count one-two-three-four. This, of course, quite aside from the vocal discipline (making a trained voice out of an assemblage of powerful sounds).

That experience taught me a good deal, I think. Interference with the lives of others (even in the best of intentions) is always wrong. If a man wants to sing he will find ways and means. He may even find somebody who will send him and his wife to Milan for a year with the best teacher there is. But he *does not wait for somebody else to do it for him.* My *Pagliacci-Bohème* tenor was merely somebody with a set of vocal chords, glands and diaphragmatic development which enabled him to emit very loud, high noises, which delighted and surprised his neighbors. Since he had nothing whatsoever in brain, heart or temperament to go with these noises or put them to use, he was merely another in the endless pilgrimage of the would-be singers to Milan. They do not wish to sing; they wish to "be singers." They have no desire to express anything but only to exhibit something. And, most of all, what the episode proves is that without brains of some kind (not exalted, but applicable brains) there can be no singing. We have all known many quite brainless singers, and Chaliapin himself was one of the most glaring examples, but this only means that every ounce of intellection in their organisms went to their work, with nothing left over for the brainwork of ordinary life. A person who cannot learn to count one-two-three-four or to pronounce a word correctly can never be a singer, no matter what noises come out of the throat.

7

The broad high meadows of Verdi's best work, which is to say the best of all Italian music and the best of all opera, were never mine in Italy: they were reached by another route. To this very day I have never heard the Verdi *Requiem* in Italy, although it would suit my thesis of church-and-theatre very well to say so. On Washington's Birthday (the day on which I write this) I must be particularly careful not to tell a lie. I have heard *Falstaff* all over the world except in Italy; I have heard the Verdi *Requiem* most of all in New York but stupendously first, tremendously and overwhelmingly first, in Salzburg; and I have heard *Otello* only in New York and London, or in the snowbound silence of a farmhouse in Vermont, and oftener still in my own mind both asleep and awake. None of these things, the highest achievement of the Italian genius since Dante, have come to me in Italy itself, as it happens—circumstance is frequently perverse enough to play these tricks on us.

Never mind. It was in Italy that I made my way toward them and began to understand the logic of their being. In the lake and the mountain I saw their deep, glistening honesty; in the Scala theatre at Milan I heard the lesser works of their sincere and true creator; when the time came (in Salzburg first of all) I was ready. The pinnacles of the Milan Cathedral pointed to the fugal farewell, the comedy in counterpoint, which is *Falstaff*. And I think it was perhaps Violetta's cry as she looks into the glass—*"Ah, come son mutata!"*—that made it possible for me to receive into the innermost depths of my being the greater and later cry, *"Libera me Domine de morte aeterna."*

6 : *Fidelio*

My older daughter must have had a great surfeit of music as she was growing up: it used to surge and pulse through the whole house at all hours of the afternoon, evening and night, although I rather doubt if it gave much trouble before noon. She acquired a repulsion —not a prejudice only, but a sincere and deep repulsion—toward it, and since I have never believed in the possibility of overcoming a natural taste or distaste, I accepted this fact for what it was and let it go. One day in our farmhouse in Vermont there was a guest at lunch time who fell into a discussion of certain works of Johann Sebastian Bach and their characteristics; I think it was on a Sunday and we had been playing organ chorales on the gramophone while the children were outside pursuing their own high purposes. I suddenly realized that all this talk about Bach must sound like a Chinese dialect to my anti-musical daughter, and I stole a glance at her as she demurely kept her eyes on her plate.

"I expect we'd better change the subject," says I. "I really doubt if Linda has the faintest idea who Bach is or was."

She looked up with a flash of amusement, not at what I said, but at me. (I think she was about ten at the time.)

"Oh, yes I do, Daddy," she said confidently. "He's the guy that invented music."

She was inordinately proud of her command of the American language; it had the charm of novelty since she delved into it only during the summer holidays from her school in England. The word "guy" did not, therefore, occasion surprise, although it seemed almost to require quotation marks in her very English voice, but I was startled to find that she had such a conception of the true historic position of J. S. Bach. It reminded me of Mr. Pontifex in Butler's *Way of All Flesh*—remember?—who hated what he called "modern music" and never stopped delivering lectures about its iniquity. Once somebody asked him where he put the beginning of this degeneration. He said, solemnly, portentously, with the full awfulness he gave almost every utterance: "Modern music begins with Johann Sebastian Bach."

It amused me vastly to find that my very young daughter, across about a century of time and almost innumerable differences of circumstance, should be found in the same lobby with Mr. Pontifex. It could never drop out of my memory because, essentially, it is so true: "Bach is the guy that invented music."

It is true, that is, for me. (No other canon of truth has a firm foundation in such matters.) The music preceding Bach is sometimes of the most heavenly beauty in certain stated performances by specialists. They have to make up their own way of doing it, naturally, since nobody nowadays or for a long time past has really known how seventeenth-century music should be performed. The orchestrations differ in every performance; the depth and strength of harmonization may vary widely; the ornamentation even for the voices is more or less optional; the true intention of the composer cannot be penetrated except by happy divination, sometimes unattainable. Sincere and noble musicians have devoted their lives to this early music; I respect them most profoundly. I have even had the honor and privilege of long conversation with Mlle. Nadia Boulanger, one of the finest of these musicians, on the subject of Monteverdi, and at this or any other moment any performance of anything by Monteverdi arouses my interest to the extent of my final kopek. That same final kopek would be expended for Vivaldi, too, or conceivably several others: I speak, of course, as a member of the public, a listener to performances, not as a student of scores or a philosopher of music.

And yet the simple truth is that which my daughter enunciated so plainly. Modern music, and this in effect is to me all music, began with J. S. Bach. It is impossible for all but a very few specialists to understand the musical language of Bach's predecessors, with the single exception of the luminous Handel who may, for our purposes, be regarded as an elder brother. The earliest music is almost indecipherable, and to me is totally so: the work even of Handel himself must be rather freely treated nowadays to be susceptible of performance. With J. S. Bach we come into the realm of true communication between the composer and the public. He wrote most of it down himself, with pen and ink and on paper, so that there could be no mistake. All the cryptic signs and symbols of an earlier day had been, by now, translated. (The figured bass, naturally, remained.) Moreover, the instruments of performance had been brought to a high level of perfection—in the case of the violin, the viola and perhaps also the violoncello, to a perfection never attained thereafter—and the training of the human voice had not only progressed very far, but, regrettably, too far, so that it almost ceased to be human and had to be brought back to reality by hard black notes on white paper. The liberties allowed to singers in even the late eighteenth and early nineteenth centuries would be regarded as insanity today, and the craze for artificial sopranos (men whose voices were whitened, dehumanized and elevated by physical castration) made the composer's contribution to much of his own work little more than perfunctory. The *castrato* in the eighteenth century made up his own music in the great showy scenes—not only cadenzas and ornamentation, but actually long cardinal passages contrived to exhibit the peculiarities and individual proficiencies of the singer. Instrumental performers before Bach had also much the same liberties upon occasion, since in their case, too, a good deal of the music was indicated rather than fully written.

This, however, is a mere historical divagation compared to the essential fact that the music of Bach speaks to us directly. It only really dropped out of the consciousness of mankind for a brief period, possibly fifty years at most. The greatest of his children, Mozart and Beethoven, were tremendously aware of him. If the musical public had to be reminded, some decades later, by the performances given by Felix Mendelssohn and the critical writings of Schumann, among others—and if there were difficulties even in our own time in hearing enough of these works, especially in their larger forms and aspects—is it not the fault, chiefly, of the musicians? They have their waves of direction and intention, just as all other humans do. They are not wholly governed by public taste, by any means (if, indeed, anybody knows anything about public taste). They are governed chiefly by their own taste, which varies from decade to decade. An artist like Miss Rosalyn Tureck, who at this moment gives unprecedented performances of the music of Bach on the piano, would probably not have been possible fifty years ago. That Bach is contemporary, that he is "modern" in the highest degree, that he is the most modern of all moderns, was a discovery made, as I remember, only about thirty years ago—Stravinsky *stentator*—and those persons who, in my youth, performed Bach recitals did so chiefly upon the harpsichord, which, as Mozart so instantly understood, was a mere forerunner or adumbrator of the pianoforte. (I tread on dangerous ground—the harpsichord has its fanatical devotees even now —but I am sustained by the august shades of Mozart and Beethoven. If Bach had possessed a pianoforte he would have composed for it also.)

One more point, before I get to my onions: has anybody now alive failed to notice how much of the work of Mozart is being performed all over the world in the year 1956? Why? Because it is the two hundredth anniversary of his birth—that is the reason given. It may be a reason but I think it is only an excuse. At the present moment every artist in the world of music, with no exception I can readily call to mind, has a vast Mozart repertoire. Every pianist, violinist, chamber-music player, orchestral conductor, singer and virtuoso of every description has Mozart treasure to give forth. Without the slightest difficulty you can get up a good program of Mozart's music anywhere on earth where there are musicians. It could not have happened even so much as twenty-five years ago. When I was growing up, and indeed until I was in my thirties, there were hardly any opportunities offered to hear Mozart's work in the opera houses; the symphonies and some chamber music were currently performed, although not as they are today; and as for the piano, everybody knows that the programs of our youth (I mean this century up to about 1935) had a much heavier reliance on Chopin and Liszt than they do now. This is no denigration of the work of other composers, least of all of the wondrous Chopin; it merely means that in fact Mozart's compositions were not performed as much some decades ago as they are now. Why? I think it is the choice (or the taste) of the musicians themselves. They are all soaked in Mozart today. So are the singers. They were not soaked in Mozart when I was growing up, and I believe I was about twenty-two years old before I heard that first Mozart opera—a *Figaro,* and in Duesseldorf as I have described —which remained unique for years. At the Metropolitan Opera House in New York, the Scala in Milan and the Paris Grand Opéra these masterpieces hardly ever received a performance during the 1920's. No Mozart opera received a performance at the great season of 1924 at Covent Garden, when Bruno Walter revived the glories of the past and introduced the reigning artists of the next decades. Exceptions there were—Gatti-Casazza did his long-delayed *Così Fan Tutte* in the 1920's, but in a chocolate-box manner, antiquarian to a degree—and the Paris Grand Opéra dug up *Die Entführung* during that decade (called *Un Enlèvement au Sérail*). Mozart, in other words, although he seems today the most universally admired of composers, has had his ups and downs just the same as all the others, and there is no use supposing that because he is the most popular composer of 1956 he will necessarily be the most popular of 1966.

Bach, initiating this period of direct communication between composer and public—the most direct form of speech existing in human experience, I believe—was by every test the master of everything since. The word master, as here used, is equivalent to the Hindu *guru,* the old man teaching the young; or it is like Socrates asking questions; or it is like the Pope blessing "the city and the world." The chances are that Bach had not the vaguest notion of what he was doing. He was a musician like everybody else in his family, before him and after, and he wrote his music about as instinctively as the beaver builds a dam, and about as industriously. He had a marvelous adaptation to his own language, that of musical idiom (harmony, counterpoint, polyphony), and the stories about how he could use it are numerous and generally known—a fugue on the letters of his own name, for instance, and other musical jokes of an erudite nature. We know how Frederick the Great, the old fox, tried him out, and how quickly any other local emergency could produce from Papa Bach the required response. I have always thought the funeral of the burgomaster's widow, for which he quickly wrote the immortal *"Jesu, Meine Freude,"* was the highest point of this instinctive or natural capacity. There are many, many others.

However, if Bach had been merely an extraordinary manipulator of the musical idiom—a man who could put anything into counterpoint—a man who could give an answer to any conceivable musical difficulty of the time—erudite, skilled, proficient to the point of automatism—modern music would not have flowed as it did, powerfully and inevitably, from his invention. What he put on top of the erudition and facility was an expressive gift which had never existed before or had never been written before. It was on top in many cases, but it permeated the entire composition in many other cases, so that the slightest toot of the bassoon has an expressional or expressionistic relation (not merely by harmony or counterpoint but by sound as governed by feeling) with the prevailing utterance. This is what originated modern music. Not, that is, either harmony or counterpoint, and not the greater facility of writing them; not the increasing perfectibility of the individual instruments; if these had been the creative elements, many others—even Dittersdorf!—might have been Bach. The distinctive and seminal flow, bathing the subsequent centuries, was the music that expressed ardor, despair, aspiration, the experience of the human soul. That is why we respond to a speech originating so far away from us in every respect. The elementals, such as, for example, joy, are independent even of language, any language. They speak to the innermost being. Until music had become capable of so speaking across every intervening obstacle, of transcending, that is, every known difficulty of communication and reaching the absolute heart, yours and mine, it was not music.

Two objections arise immediately: first, there was "expression" in music before Bach, and, second, all of Bach's music is not "expressive" by any means. Some of it is mathematical and abstract in effect as well as by intention.

This, of course, is true. Neither music nor any other creative activity of mankind goes by a system of red-and-green lights. Expressivity of instruments and voices, the use of sound to touch or move the listener, arose long before Bach and must, indeed, have been one of the original wellsprings of even the most primitive music. Furthermore, we see in Bach himself a mass of abstract music (the *Art of the Fugue,* for example) in which whatever stirring of the listener's pulse may take place must be the result of idiosyncratic adaptations, a love of musical arithmetic, an admiration for structure or a glow from actual performance. There is a further mass of Bach's music (the *Musical Offering* and the *Brandenburg* concerti are examples) in which an expressive content, sometimes very strong, depends on the listener's receptivity and willingness to be swayed by sound as well as structure. In other words, the muse did not suddenly manipulate the traffic lights of history and declare: "Here is Bach; from now on there will be expression in music, and music will become primarily one of the arts of expression." Such sudden scene-changes and transpositions of purpose do not occur even in political history, still less in music, literature or painting. Things flow rather than jump. It takes a long time, a century or two in retrospect, to perceive that at some moment the tide really did change, and a new direction did set in. It was in Bach's work that the ebb and flow and the final power of the victorious tide can be seen, that is all: and it is in this sense that both Mr. Pontifex, in Butler's novel, and my daughter in her own way, set a finger on the truth.

I have an idea that we make our way to this original alma pater through many highways and byways. I have myself known persons (several) who arrived at a mighty predilection for Bach through modern American jazz music, more or less skipping everything else that has been written. We are all very familiar with the critics and musicians, generally under thirty-five years of age, who arrogantly condemn all music between Bach and Stravinsky. They were far more common in the 1920's and the 1930's than they are today, but they flourish in the freshman and sophomore years at any university even now. With some critics, such as the late Constant Lambert, this was a thoroughly reasoned position: he considered that all music beginning with Beethoven was a deviation, and said so often. He would willingly have forgotten the whole nineteenth century in music. Some of our young absolutists do not have Con-

stant Lambert's thorough musical knowledge—far from it: they scorn a great mass of music which they have not heard and which they declare they "couldn't possibly listen to." This is an attitude of mere faddism and would not be worth mention if it had not become so widespread among intellectuals—who, in my long experience of them, do not really like music anyhow and are delighted at any excuse for reducing the quantity of it which their mysterious standards oblige them to hear.

The most ordinary way to the springs of music is, I think, roughly analogous to my own: that is, we go backwards in time as we grow older. My own musical experience may be special in one respect, in that it had for a long time (still has, although less) a heavy dosage of music for voices with orchestra, chiefly opera; this may be common, but it is not general enough to be called universal. What does seem to be universal is the way in which all who really love music and make of it a highly valued element in life (essential to it) tend to progress forwards and backwards at the same time—getting older in years and in actual acquaintance with works written and performed, and yet at the same time becoming more and more addicted to the earlier of them. It almost seems that with an extra decade of years added to our lives we take one off in our musical preferences. That, of course, is a manner of speaking: we cannot add and subtract quite so simply. The "discovery" of even the earliest music can come to very young people: I know a young girl with such a Dolmetsch-Trapp upbringing that almost any music after Bach sounds to her like an air raid. I once deliberately played the *Meistersinger* prelude on the gramophone in her presence to see what would happen. She seemed stunned into insensibility and a kind of incredulous horror. Once I put on some early recordings of Caruso (Neapolitan folk songs) and she shut her ears tight with her thumbs. I need hardly say that she was a devoted player of the recorder and other premusical proto-instruments.

However, these are the exceptions and my own awkward and bumbling progression seems far more the rule, so far as I can tell, in that vast musical public to which I belong. The whole of music is presented to us at once, from childhood: that is, almost any program to which we listen anywhere in this world begins with early music and ends with later works. It is iron custom. And yet for some

complex of reasons the later work "speaks to us" first, and it is only
as we grow older that we pierce the barrier and go back, through
the early nineteenth century, into the eighteenth, and sometimes
(many of us) beyond.

Bernard Shaw says there exists a short story by Richard Wagner,
somewhere in his immense collected works (I have never been able
to find it), in which a dying musician, visited by a spiritual adviser
on his deathbed, makes a confession of faith. "I believe in God,
Mozart and Beethoven," he says.

2

The soft, rainy summers of Salzburg before the war were hospitable to a musical audience which came from more or less everywhere
on earth. Mozart's birthplace has its own charm, regardless of music,
and would be visited by travelers in the travelers' season whatever
happened; but the festival, originally only of Mozart's work, has
brought about an increase of the amenities and no doubt an exploitation of the charm. There was a Mozart festival before 1914, created
largely by the efforts of that fabulous singer of an earlier day,
Mme. Lilli Lehmann. John McCormack used to tell me about one
of the regrets of his own career as a singer: he wanted to sing Don
Ottavio at Salzburg. It was all arranged for 1914, in one of the most
remarkable casts ever assembled: Lilli Lehmann herself was to
undertake Donna Anna, with Mme. Gadski as Elvira and Geraldine
Farrar as Zerlina. John was to sing Don Ottavio with Antonio Scotti
as Don Giovanni and Chaliapin as Leporello. The unimaginable
sextet, with the Vienna Philharmonic, was to be conducted by Dr.
Karl Muck. Along came the First World War just as they were getting ready for it, and the event never occurred: it was one of the
most brilliant of the might-have-beens in music.

In the mid-1930's another realization took place at Salzburg, not
quite so preëminently in many voices, perhaps, but on a plane of
total excellence which in my own experience has not been surpassed, and which, truth to tell, it would be difficult even to equal at
another time or place. The Vienna Opera and The Vienna Philharmonic were the workers in the vineyard, as they had been
before, as they are now, and as they will be, we all hope, far into the

future. To their resources were added the gifts of a considerable number of extra singers from Milan, Berlin, Munich and elsewhere, with concert soloists and virtuosi on special occasions and with the conducting skills of Bruno Walter and Arturo Toscanini besides Vienna's own.

Bruno Walter was the moving spirit of the festival in those years and took all the Mozart performances, along with a memorable production of Gluck's *Orfeo*. His wondrous musicality, never rigid or inhuman, glowed through all the works that came under his command, and I have never doubted that the revelation of Mozart's stage music came to me then and there, under his direction. He also invited Arturo Toscanini to conduct symphonic concerts and certain other works at the festival during three momentous years (1935-1938), and it was thus that we had bestowed upon us the revelations of the Verdi *Requiem, Falstaff* and Beethoven's *Fidelio*. Between them, Walter and Toscanini made the little town in the Salzkammer hills a world capital for three summers.

They were enchanted summers, even though the weather in Salzburg is about as undependable as it could be anywhere. Rain or shine, there was a halo of rare excellence over the days as they passed, and I think even the country folk of the Salzkammergut, who never went near the musical performances, were aware that these times could not often occur and would not come again. For myself, by 1935 I was already extremely uneasy about the shadow of Hitler, which, only three years later, was to obliterate Salzburg and Vienna for us in the West; in 1937, our last summer there, the premonition had become a certainty.

What made the unique quality of these last festivals at Salzburg before Hitler? It was not, surely, just because the pretty little baroque town was Mozart's birthplace. That was the hook on which everything else had to hang, but it was only a hook. Both before and afterwards there were Mozart festivals in Salzburg without the same magic. I shall venture to suggest that the mysterious genius of Toscanini was at its very height during those years—even though I know it had two more decades of unexampled power before it. To say that Toscanini was ever less than supreme is a crime in the eyes of his idolaters, and yet it seems to me that his greatest wizardry invested those Salzburg performances. Perhaps he was himself happier, musically speaking, in Salzburg than anywhere else: the conditions for work were ideal and he never had any of the minor annoyances which, as sometimes in Milan or New York, made things difficult. He had wonderful instruments, the beauty of the Vienna Philharmonic at its very peak, an audience which had traveled far with bated breath, singers unequaled for the tasks he gave them. The baroque town itself contributed its own evocation. And then, finally, I believe that the actual sense of gathering doom—the grim shadow of Hitler—may have intensified the keenness, the exaltation, of the work done there, and our own reception of it. Such things are so intangible that it would not do to insist on them, and yet we all know they exist. We were more or less obeying the injunction of the Prophet Mohammed—Upon Whom Be Peace!—in living each day as if it might be our last. That must have made some difference.

My way of going to a festival was to go to it, all out, one hundred percent, or as near to it as twenty-four hours a day will allow. That is, I went to every symphony concert and every performance of every opera during the two or three weeks I spent there. It might be a method conducive to indigestion at most festivals, but in the Salzburg of those days it was all delight. I cannot remember having been tired even by midnight on a day filled with various offerings. There was chamber music in the afternoons and often in the mornings; recitals were in the late afternoon; the symphony concerts were at eleven in the morning; the opera performances were at seven o'clock in the evening. My first and most memorable hearing of the Verdi *Requiem* was at eleven in the morning, and my first hearing of Miss Marian Anderson at four o'clock in the afternoon. These would be strange hours in any of the great cities, but after one day in Salzburg everything fell into place and assumed its own inevitability. Since we had come there for the festival, the rest of life conformed. I think if we had been, for any reason, summoned to an opera or a concert at three o'clock in the morning we would quite eagerly have made our arrangements to do so. Common sense was in abeyance.

Now, twenty years later, the repertoire of all opera houses and concert halls has changed so very much, largely as a result of these performances I am talking about, that what we heard at Salzburg can be heard with some frequency in all great cities. It was all "old music." A critical retrospect might make that into an accusation: Where was *Wozzeck?* Where were the twentieth-century composers? (I think they were represented in the chamber-music concerts although nowhere else.) But the young, or those who came to maturity after 1935, can hardly imagine how new this "old music" was to us. Mozart was, as I have said before, very little performed in our opera houses and figured much less in our concert programs than he does today. *Falstaff* and the Verdi *Requiem* were both completely new to me; an assiduous consumer of music for more than fifteen years before 1935, I had never had a chance to hear either one of them. *Orfeo* had not been heard in New York or elsewhere when I was on hand to attend. *Don Giovanni* had only just returned to New York after a very long absence from repertoire, and *Figaro* was seldom heard outside of Germany (it reached New York in a revival one year later and has remained). *Fidelio* I had heard in the solitary, and quite unsuccessful, revival of some years before at the Metropolitan under Bodanzky.

Nowadays you can hear all this music, or most of it, in New York, London, Chicago, Berlin, Milan and even sometimes in Paris. In 1935 such a repertoire of masterpieces was regarded as suitable only for special occasions, anniversaries, festivals and the like: the notion that the public in general really does like good music had not yet been born. It made its way, to a very considerable extent, as a result of these Salzburg performances; people went to Salzburg and returned home demanding something better of their own native operas and orchestras than they had received before. Furthermore, after this Salzburg conflagration, the Glyndebourne Festival in England began, the gramophone companies started giving more attention to masterpieces, and the result is that now you can hear almost anything you want to hear without stirring from your own fireside. Whole operas by Mozart are within reach of your hand, whereas twenty years ago even a solitary show piece out of one of them was hard to find. Salzburg may not have been a principal cause of this revolution in repertoire and public taste, but it was at the very least an early and most conspicuous symptom of the change and thereby helped to accelerate it.

Bruno Walter's way of performing Mozart was such that it would have been difficult for anybody neither deaf nor heartless to resist it. He had not one trace left (if he had ever possessed it) of the metronomic and routine quality which is so common in the opera houses of Germany. He did not give in to sentiment, but he molded the phrases with a sort of plasticity which allowed every meaning to come forth and yet kept the whole within the limits of time, structure and form. It was the best Mozart, both in the concert hall and the opera house, known to the period; it was expressive music, truly enough, but strictly contained in classic form; and although there was thunder and lightning on occasion, most of what it had to say came to us with that smiling grace which belongs to it by nature. There are conductors today who approach this most natural of all composers with a portentous, frowning piety which magnifies every difficulty; like the "precision" choruses so much in vogue at the moment, their aim seems to be to frighten rather than to delight. No matter how difficult any passage might be, it was Walter's accomplishment to make it seem as easy as sunlight on a waterfall, and that, it seems to me, is the only right way for Mozart.

Don Giovanni and *Figaro,* known to me in very few performances (two of each? scarcely more than that) scattered over fifteen years and two continents, became familiar and beloved works during those seasons in Salzburg under Walter's ever skillful hand. Ezio Pinza sang both parts: still a trifle vociferous at the beginning, and more than a little vulgar, he made an extraordinary adaptation to the style, so that in the end at Salzburg (and afterwards in New York and elsewhere) he was a remarkable performer of this music for which he had small natural affinity. Born for Verdi and Rossini, he evolved into Mozart, and if he lacked, to the very end, the full *grand seigneur* quality of Don Giovanni, he made up for it by a vitality, not to say sexuality, which did a great deal for the drama. The soprano Dusolina Giannini—an excellent Donna Anna—and the tenor Dino Borgioli were among the other notable elements of Walter's triumph. In *Orfeo,* broadly and nobly done with a particular beauty in the final scene, the protagonist when I heard it was always Mme. Kerstin Thorborg from Sweden, then in full control of her grand contralto.

Sitting over the beer at the Café Bazar or dawdling on the bridges across the swift little river, we were always, so to speak, in the festival house or one of its subsidiary concert halls; these conductors and singers and performances were forever discussed. I know, therefore, from the amazement of others as well as from my own, what a profound impression was made in Salzburg by the apparition of Miss Marian Anderson. Rumors had gone forth from the Soviet Union and from Berlin, where she had been heard before she came to Salzburg, but on the afternoon when she was first made known to us she was quite new and utterly unexpected to that audience. It was an invited audience consisting of the very great (Toscanini, Lehmann, Walter) as well as of many lesser lights from the Vienna Philharmonic and Opera; it included the Archbishop of Salzburg; it took in a sort of cross section of the festival visitors, myself with bride among them. With all this it was still a very small audience and behaved with a singleness of response which, perhaps, only small audiences can feel. When there was applause, for example, it was an outburst, but when there was no applause—which was most notable after the spiritual on the Crucifixion—it seemed an electrical silence. I was myself paralyzed and could not have applauded if I had wished to do so; but it was a surprise, when I had time to think of it, that everybody else was in the same condition. Anderson's incomparable voice and intensity of purpose, her rapt and trancelike absorption in the music, her dark, angular beauty, all made the experience unlike any other, and no matter how many times it was repeated thereafter, that first occasion remains one of the rarest any of us there present can remember. A mantle of tragedy—that of an individual, of a race, of a destiny—seemed to envelop this artist and set her apart from all others. She was exquisitely capable of pure singing without racial color or sadness— the Schubert *"Ave Maria"* was a case in point—but her own personality, however suppressed, dwelt in the music just the same because it came from within her. The quality is hard to analyze or describe because it is excessively difficult to understand; it can hardly be called "racial" because no other Negro singer has ever possessed it; at the same time it is scarcely to be found in the music alone; it is like all art at its height, a mystery beyond our comprehension. The enormous audiences which thereafter applauded Anderson throughout the world must have felt a great deal of this, naturally —I felt it myself even in such vast places as the Metropolitan in

New York and the Paris Grand Opéra—and it is a quality which also can be heard through mechanical contrivances such as radio and recordings. After twenty years of intermittent reflection on the subject, I came to the conclusion, a year or so ago, that it is essentially a religious phenomenon. Some of the Bach arias obtainable on the gramophone (*"Es ist vollbracht,"* for example, or *"Bereite dich, Zion"*) contain it in a remarkably pure form, but I also distinctly remember hearing the same thing in *"Ah, mon fils!"* from Meyerbeer's *Prophète* when the artist sang it once in Paris. To call the quality "racial" is a fallacious way out of a difficulty—it suffices to repeat that no other singer of any race has had it. It shows in Negro spirituals strongly, of course, by the nature of that music: but it shows equally strongly in Beethoven's *"Die Himmeln rühmen des Gottes Ehre."* Unexpectedly, it is to be heard in songs by Schubert as well as in clearly or obviously devotional music. In short, a religious artist is a religious artist, whatever subject may be undertaken, and the point may be made a little clearer by an analogy from painting. Certain painters of the Italian quattrocento would have given a religious feeling to any subject, however profane, and certain others of a later period (Titian, for example) gave a sensuous and worldly feeling to any religious subject they attempted. The personality of the talent determines, and the subject in such cases must be treated as that inner mystery has dictated. After a great many years of listening to this unique artist, I finally concluded that with her, no matter what the material, singing was and is a form of prayer. It may seem obvious once it is stated. It was not at all obvious—it was startling almost beyond belief—when we first met it at Salzburg. I count myself very lucky to have heard it first (no matter how little I understood it) in that company which instinctively bowed, as I did, before the mystery.

3

Toscanini's long and profoundly useful life began under the star of Verdi. He actually, as a very young man, played the violoncello in the Scala orchestra on the first night of *Otello* (February 5, 1887). The publisher Ricordi took him out to Santa Agata later on to see the old man, the glory of Italian music, and in 1902, on the first anniversary of Verdi's death, it was Toscanini who conducted the tremendous open-air performance of the *Manzoni Requiem* for his memorial. Thus in two lives, both far longer and more fruitful than is given to men in general, almost the whole story of the Italian lyrical stage can be told.

Perhaps in filial piety toward the master of his youth and perhaps out of sheer patriotism—an emotion so natural in Toscanini that even Fascism could not kill it—he would have chosen Verdi for that apotheosis in Salzburg. Perhaps. I prefer to think that these were contributory rather than primary causes. Primarily, Maestro Toscanini was concerned to give the best possible presentations of works which he intimately knew to be masterpieces, but which, through neglect and their own intrinsic difficulties, had not been well or widely performed for a long time. In *The Times* of London yesterday (March 5, 1956) my eye falls upon a sentence which expresses some reasons for that neglect: "Verdi's *Falstaff*," the critic says in writing of something else, "has been criticized for its excessive speed, and it is an opera that works out right on the stage only once in twenty times."

Once in twenty times (if, for the moment, we accept this statement) is nowhere near enough for a hard-working repertoire company, and it may be understood that *Falstaff* is regarded as difficult to fit into any ordinary season. Some of its very best effects can only be attained by careful rehearsal and a kind of telepathic communication between conductor and stage artist. The difficulties are musical rather than vocal. That is, no strange or unusual voices are required—it asks for no freakish high or low notes and no phenomenal power or agility in the singing parts—but everybody on the stage as well as in the orchestra is obliged to deliver the music as written, in time and tune, with an exactness seldom achieved or even expected in opera. If they do not all deliver their music precisely on the dot of time, they can, any one of them, ruin the brilliant freshness and joy of that incomparable part-writing which, all-Italian and all-Verdi as it is, must have the clarity of Bach.

This musical precision is hard in an ordinary opera house. It may often be impossible. With one or two good soloists you can get an acceptable performance of *Tristan und Isolde,* even though the rest of the performers be very bad; we can all remember such. In *Fal-*

staff everybody has to be good, musically speaking, although the vocal sounds may vary in beauty. (Good voices are desirable, but good musicianship is essential.) And somehow or other the much-abused public can always tell when a performance is muddy or in-effective, although the reasons may not be apparent. Thus we have the strange history of *Falstaff*, a masterpiece which has never failed to arouse enthusiasm when it is properly performed, and yet goes for years without a hearing. It takes too much work—in a word—for just the ordinary dog days in an ordinary opera house.

Festival conditions, with one of the best of all possible orchestras, with singers eager to offer their services and with rehearsals at will, gave *Falstaff* in Salzburg the chance to unfold its special excel-lence. There was over all the phenomenon of Toscanini, at full blaze, welding every element into a fulfillment of Verdi's inven-tion. In the result, we had there a series of performances the like of which could hardly exist in any other conditions. I should never dream of comparing Toscanini's *Falstaff* at Salzburg with another performance of the same work or possibly of any work. Malcolm Sargent said—and I remember that he was quite pale with awe—after the first one: "I think it is simply the best performance of *anything* that one has ever heard."

The Falstaff in all performances was Mariano Stabile, not, per-haps, a great singer, but one ideally suited to this part, which he had absorbed thoroughly and knew beneath the skin. Even Stabile, I found out afterwards, was not as good elsewhere as he was those seasons in Salzburg. I heard him sing *Falstaff* later under other con-ductors and the same miraculous precision was not attained. Ex-ample: the Honor soliloquy. In this brief outburst one of the most astounding things at Salzburg was the way in which singer and orchestra seemed one instrument in the staccato repetition of "No!" This seems a simple enough thing—the pause and then the single word "No!" on the same tiny nick of time as the staccato chord in the orchestra. Every time it happened in Salzburg it seemed like some kind of minor miracle. I never heard it like that anywhere else afterwards: it may be only by a hair's breadth, but the voice and orchestra are always separate. The eight parts in Act II, again: where else have they been so distinct and yet so together? Or the fugue at the end, indeed?

It was in these hours of astonishment (for I went to every *Falstaff* given while I was there) that I perceived the final greatness of Verdi, the height of mastery combined with humanity which crowned his incredible old age. Other works for the stage might be different but none could ever surpass it.

The *Requiem,* Verdi's memorial to Manzoni, was the reverse of the shield, if you like, in a mood as different as night from day, and a work of almost twenty years earlier. (It was finished in 1874, three years after *Aïda,* and *Falstaff* in 1893.) It has always seemed probable that the *Requiem* was intended to be—as it very nearly was— Verdi's farewell to the composition of music and to the world. Many years passed before he was willing to compose in any large form again; his letters contain a good many indications of his belief that it was all over for him, and good riddance. Boito, that strange creature, by some combination of persuasion, tact, persistence and a selfless immolation of his own gifts, induced the old man to come back once more—after sixteen years away from the theatre—with *Otello,* and then again, at the age of eighty, with the miraculous *Falstaff;* but readers of the Verdi letters know what a tremendous amount of persuasion was required. In saying his farewell to Manzoni, which was simultaneously a Latin prayer for the dead and for the human soul, Verdi entered upon what Mme. de Sévigné calls *les délices d'un adieu,* a state of mind in which the world has little left to offer and has in many respects already perished. The letters do not make this so explicit, but what they do not say the music does.

And, as I learned first in Salzburg from Toscanini, it is music of the Latin genius in which church and theatre become one: there is nothing like it in existence, either in the work of Verdi or anybody else. Verdi emphasized its devotional character by performing it first in a church, but actually nothing less than a symphony orchestra, a first-class professional chorus and a quartet of highly gifted singers can give its stormy grandeur a true hearing. At first in Germany—where it is now performed as often as anywhere else—it was a kind of shock: it is called "operatic," as a term of abuse; only Brahms, at first, knew it for what it was. (His own *Deutsches Requiem,* I always think, is the Protestant version of that same state which here receives a Latin and Catholic expression.) Repeated hearings over the years have never diminished its power to awe and exalt; for me it is without doubt an intimately congenial form of religious passion to begin with (Catholic childhood?); in its despair as in its hope, the questioning that brings in fact no definite answer, the cry for help at the end, its drama seems more real than anything that was ever set upon the stage. It is not in the least "ethereal" or angelic and bears no resemblance to the floating tranquillity of tone we hear sometimes in Anglican cathedrals. Small boys could never sing it. It is human from first to last, a long and stormy meditation upon the soul by adult human beings who are all, all sinners and every one afraid of eternal death.

Toscanini was supremely in control of this music and he had results in Salzburg, in that performance which was my first hearing of the work, such as even he never surpassed afterwards. The drums of the Vienna Philharmonic (in *"Dies irae"*) are said to have been reinforced by an extra layer of skin for that terrifying climax he exacted of them. Orchestra and choir were on the razor's edge of training, tension, response; the soloists were, so to speak, sustained by the toe alone, keyed up for flight. The soprano, upon whom so much depends, was unknown to that audience: she was Mme. Zinka Kunz of the opera company at Zagreb, in Croatia, and this was her first incursion into the great music world of the West. She was to adorn it for a good many years afterwards under the name of Zinka Milanov. Her voice, one of the loveliest of our time, produced, in the B-Flat pianissimo (*"Requiem!"*) such a sound as seldom can be heard. Mme. Milanov continued to sing the *Requiem* thereafter, always with the most ardent beauty; in 1951, with Bruno Walter, she achieved perhaps an even more perfect vocalization; but I might hazard a guess that she, too, thinks of that first Salzburg occasion as one which could not be reproduced. At the end when she said—said? or sang?—*"Libera me Domine de morte aeterna"* she seemed to me to be praying, and no doubt she was. Most of us in that hall, musicians or audience, shaken to the very depths, were doing exactly the same thing.

4

Lotte Lehmann, to whom this book is dedicated, and who afterwards became my especially cherished friend, was the reigning queen of the Vienna Opera at that time. Vienna loved her for appearances in many operas she never sang in countries farther west—*Manon* and *Bohème,* for example, *Eugen Onegin* and several Italian works—as well as for the pieces by Strauss, Beethoven, Wagner and others which she sang in London and America. She had beauty, voice, style, intelligence, everything a singer may need in that arduous career, but along with it she had some very particular gift of emotional communication which it would be as difficult to define as to acquire. You have it or you do not have it; it comes, apparently, from on high, and in my own life I have never seen or heard anybody else on the stage with whom it was a sovereign and compelling quality as it was with Lehmann. Later on, after she stopped singing in opera, this capacity to communicate feeling in every shade came to another fruition and she had a whole new career as a Lieder singer—the best of whom I have knowledge, in the entire German literature from Beethoven to Wolf and Strauss. In 1935 she was hardly beginning as a *Liedersängerin,* and her one recital in Salzburg, with Bruno Walter at the piano, was only an adumbration of what she could and did achieve afterwards. (This is in retrospect: at the time we were all enraptured!)

Lehmann's fame in the West, already great, was based chiefly upon her incomparable Sieglinde—far and away the best of the time—and beautiful impersonations of Elisabeth, Elsa and Eva; upon *Ariadne auf Naxos;* upon an occasional Italian foray such as her Desdemona in London; and, most of all, upon the Marschallin in *Der Rosenkavalier,* which had been all her own for about ten years. Some of her triumphs in Strauss works—*Die Frau ohne Schatten* and *Arabella,* for instance—never reached England and America except as echoes from central Europe, and the kind of season customary in London, New York and Chicago gave no opportunity for her to sing her whole Vienna repertoire or even much of it. Four or five parts were all that most of us had heard from this unique artist, but they were enough to establish our regard for her in a very high and special place with a firm foundation.

Toscanini chose *Fidelio*, with Lehmann as Leonore, for his first performance at Salzburg. Her Leonore in Vienna nine years before, under Franz Schalk, had been acclaimed by all of central Europe during the Beethoven celebrations of 1926, but fame alone, or public recognition, never swayed Toscanini in his choice of a leading artist for any great work. On the contrary: he frequently delighted in excavating artists hitherto unknown and showing what they could do. Sometimes he even seemed to have a prejudice against singers who were too famous or too established, I thought in after years, and insisted upon his unknowns even when they were not the best he could have had. In the case of Lehmann he was swayed not by her fame as Leonore but by his own ardent admiration, which on one occasion, I was told, led him to declare at the end of a difficult passage in rehearsal: "You are the greatest artist in the world."

Well, she was. The sheer ecstasy which she and Toscanini between them got into certain passages of *Fidelio* could not otherwise have come into being. I mean, for example, the part of the *Hoffnungsarie* beginning *"Ich folg' dem innern Triebe,"* or the duet *"Namenlose Freude."* For my own part, I held my breath in those passages every time (I have no idea what Lehmann did) and to this day I am unable to say what the secret was. With other singers (Flagstad, for example, who sang it with Walter later on in New York) nothing of the kind occurred although the notes were the same and were taken just as fast. In fact, it is my conviction that in the complete *Fidelio* recording which Toscanini made some years later he took those passages even faster than he did in Salzburg, but the ecstasy is not there. Ecstasy is not a matter of speed. Nor can any time-beat account for the magical tranquillity of that first-act quartet as Toscanini, Lehmann and the others did it in Salzburg (*"Es ist so wunderbar"*). There was an element in this *Fidelio* at Salzburg which defies technical definition. It was not perfect—not as, for example, *Falstaff* was perfect or nearly so—because in this *Fidelio* there were singers who were not physically able to reach the exalted mood in which Lehmann and Toscanini performed. The incandescence of the conductor and the soprano produced the very curious effect of making one pass over these imperfections almost without noticing them—noticing them, that is, afterwards or remembering them with a certain childish wonder, but paying them no real heed during the performance.

Fidelio is certainly not a work for ordinary repertoire—it requires much too much; it leaves its best participants purged to extinction; when it is really recreated as it was in Salzburg, it leaves even its audience much in need of food, drink and sleep. But just the same it does not deserve the reputation it has had for a century or more of being "unsingable" or "undramatic" or " unoperatic." The main line of the drama is absorbing and the music sets it forth with the passion and skill and sincerity of a master. The central soprano part has long been reserved, in Germany anyhow, for those mammoth voices which otherwise sing only Brünnhilde and Isolde. The general idea is that unless a woman has a voice suitable for a fire engine she cannot sing the part of the faithful wife. I am sure Beethoven had no such notion, and Lehmann supplied the proof—if it were needed—that a richly human voice, warm and full, has far more to offer in this music than any *hochdramatische* goddess. Most Leonores look like the Soviet women competitors in the Olympic games, with sound to match. Lehmann was not a sylph in 1935, but her appearance in that ungrateful costume was more convincing than any other I remember, and every note of her voice conveyed the meaning of the part. Her speaking voice, for instance, had a slow tenderness (sounds like *"kühl"* and *"schwül"*) which extended the beauty of the music even to that part of the drama which is now, I think unwisely, so often omitted. Those who remember Lehmann's Leonore in all its moods and tenses, its whole range, must know very well that this music is not "unsingable" and the character not at all beyond the acting range of an authentic talent.

True, the tenor part does seem more or less unsingable, but only because we have never heard it sung properly. Some day a tenor will come along who has the resources and the skill to do it. In the meantime, when we can get a Leonore like Lehmann we find the tenor's shortcomings obliterated in the general blaze of great music greatly performed.

Blaze is the word that comes to mind most often in thinking of this collaboration between Lehmann and Toscanini. They seemed to take fire from each other; the resulting conflagration warmed

all of us for as long as memory can last, but I never shall know
what caused it.

5

One of the pleasures of life in the festival atmosphere is that the
music-makers and the audience tend to get a little bit mixed up,
owing to close quarters and common preoccupations. In the ordinary
way you could live twenty years in New York and never meet an
opera singer, conductor or an orchestral player—unless, that is, you
happened to be addicted to such company and went out of your way
to seek it. At Salzburg some relaxation of the stern barriers of the
guild system was more or less inevitable. The players of the Vienna
Philharmonic frequented the same beer-drinking place beside the
river—the Café Bazar—which commanded our adherence. I call it
a beer-drinking place, but I have seen many a man sit there all
afternoon over a single cup which had once contained coffee. We
used to see Rudolf Kommer there, and whoever saw Kommer was
introduced to whoever else happened to be in the neighborhood.
There were conductors and singers and musicians of all sorts in the
actual audiences at Salzburg, quite aside from those who performed.
During those summers we used to see Sidney Beer—who had conducted the Vienna Philharmonic and knew many of its players—
Malcolm Sargent and Herbert von Karajan, and it is perhaps from
those days that I derived the impression that nobody gets so excited
over a good performance as a conductor. Karajan, especially, young
and very eager (he stammered in those days, at least in English,
although this has since disappeared) went to every Toscanini rehearsal and was incapable of getting a coherent word out, in spite
of frantic struggles, after any of the supreme performances.

With them, or with others, or merely by the operation of chance
in a music festival, we met a considerable number of music-makers,
actors and others connected with the work of the stage. (Actors
because Max Reinhardt's productions were going on all this time,
although I did not see them when they conflicted with anything in
music.) It was probably the first time in my life that I had ever
been on conversible terms with the actual artisans of these occult
pleasures. I did not have much to say to them but it was one form of

enlightenment, anyhow, to discover that they were not much different from the rest of us when it came to such major considerations as weather, money, nutriment and jobs, the main subjects of ordinary talk. A player of the E-Flat clarinet in the Vienna Philharmonic, I learned to my amazement, got just as wet in the rain as an itinerant scribbler from New York.

Among the acquaintances made in festival time there were, too, some of the actual idols of my *Schwärmerei*. *Schwärmerei* is a peculiar disease (does it not mean, literally, foolishness?) prevalent in opera houses and concert halls, which shows itself in breathless and senseless adoration of either artists in general or of some artists in particular. I suffered from it to an extreme degree at that time and shall never wholly recover, although since then I have known a large number of such demigods and some pretty well. It is a malady of romanticism, in all probability, and consists in the inability to distinguish between the person and the impersonation—that it, between the ideal figure of poetry and music, *la princesse lointaine,* and the living woman of flesh and blood who by aesthetic skills has represented the ideal. I do not think I ever had the kind of *Schwärmerei* which attaches itself indiscriminately to anybody bold enough to set foot on a stage; such wholesale foolishness was beyond me; and I had very little of it for the personages of spoken drama (that is, for few, very few). My *Schwärm* was specialized, but upon those whom it singled out (all singers or musicians) it shed a fantastic radiance which set them apart from other mortals and had the effect of reducing me, a fairly experienced adult, to tongue-tied and agitated adolescence.

In Salzburg it happened more than once. At Anderson's debut, for instance—debut so far as Salzburg was concerned—I was presented to both Lehmann and Toscanini and could not utter a word to either. As a matter of fact I never have been able to originate any remark to Toscanini, although I met him fairly often for the next twenty years; the most I could ever manage was the mumbled conventionality of hail and farewell. Once in New York we were left alone in the same room together for well over half an hour (perhaps deliberately) but I did not dare to speak, and he finally took up a book and read it while I looked at some photographs. This is the limit of imbecility, of course—there are innumerable things I have long wanted to ask him—but the effect of *Schwärmerei* upon me is something akin to paralysis. I do not have it with the ordinary great of the earth. As a journalist I talked often and freely to presidents, prime ministers and the like; neither Mr. Roosevelt nor Mr. Churchill nor Mr. Nehru ever had such an effect upon me in public or in private, and I had quite long conversations with all of them at different times; it seems to afflict me only with these idols of the unconscious, the wizards of my might-have-been, necromancers and magicians as they seem to me, prefiguring unseen powers I have long felt and cannot define.

Lehmann got over all this by her own vivid warmth and compassion; even in Salzburg, at the very beginning, she extended her humanity, with a word and a laugh, to a total stranger. She and her husband Otto had been consulted, by our friend Marcia Davenport, about ways and means of getting married in Austria, which is by no means an easy enterprise. Marcia relayed the information and my wife and I were duly sanctified by the Austrian State at the Rathaus in Vienna (between a *Falstaff* and a *Fidelio,* as I remember). Lotte has ever since contended that she "married" us, which perhaps she did, and at all events her contribution to that result made our acquaintance something different from that of the great artist and the humble admirer. We had, so to speak, a past to share, and acquired it before we met. In spite of that it took years for me to overcome my awe of her enough to speak as if she were a mortal too. (I am not sure that I can even now.) Leonore and the Marschallin got in the way, I suppose, and their totally contradictory personalities may have doubled the witchcraft.

Chaliapin in Salzburg was something else again: it had been years since his *Boris* had shivered my timbers, and although it was impossible not to remember it when I saw him, the case was simplified by the fact that he seemed to have forgotten it himself. A great, roaring Russian genius of the most childlike simplicity, quite unconscious of most things in the daily life of this world, he delighted me most of all by the homogeneity of his character, its pungent separateness from all others, so distinct and monolithic that it seemed invented rather than simply evolved. In a countryside with dozens of lakes and hundreds of churches he once sent a message to his daughter Marina, our friend: "Meet me at four o'clock in front of the church by the lake." If he thought about it at all, he simply knew that by hook or by crook she would get there, whatever the lake and whatever the church. Afterwards in Paris when he was dying he told me that he was perfectly well; "only the heart doesn't go." He said to me about Toscanini: "I know him well—he used to conduct for me in Milan." If you put a character like Chaliapin in a novel I think he would become unmanageable to writer and reader alike, because there was at the same time too much consistency (bold and absolute) along with too much *largeur,* sheer size. In his case I could never quite forget *Boris,* and he always remained of that race apart, half here and half there; but one roar from his capacious lungs was enough to dispel the moon dust and—by means of laughter if nothing else—bring me right down to earth. He had, like Mary Garden, a bold and unconquerable reality in life which was as irresistible as the quite different illusions they had spun upon the stage.

The whole business of human relationships for such artists as these I have mentioned must be far more difficult than it is for others. Their work alone makes them supremely self-centered (they cannot be good unless this is so) and they are surrounded by the kind of *Schwärmerei* I have tried to indicate, which makes a good, solid, truth-telling friendship more or less impossible. For a long period I thought my painful embarrassment in their presence was a private trouble, as you might say my own funeral, but gradually, incredulously, in the face of the mounting evidence, I came to perceive that it was also theirs. They have self-consciousness forced upon them by the behavior of their admirers; the world treats them in such a way that nature must inevitably be lost in the parade; and, above all, the most intimate transaction of their entire lives, that by which they weave the illusion and embody our dreams, is one in which, after their salad days are over, no other person can help, hinder or enhance. Wonderful combinations of highly complete aesthetic phenomena do occur, of course—as in the Lehmann-Toscanini *Fidelio*—but each must be complete and ready or the spark will not fly. Toscanini himself could not make great artists out of the numerous gifted young singers whom he used in his later years for his broadcasts and recordings: a study of those recordings will show conclusively that the most inspired conductor cannot bring out what is not there already. The readiness is all—and this readiness is what must be prepared with toil and tears, in secret, through the long pilgrimage which is the artist's life. I think the reason why the novels and plays which have dealt with great musicians or singers are failures—fail to convince, move or make real—is simply this: that the mainspring of the subject is too private, too secret, for any writer's skill and cannot be shown on any stage. It is a transaction, essentially, between the artist and God, using God as the terse, comprehensible term for a higher power which any artist worth the name must consult and obey in the hour of creation.

Now, if your most intimate transaction is so solitary, if it is at most a sort of dialogue with the unseen, what is left for beer and skittles? What butters the parsnips? Where do the "loved ones" come in and where do they get off?

When Shelley walked into his wife's luncheon party stark naked, that day in Italy, he had undoubtedly been engaged in a dialogue with the unseen and had not yet adjusted his mind to the realities of life with Mary. Humiliating, really, for poor old Mary, but she, anyhow, knew what she was getting into when she married him. Most of the musical artists I have known—I speak only of the very great ones: lesser phenomena have lesser troubles—must do without real comprehension in their lives as human beings; they are compelled to accept worship as a substitute for love.

6

The Vienna State Opera is much younger than the Scala in count of years, but its place in the life of the city and country is no less central: it is perhaps even more so. When the Opera burned (on March 12, 1945, the seventh anniversary of the Anschluss) as a result of incendiary bombs scattered by a returning mission of the American Eighth Air Force, the starved and shattered city regarded it as the most appalling catastrophe of the whole war. I have been given graphic accounts of how the news traveled through the whole mourning metropolis, and how men and women who had far more personal tragedies upon their minds forgot everything to rush to the center. This was not only because the Opera was a big edifice in the middle of the town: the Bristol Hotel, across the street, is also pretty big and equally central, but its destruction would have meant nothing in particular in the midst of such general disaster.

The reopening of the Opera as rebuilt (November 5, 1955) was the occasion for an outburst of rejoicing just as remarkable. Crowds stood in the streets leading to the Opera all through the day and most of the night, weeping and cheering. At night the illuminations and the general festivities reached a multitude of Viennese and Austrians who could not get into the Opera house and who perhaps (many of them) never will set foot inside it. The American Secretary of State and some of our ambassadors to European countries were there, along with all the potentates of the Austrian State so recently freed from military occupation. The vast crowd listened to *Fidelio* as it came from the loud-speakers in the center of Vienna, and during the hours of the performance I have been told that hundreds of thousands stood in silence broken only by tears. Such a thing is impossible to imagine anywhere else.

Lotte Lehmann went to the reopening of the Opera, from her home in California, as a guest of the Austrian State. Eighteen years had passed since the terrible day, March 12, 1938, when Hitler occupied Vienna. It so happens that I was lunching with Lotte in New York on that day, the day of the Anschluss, of which none of us there present knew anything. She drove us downtown in her car after lunch; she was on her way to the hairdresser's, and I believe it was there that she heard the news. What it did to her can be imagined; it was the end of one whole life, certainly; she was ill for days. After that she became an American citizen, a condition which suits her perfectly, but she never returned to Austria until the rebuilding of the Opera called her there. (Lehmann was not in the least political, by the way, nor was she in the least Jewish—she was "German-Aryan" to the utmost, born in Hamburg—but the whole Nazi phantasmagoria filled her with disgust.) On her return to Santa Barbara she wrote an account of her Vienna visit and read it, or spoke from it, to an audience in the Music Academy of the West. She allows me to quote from this document, composed in English, and not without a certain pride: for our Lotte has never been content to be merely the finest singer of the age, its purest and truest artist on the stage; she also writes, paints, models in clay; if I ever hear she has taken up theoretical physics as a sideline I shall not be surprised. It may irritate the reader to have her account of Vienna delayed, but I must here relate a brief conversation we had in New York a year or so after our first meeting in Salzburg. I was put next to her at dinner one night at Marcia Davenport's, and the guests were few, so I am sure Lotte knew exactly who I was even though she might not have remembered me offhand. At that time her English was not as accomplished as it has since become. She started the talk by saying to me: *"Was tust du, Mensch?"* (What dost thou do, human being?) I replied: *"Ich schreibe."* She nodded and said: *"Ja, ich schreibe auch."* (Yes, I also write.) I said: *"Doch, ich singe auch."* (Then, I also sing.) We looked at each other and laughed so hard that it must have sounded a little immoderate to the others; we have been friends ever since.

Lotte made a motoring trip through Italy on her way to the re-opening of the Opera and acquired on the way a chauffeur with a floridly Italian (or at least histrionic) temperament. On her first night in Austria, at the border town of Villach, she experienced a foretaste of what was coming: the innkeeper brought her flowers, there was a cluster of eager townspeople around the car in the morning to see her off to Vienna. In her account she says: "I would never have thought that I would be so sentimental to feel tears in my eyes, just because I am on Austrian soil again."

Everywhere the car stopped the same kind of thing happened. In a village where the waiter asked her to sign his memory book she asked him, in some surprise, how he could know her after all these years. He said, all offended dignity: "You think I cannot recognize Lotte Lehmann?" (It was as if she had questioned his literacy or even his Austrian citizenship, really.) Two days at Semmering, and then Lotte with her companion and her flamboyant chauffeur arrived at the Ambassador Krantz Hotel in Vienna, in the royal suite. She goes on:

"I am sure you know that in Europe and especially in Vienna one has always very many servants. Domestic help is no problem over there. So my maids from former years had made enquiries when I would arrive. And there they were—all of them. They had decorated the door of the apartment with garlands and had put a big sign above it: 'Welcome home in Vienna.' I don't know what the Hotel Manager had thought of it, but in any case he had not forbidden to put nails into the door frame. My rooms were so filled with flowers that it was difficult to put anything down. Two of my maids who had always been terribly jealous of each other continued exactly the same thing after these apparently quite unimportant eighteen years. Each of them wanted to come every day to press my gowns and wash for me and make order and whatnot. Being rather independent, I was not at all delighted. I explained to them how easy it is nowadays to take care of myself. They paled. They looked at each other and then at me with stricken eyes. They whispered: 'You wash your stockings yourself?' and when I, blushingly, said, 'Yes,' they protested with flashing eyes. . . . I really felt totally destitute and pitiful. What could I do without hurting their feelings? So I decided like the wise old Solomon that they should come on alternate days so that each of them could make my life easier. My old hairdresser was there—eager, like in old times, to come each morning to dress my hair. Her face fell when I said that I really do that myself now, and quickly I added: 'But I would be very happy if you would come and do it here.' My former chauffeur appeared, he has since seven years a very good job; but he offered to leave his boss immediately if I would take him back for the short time of my stay. This I refused with much energy, and I believe that he was the only one who left me with a disappointed heart.

"Eighteen years ago I had some special fans who followed me everywhere. They were young at that time and they lived, apparently, only for the purpose of waiting for me on street corners, shouting '*Hoch Lehmann!*' whenever I appeared. They are now middle-aged, married, have children. But there they were—with shining eyes, hands full of flowers. As in old times, they peered round the door, giggling and laughing. I stood there, really speechless. At last I said: 'Are you crazy? All of you? Eighteen years have passed. You are no flappers any more.' Jubilant laughter, radiant protest: 'Oh, Madame Lehmann, you are the same; only we have now an addition, our children who will adore you too.' You see, there is a very strong bondage between the audience and the singer—stronger than in any country, I believe. Music is so very much a part of their lives. All the people feel music in their own blood, necessary for them like the air they breathe. And the artist who brings this music to them becomes much more an idol who, in a certain sense, is their own, a part of their lives. Therefore their adoration is a very personal one. For instance, and you will understand how deeply this moves me, in all those years some of my loyal young friends have gone out to the cemetery on anniversaries to bring flowers to the grave of my parents. They did so through all these eighteen years. I cannot tell you how humble and grateful I felt."

The official opening of the Opera took place in the morning of November 5th—a ceremony of great solemnity for invited guests, with the President of the Republic and all the officials present. Mme. Lehmann seems to have been even more moved at the ceremony in the morning than at the first performance (*Fidelio*) that night.

"It was an unforgettable moment when the iron curtain rose," she says of the morning. "Even now in memory, it chokes me. This wonderful old house which has served only beauty, which has given joy and uplift to thousands of music-loving people, had been mute for so long. Now it lives again. Now the old times will come back again; and I am sure of that. I don't belong to those people who always sigh for the past. Nobody is irreplaceable. Wherever some beauty dies, some new beauty is being born. Much glory lies ahead of this beloved house. If I would not believe this, I would think, 'There never will be a time as we have lived through in the past,' it would make me very unhappy. Today the house is yet echoing with voices of the past. But soon those voices will fade away in the glory of new voices, as beautiful as ours were. Oh, I am sure of that!

"There were a lot of speeches, and when Ministerialrat Marboe, the General Manager of the two theatres, Opera and Burgtheater, greeted the guests of honor, I felt proudly the surge of love and loyal admiration which came up to my box in big waves of applause. In the end the wonderful Philharmonic Orchestra played the Prelude of the *Meistersinger*. It almost killed me. I was dissolved in tears. I sang at a kind of 'trial performance,' Eva, as a guest, coming from Hamburg. Standing on the stage behind the closed curtain I wanted to listen to the Prelude. But when the first bars sounded in all their splendor I had the sensational feeling that I had never heard it before. On the wings of this orchestra the music sounded almost unearthly beautiful to me. That was in the year 1914. And the same awesome shock gripped me again now forty-one years later when I listened to this orchestra again.

"In our box of honorary members sat also the first ballerina of former years: Gusti Pichler, now in her sixties, looking simply ridiculously young. I remember so well her birdlike grace, her elflike figure, her radiance. She sat there, tears shimmering in her eyes; and suddenly she leaned forward, touching my hand and whispering, 'Your Eva.' It moved me very much. After the Prelude, Director Boehm gave an encore which was received with much delight—the 'Blue Danube.' Oh, how this orchestra played the waltz! And through the music, through the veil of my tears, I saw in my memory the graceful form of Gusti, soaring in her lovely dance. I leaned forward, and, touching her hand, whispered: 'I remember you.'

"This morning was rather exhausting with all its emotion. I had to go home to the hotel and take a rest in order not to look too terrible in my beautiful gown. I was asked to open the ball of the Philharmonic Orchestra after the *Fidelio* performance that night, but I was sorry to have to refuse. I am accustomed to a quiet life, and three times a day being moved to tears is a little bit too much for me.

"When I came down in the hotel in the evening it felt like old times; I knew that I looked well—and you know how that can give one all the necessary poise and dignity. The whole square before the hotel was black with people who wanted to see me and there I went, exactly like a queen, through the cheering crowd.

"Arriving at the Opera I was quite amazed at the efficiency of the reporters and photographers. We walked through a battery of cameras up to the box; and the delight with which my name was said again and again awakened in me a delight which certainly matched that of my old admirers."

Lehmann was so stormed by emotions of every kind that she seems to have been unable to give full attention to the performance of *Fidelio*, which, in any case, heard after these momentous eighteen years, must in itself have set her mind and heart wandering. I have been told by persons who saw all this that she was in tears most of the time, and I can well believe it. As she says, "Beauty had awakened in ruins," and "the heart of Austria was beating again." I have also heard that the singers and musicians themselves were so shaken by emotion on that night that they could not give the best account of themselves or of the music, which nevertheless sounded like the wonders of paradise to most of those who listened inside and outside (most of them outside) the house. As Lotte also says, "It was a holy day, a day of deepest thanksgiving."

The ending of the performance provided a challenge to Mme. Lehmann which she dealt with in her characteristic manner. This is how she tells it:

"Will power is really all we need when we want to succeed. You see, I have a rather bad arthritis in my knee and walking down a stair is very difficult for me. After the performance I had a moment of terrible panic. I had to walk down the stairs which were flanked on both sides with photographers and reporters. I said to myself: 'This I cannot do. I cannot show them that I am so handicapped. I just have to walk as if nothing is the matter with me.' *And I did!* I just walked down as if going on clouds. I really don't know how I did it. When I reached the ground my knee hurt me like the devil. But never mind . . ."

The Italian chauffeur provided comic relief to all the deep feeling aroused in this rebirth of the Vienna Opera; he discovered, on arrival in Austria, that "Mme. Lotte Lehmann" was a great singer and a national glory—he had previously thought her a painter because she sketched all the way through Italy—and now he took full advantage of the fact. He obtained free seats at theatres, disobeyed traffic rules, discarded his old clothes for new, and did everything he could to take advantage of the fact that he was chauffeur to the great lady. On the night of the *Fidelio,* when Lehmann's name was mentioned on the loud-speakers and the crowd in the streets outside cheered, he rose and made a speech as being her chauffeur. And on his last night in Vienna he was given a farewell party by all the new acquaintances and friends he had made—forty people were present, he told Lehmann proudly.

I know more or less how the chauffeur felt. Between Lehmann and the Viennese, in their prolonged love affair, some special excitement was always released in the atmosphere, and the chauffeur would not have been an Italian if he had not felt it too. When I arrived in Vienna some six weeks later the people there were still talking about Lotte and about all the strange and wonderful events which surrounded the reopening of their Opera. I found that a popular brand of cigarettes (from the Austrian State monopoly) had put out a series of picture cards, one in each package: "the great from the brilliant days of the Vienna Opera." (The word I have translated as "brilliant days" is *Glanzzeit*.) Number one in this series of cigarette cards is Lotte Lehmann as *Fidelio*.

7

Number One she was. It is true. I think everybody who either participated in or witnessed the great performances of the 1920's and 1930's would agree. And yet there were also others of special quality who hold a most exalted place in any record of the time: Elisabeth Schumann, for example, a pure vocalist who could also give a stage performance as lively as any musical comedy soubrette. There were the lyric tenor Alfred Piccaver, the coloratura Maria Cebotari, and a dozen others who deserved well of their profession, including always the admirable Richard Mayr. But what was true of the *Glanzzeit* is again true, possibly not quite so "brilliantly," at the present moment: the new voices and talents, the new conductors, the wonderfully rejuvenated and deeply renewed orchestra, all reassure the visitor about the Vienna Opera and give him a positive bond to the effect that, as Lotte says, "Whenever some beauty dies, some new beauty is being born."

Ten million dollars of the Austrian State's money went into the rebuilding of the Opera, and for the moral fortification of the country every penny of it was well spent. It is the most modern theatre in existence, and during a tour of all its machines, stages, electrical and hydraulic devices, rehearsal rooms, television screens I was not only bewildered (as a chronic misfit in the machine age) but also saddened to think that this was possible in one of the poorest of the great world capitals, whereas our New York, so unimaginably rich— and our London not much less rich, after all—cannot find it socially necessary or desirable to do the same. The same? They cannot afford, which means that they do not find it necessary to afford, even a small fraction of such expenditure. The society does not demand it, does not feel deprived or humiliated if the opera house has no proper machinery and no space and no decent dressing rooms or even a proper floor on the stage. I have never been backstage at the Vienna Opera or the Scala without contrasting those ample quarters with the exiguous and tattered alleyways of the Metropolitan. To look at the stage machinery in Vienna—where the next opera and the next and the next are neatly stacked above and beyond the one now ready for performance—makes me positively dizzy. Even the Scala, which was rebuilt earlier and with less expenditure, is incomparably more modern in such respects than the Metropolitan or Covent Garden. These are the responses of a social organization to the demands from its own vital components. Our vital components make no such demands.

The Vienna Opera this winter made no use, so far as I could see, of the technological panoply at its disposal. Perhaps it takes time to learn such a staggering amount of machinery—six, or is it twelve, stages, all of which go up and down and around?—enough dynamos to supply electricity for weeks if the municipal supply goes off, and enough storage batteries for other weeks if the dynamos are struck by lightning—almost endless rehearsal rooms and chorus and orchestra and organ rooms—perhaps it is too much all at once. At all events, I saw no very noticeable result in the actual performances; the stage designers and directors have yet to accustom themselves to their new powers. *Don Giovanni,* for instance, was done in a single set, just as at the Metropolitan (it was a better set, but otherwise nothing was different). The principal singers at Vienna also sing at the Metropolitan, Covent Garden and other opera houses, so that the principal novelty of the freshly produced works in the spanking new houses was—as indeed it always has been—the heavenly beauty of the Vienna Philharmonic.

And here I think my favorite thesis, that there are just as good fish in the sea as ever did come out of it, is abundantly proved. For this Vienna Philharmonic is not made up of the same men as the one Toscanini conducted with such celestial fire twenty years ago. At some performances this winter I sat very close (in the first row), which on one side or the other, strings or woodwinds, gives, at least in Vienna, a somewhat intimate acquaintance with the orchestra. I got to know their faces well enough to recognize a considerable number of them. The orchestra pit, also, like everything else, goes up and down and around, in sections, but when I was there it seemed to be fixed at more or less the same altitude, rather high as compared to the Metropolitan or Covent Garden. And I can take my oath that there are more young men than middle-aged or old ones in that orchestra—some of them clearly very young. Whether it is the conditions of their life and work, the kind of rehearsals they get, the high quality of their conductors or merely the influence of life in Vienna, I do not know, but they play as beautifully as their forebears did and I know of no opera company which is upheld by such a body of musicians.

I noticed a number of rather curious things, too, which have their place in any reflection on the subject: for example, in Vienna these orchestra men listen to the music and also to the singing when they are not themselves engaged. At the Metropolitan I have watched unengaged players reading books, doing crossword puzzles or even writing letters while the performance is going on. Last spring at the revival of *Orfeo* a trumpet player who was directly in front of me (and much below, but I could see it all very plainly) was working crossword puzzles out of a book at all times when he was not obliged to play, which was most of the time. As Orfeo, on a ramp directly above him, as he could have seen plainly by casting his eyes up, began to sing *"Che farò senza Euridice,"* this man finished his crossword puzzle, closed that book and started at once on another book of the same.

In Vienna I observed that the unengaged players took a lively interest in what went on on the stage, even craning their necks at times to see as well as hear. Once I sat over the French horns in *Don Giovanni* and saw that these men, all young and with not much to do in that orchestration, had a sort of silent discussion with each other about the merits of singers in the great Mozart arias. They did it by means of lifted eyebrows, pursed lips, nods of acquiescence and the like, but the conversations were as clear as if they had been spoken: so was their interest in the performance. Even those who did not trouble to communicate with their fellows generally lifted their heads and obviously listened (looked, too, if they could) while they were not themselves obliged to play.

Then, we must suppose, the attitude of all Vienna toward the Opera, the orchestra and music in general has a great deal to do with it. Social consideration attaches to those who engage in these pursuits; every musician in the orchestra is addressed as "Herr Professor." The great city, in its historically anomalous position—once the polyglot and multiracial capital of an immense empire, now all head and no body in its tiny state—has seen so many glories vanish that it clings with more obstinacy than ever to its musical supremacy and pride. It sometimes seems to visitors in Italy that every street or square is named after a poet or a painter; in Vienna it seems that many such bear the names of composers; certainly in the mind of Vienna there is a place given to music, all music, which it does not occupy so indisputably in any other capital. That is part of the reason for excellence in the orchestral performances, vividness of interest on the part of all concerned, pride in the result.

We saw it plainly enough in the Lehmann-Toscanini years at Salzburg, but it was heartening indeed to perceive this past winter that all the years of war, hunger and devastation have not eradicated it from Vienna. The Vienna Symphony (*Wiener Symphoniker*) in its concerts at the great hall of the Friends of Music, as I heard it under Hermann Scherchen and Herbert von Karajan, had every bit as much eagerness and pride as the Philharmonic, with the same glowing response to every demand of the conductor and the music. The hall of the Friends of Music (ugly if you like, certainly Victorian) required no restoration after the war, and its acoustical properties are such as they were when Brahms first introduced his *Requiem* there in its completed version. Paul Hindemith's violoncello concerto, not a traditional work by any means and not a part of "old Vienna" by nature, received as warm a welcome and as vivid a performance as anything in those superb concerts.

The obstinacy and pride of Vienna were probably most in evidence in a somewhat darker period, just the same. I was there for some weeks toward the end of 1947 when the material conditions of life were not actually very favorable toward even the luckiest or most privileged of Austrians. Scarce, bad food, poor clothing and a suffocating difficulty of transport within the city were the ordinary day's experience. Private motorcars did not exist; the Austrian authorities themselves had few for public use; the tram and bus systems were crippled and the crowds that waited to employ them were pitiful to behold. It was December, both wet and cold. The Opera House was, of course, a twisted mass of ruin, and the company was giving its performances in the old Theater an der Wien (the one where

Fidelio had its first night in 1805), which was substantially without convenience for scenery, properties, dressing rooms or anything else. Some performances were given in the Redoutensaal, and of course some of the artists who sang or played in these works were also employed in other works in the Volksoper. (The use of the same musicians or singers both in grand opera and lighter or smaller works, including operetta, is a healthy aspect of the Viennese system.)

During that visit one of the American officers concerned in particular with the revival of Austrian culture—much good work in this respect was done by a section in General Mark Clark's headquarters —arranged a gathering where I met a large number of artists. They all seemed happy as grigs; there was a great deal of American food and drink at the party, which may have helped, but I think most of these men and women could have been just as merry on water; there was something rather heroic being demanded of them just then, and they knew it, and it made them feel rather splendid that they were able to deliver the goods. I had some difficulty digging out of some of them (one by one, of course) what the day had been, that very day, and what life every day was like for members of the State Opera and Philharmonic Orchestra.

I think that aside from the privations with respect to food and clothing, which had grown into routine, the principal hardship of their lives in my own view was that of getting about the cold, wet, half-ruined city. I stumbled onto this whole problem (which took up a large part of each day for them) more or less by accident, merely by asking questions like, "And then what did you do? Where did you go next?" Actually they were so used to these struggles that they would not have told me, of their own accord, about matters they considered so ordinary. Some of the singers were performing two nights a week at the Volksoper and two nights a week at the Theater an der Wien, with rehearsals at one or the other between times, and sometimes rehearsals at the Redoutensaal as well. If you have only to take a taxi to get from one of these theatres to the other, as you do nowadays, there may be some time wasted but it is quite endurable; in the trams and buses of Vienna in 1947, in all those patient crowds, it was an ordeal for body and soul. One plump, jolly contralto—it was the Hungarian Rosette Anday—gave me an uproarious account of her day spent between the three theatres, and I knew that she had only a very slight notion of how funny and how sad it all was.

If you asked these hard-working and underpaid artists for their complaints, as I did—simply asked them what was hardest to bear in their harassed lives—they always had something of the most rock-bottom professionalism to offer in reply. Insufficient supplies of good cosmetics, poor quality in costumes, not enough rehearsal time or room, too much public work, not enough "leave of absence" for lucrative engagements elsewhere (which were just then beginning to be offered): this was the kind of hardship that irked them. But their spirits were extraordinarily high and their pride was irrefraga-ble. At one moment I was talking to Mme. Elisabeth Hoengen, the leading contralto, about the Metropolitan Opera, to which she had just been invited. I told her—breaking it as gently as possible—that she would not have as many rehearsals there as she was accustomed to, and that I had personally known a good many artists who made their first appearances at the Metropolitan not only without rehearsal, but without ever having set foot on that immense stage before. She stared as if she thought I had gone insane. "Can I be-lieve what you say?" she asked. I doubt if she could, really, because by her standards it was far more important to have adequate re-hearsals than it was to have adequate food or clothing.

It was during that 1947 visit that I heard some of the most mem-orable performances I have ever heard in Vienna. Queerly enough, these opera and orchestra lunatics seemed to thrive on poor rations. Perhaps, after all, the severe material limitations of life threw them more utterly than ever into the pursuit of their art—they worked harder, so to speak, because there was literally nothing else to do, and since the ordinary satisfactions were brutally restricted, the sat-isfaction of making music had to take the place of almost everything else. The most spirited *Boris Godunoff* for years was the one pro-duced that December with Paul Schoeffler singing the Czar and Elisabeth Hoengen as Marina; the Russians flew down a quantity of magnificent clothing, gold brocades and heavy museum jewelry and the like, straight out of the Kremlin, to make splendid that rickety old stage; all the other occupation authorities vied with each other to contribute something. It was a superb performance from every point of view and the poor old Theater an der Wien, so much smaller than the big opera houses, probably came near to collapsing from the full body of rich sound. One anomalous detail was the omission of the final scene; the Russian occupation authorities decided that the burning of Moscow and the downfall of Russia were not suitable representations for this audience.

At the Friends of Music, along about this time, Wilhelm Furtwängler conducted a performance of the *Deutsches Requiem* which surpassed any other I have heard before or since. The chorus of the Friends of Music is made up of unpaid volunteers capable of rehearsal without end; the orchestra was the Philharmonic; the soloists were the exquisite soprano Elisabeth Schwarzkopf, then new to me, and Hans Hotter. Furtwängler was sovereign in this music; he was at all times a conductor of the supreme category, with few equals and only one superior; his bad reputation in America, where he was supposed to be a "Nazi" and had been rejected from our orchestras, was never, in my opinion, deserved. (The whole question of "Nazis" in music was weirdly confused for years, and in a later place we shall have to try to think it over.) So great a conductor, with the materials here at his command, could not fail to give a performance which for mystery and tenderness, grace and command, brought forth everything Brahms had written. That wonderful music has never sounded more irrefutable in its masterly sincerity, its humble (and so Protestant!) greatness. It was startling to me, afterwards, to find that the maestro could do this with apparently no wear and tear on his nervous system—no wilted collar, no wild eyes, no exhaustion—and if there were such a thing as a man of iron, this was what he suggested. He received me in the director's office—Brahms' office— seated at Brahms' desk, underneath a big picture of Brahms, and there was not much chance of talking about anything else. I remarked that one thing I hadn't been able to understand was where that canal was, the canal over which Brahms walked every day from his boarding house to this office. Furtwängler said flatly that there wasn't any canal. I protested: "But, Maestro, it's in his letters—it's in all the books—he made the same walk every day for many years— it's all described." Furtwängler said, "Well, I came here first over thirty years ago and there wasn't any canal then and there never has been any canal." There was something so unutterably final and

Germanic (however wrong-headed) about this statement that it was useless to dispute the point, which mattered very little anyhow. I found out, of course, that the canal had been filled in and turned into a street sometime before Furtwängler arrived. Because he had never seen it, there *could* not have been a canal. This dogmatism of mind, along with his ramrod appearance and his imperturbable self-confidence, I suppose, gave Furtwängler that ultra-Teutonic external semblance and manner of address which Americans and other Westerners tended to dislike. He *looked* like a Nazi, poor man, and acted like one too in private interviews, although we all know that he went to great lengths to save his Jewish musicians and to preserve the values of German music through the nightmare years. I think he was almost pathetically aware of his own stiffness, his lack of grace or charm or human warmth, and, as a very shy man, he made some rather hopeless attempts to remedy a situation which by this time was beyond repair: I remember he went out of his way to make some laudatory remarks to me about American orchestras. In two or three talks with him I came to the conclusion that although there certainly was, underneath this forbidding exterior, the heart and mind of a very great artist, it would never be perceptible to me except through his work.

There is something more than usually contradictory about the contrast between Furtwängler's art and his personality: I have never seen anything quite like it. It is worth recalling that some of his most irresistible musical passion went into opera—*Tristan, Otello*—and even his *Carmen* in Berlin years ago was unique; but these hidden fires never gave off the faintest flicker on the surface of the man.

In all the ups and downs of musical life in Vienna, as centered upon the opera and orchestra, I believe the ruling character of the performers themselves has been an utter and unquestioning professionalism combined with a peculiarly Viennese sort of good temper. This does not apply to composers, of course; they are all intellectuals of one kind or another, by definition, and the terrible dramas of revolution, dictatorship and war could not fail to uproot them and alter their view of the world. Almost every Viennese composer of rank (Jewish or not) left Vienna after the Nazis came. Singers and violinists and horn players are a different breed. They may not have liked the Nazis much, and I have an idea most of them did not; for one simple reason, most of them had Jewish friends; but they were employed in state enterprises with the guarantee of an old-age pension at the end of their service. "Work or starve," they say. And aside from the internationally famous artists (never more than a handful at a time) who could take their pick of engagements anywhere on earth, the great solid ranks of the employed in opera, orchestra, conservatory and other musical institutions have little to say and nothing to choose.

There was a big basso in the opera during those years—I met him in 1947—who gave me his own account of how the nightmare decade had passed. (His name was Herbert Alsen and he had sung at the Metropolitan before the war.) He told me the chief result of every political change was a sudden alteration in repertoire at the Opera —new parts to study, old ones to forget. When Hitler was having a flirtation with France (as just after Munich, with the "non-aggression pact") the singers had to learn a number of French operas in a hurry and put them on; then suddenly all the French operas were thrown out and, with the Nazi-Soviet Pact of August, 1939, they were ordered to learn a bevy of Russian works in no time at all. What with all the chopping and changing of Hitler's line during those years, it was as much as a singer's job was worth to waste time on anything but learning parts. You just got yourself into a thoroughly Russian mood, with perhaps six fine Russian basso parts—and what parts!—ready to offer at a moment's notice, and then along came the order to scrap all that and learn Italian. According to Alsen, who told it in a booming voice accompanied by Herculean laughter, the political events of the decade were known to the hard-working State Opera employee as just so many excuses for more work.

8

The ministrations of such a devoted band as we had at Salzburg—the Vienna Opera and Orchestra with Lehmann, Toscanini and Walter —led us to the heights of musical excellence; I have suggested, at the beginning of this section, that by leading us to Beethoven and Mozart they led us also "back to Bach" and gave us our most comprehensive view of all modern music.

This is, I think, true, but at the same time almost anybody could inquire, with some justification, where our own contemporaries entered the scheme of things. Aside from occasional performances of chamber music, none of the work done since Debussy and Strauss was represented on Salzburg programs. It seems odd, twenty years afterwards, that such an epochal production as *Wozzeck* should never have been heard or seen in the favorable conditions of the great festival years. Nowadays every Salzburg season prides itself on at least one new work in one of the grand forms, opera or symphony, and in fact hardly any festival or semifestival season anywhere— except such as Bayreuth, devoted only to Wagner—can get along without some homage to the composers of today and the past thirty years. During the opening weeks of the Vienna Opera (1955-1956) in the rebuilt house, weeks which were designed and executed as a *Festpiel,* the representative works chosen were *Fidelio, Don Giovanni, Die Frau ohne Schatten, Aïda, Die Zauberflöte, Die Meistersinger von Nürnberg* and *Wozzeck.* The shade of poor Alban Berg may have looked down upon this apotheosis with reasonable pride, but certainly with no surprise, for he seems always to have known— even during the years when he was working on it—that *Wozzeck* was not an "experimental" work or an atonal curiosity, but simply the best music he could write for the theatre. "I wanted to compose good music," he says himself, denying all else, "to give to the theatre what belongs to the theatre." (*Modern Music,* November-December, 1927) He did not wish to "reform" the opera techniques, give lessons to other composers or found a school. He simply wrote an opera. It is the good fortune of the period he enriched by his talent that he was able to do so where so many daring spirits have failed. I hereby declare that from the point of view of the ordinary listener like myself the precise method adopted by the composer has only the most academic interest; what I (and millions like me) want to hear is music, the creation of a world in sound, and whether it is done in whole tones, as Debussy so often did, or in twelve tones as our friends do today, makes no difference. The absence of key signatures and key relations—atonality—was never worth the fuss all the "modernists" made about it a few years ago. Music has been verging in that direction for a long time. I picked up an elementary harmony textbook in a London library a few months ago—something used for the teaching of primary students—in which several examples were given of "atonality" from piano pieces by Chopin. That is, the accidentals were so extremely frequent in these examples that it was a sort of farce to call the piece by any key-name. A Flat or D Minor or the like; it was truly atonal, it was without a key.

What we (the listeners, that is) find in the best of atonal music, as in the best of whole-tone or twelve-tone music, is simply the same thing we find in all good music. And if we do not find it we do not like it. Most of us are so ignorant that we could never tell, merely by listening, whether a composition was atonal or not, and although we all are vaguely aware of the clash-phenomenon called "dissonance," which is perhaps different for each pair of ears, we cannot rise up and label a twelve-tone composition at first hearing.

In other words, we (the listeners) are a great deal freer and more unprejudiced than professional musicians ever can be. Things which shock musicologists to the depths of their being are very cheerfully received by us, and it is only by this process—our willingness to listen to something new—that the old guard of the musical mummies, those ornaments of the museum, are circumvented at all. The "preparation" and the "resolution" of the chord of the dominant seventh, for example—in God's name, is there anybody now alive, among listeners, who ever gave it a moment's thought? I suppose I have been listening to "dissonant" chords ever since I first heard anything, and although my ear probably separated them fairly accurately from their so-called "consonant" neighbors, merely as sound, I never for a moment thought that one was immoral and the other moral. In the nineteenth century such "dissonant" chords (seventh and ninth, in particular) could not be used except according to rigid rule—prepared and thereafter resolved, like anesthesia for an operation—and anybody who just boldly used them anyhow according to his own sweet will was a mere hooligan (like Debussy). To me, and I dare say to the countless millions who feel as I do, this is the wildest kind of mandarin nonsense, akin to the old rules of Chinese decorum (how many bows to the mother-in-law and how many to the eldest sister-in-law, etc.), without any relation to music as I understand it.

Our ears must, of course, grow accustomed to a wider range of sound than that of the simplest major triad, or many twentieth-century compositions may take us too much by surprise. There is no question of "race memory" or inherited predilection involved; such notions are absurd on the face of it, and not only for our kind of music but for the other modes as well (Indian, Chinese, etc.); it is a simple matter of habituation from earliest days. We hear everything in the tempered Western scale, seven-and-five, no matter what key it is in; our consciousness of harmony is completely dominated, from babyhood, by thirds, and the common triad (C-E-G) has informed all our music for hundreds of years. It takes a little time, not much, but a little, for us to get used to anything else. Chinese or Indians born into our music and brought up in it are exactly the same; I know some among them who even compose in our kind of music with skill and naturalness, as of a fish swimming.

But—and it is a great but—during the period I represent and am attempting to describe, the changes in our music known and heard had already gone very far. By 1935, for example, when the greatest seasons at Salzburg began, all listeners to music had become accustomed to the widest possible variations in harmony and rhythm. That is, whether we knew the methods with any accuracy or not, our ears had long been accustomed to the results. I am not speaking of such minor crimes as the seventh and the ninth chords —after all, modern babies are lulled to rest by what our grandparents considered savage dissonance—but rather of the bolder harmonic and rhythmic explorations, up to and including twelve-tone composition and dissonant counterpoint or polyphony. We could perfectly well have enjoyed the best work of our contemporaries, such as *Wozzeck*: we were ready for it.

The musicians, however, were not.

This introduces a subject which gives rise to acrimonious controversy and can only be settled by statistical methods (i.e., records of attendance at concerts, and so on). My view is that we, the listeners, are far more prepared for novelties than our great musicians will admit, and, further, that the statistical evidence to the contrary is generally based upon inferior performances and consequently does not correspond to the true state of affairs.

In other words, if atonal music could be heard only from a small, earnest group of fanatics playing five clarinets and a jew's-harp in an unheated hall on Third Avenue in New York, the attendance would not be great. If an atonal composition by the same writer were played by the New York Philharmonic Orchestra the attendance would be much greater, the reception correspondingly less complete, the arguments deafening, but the statistics, at any rate, shown for what they generally are—misleading.

Speaking of great works in the great forms, which has been the general tendency of this report throughout, I believe I can say that we, the listeners, were ready a long time before the musicians and the directors of music believed it. A production of *Wozzeck* at Salzburg, directed by Arturo Toscanini, would have been an experience to throw out the frontiers of music to an immeasurable landscape, and a great many infinitely lesser works would have fallen into their proportion as regards our own lives in music. *Wozzeck* was not new—Kleiber gave it its first performance in Berlin ten years before—and 1935 was in fact the year of Alban Berg's death. Paul Hindemith's earlier operas may not have deserved the Salzburg accolade, but by 1935 his *Mathis der Maler* was available; so were the most mature and extended works of Honegger and Milhaud. The most modern work, however, of which I ever heard a discussion at Salzburg was, as I remember, *Pelléas et Mélisande,* tentatively proposed for Toscanini to conduct in his third season there; the idea was abandoned and *Die Meistersinger* selected instead.

Things have changed very much since then; almost every symphony orchestra and opera company in the world now finds a place for contemporary work. It is easier for the orchestras, for practical reasons (chiefly financial), but even the opera houses do extravagate now and then in the direction of work belonging to the present. It draws big audiences, arouses interest, curiosity and even excitement; but hardly any of it will keep on attracting a public after the novelty has worn off—that is, season after season. The Metropolitan Opera House is conservatism itself, in most respects, and yet even this stronghold of established repertoire had to give *The Rake's Progress* a few years ago; Stravinsky now has such prestige that when he composed a full-length opera (even though his talent may not be suited to it) the Metropolitan was more or less obliged to produce the result. In the subsidized (or subventioned) opera houses of Europe new works are produced every season, although a great many of them disappear into the warehouse immediately thereafter; not every composition can claim the permanence of Wagner or Verdi; it makes no difference, they take their turn and have their chance. Among the works produced in the regular seasons of regular opera houses are a good many in atonal and twelve-tone modes. And as for the symphony orchestras, not one of any importance in this world would try to get through a season without playing some entirely new music, of which much or most would have been called experimental a few years ago.

That is the state of affairs today, but it was very different only twenty years ago. Even the finest work of the past was not often produced in the most established opera houses; the Salzburg Festival repertoire was itself as novel, to most of us, as Alban Berg or Prokofieff. After all, what greater novelty can be found than Mozart and Beethoven if you have never had a chance to hear them before? The masterpieces chosen by Toscanini and Walter for their incomparable performances in the little baroque town were "established," yes—in the sense of having been safely stowed away in the encyclopedia and thereafter on the shelf; you could get through many a long year without hearing a single one of them in New York, London or Paris. Under the circumstances what we did hear was so fresh and beautiful, so splendidly brought to life, that I doubt if any of us felt the lack of the new and strange. Most listeners in 1935 had never even had a chance to hear *Fidelio;* why should they miss *Wozzeck?*

Sometimes I have wondered, just the same, in retrospect—it is always in retrospect that such questions arise—what it was that kept the finest artists of the time away from newer music. Some of the reason, naturally, was involved in what I have just said above: that the greatest works were not being performed anywhere and it was a primary duty to perform them in Salzburg. The entire world owes gratitude to those who refreshed its taste at that time. There may, just the same, have been some other reasons. I have (not long ago) looked at the orchestral scores in Maestro Toscanini's library in Milan. There are large numbers of scores there which he has evidently read or studied but has never performed for the public— all kinds of works; some of them come into the category of simple curiosities, oddities of taste and style, others into the class of worthy errors. But among them are a considerable number of orchestral works by composers whose effort was at least in the direction of originality, however near or far they came. I saw several by

Charles Ives, for instance. The numbers by European innovators were quite noticeable.

It is, therefore, not through lack of awareness of their work that Toscanini ignored these composers in public. He must, I think, have come to some point or other at which he said he had learned enough and would devote himself to the relentless cultivation of his garden. Among great composers Debussy was about his latest, his most unorthodox. He did conduct more recent work, quite a lot of it, but as a rule by Italian composers who were his friends or Americans who hoped to be. The frontier of his re-creation, his soul's green pasture, was roughly Haydn along the polar edges and Debussy toward the tropics. Having learned so much, felt so much and worshipped so sincerely, he undoubtedly came to a point at which his entire consciousness aspired toward the perfectibility of that which he already knew rather than the learning of anything else. I can very well imagine Toscanini at any age, such as the unimaginable age which he has now reached, agonizing himself over the music of Beethoven's Seventh Symphony, wishing he had done this in this way and this in that—actually discovering new meanings and new lights and shades in phrases which he has known for—lo!—and lo again!—these sixty-five or seventy years. Our imagination faints and fails at the thought of what Toscanini understands by the Seventh Symphony now, now that he can no longer conduct it, now that he must soon join its creator in the higher counties and bailiwicks set aside for the deathless spirits. It is to my knowledge that he is dissatisfied, and deeply, with everything he has ever conducted, and plays over to himself the recordings of his efforts with a groan at what he might have done, a sense of eternal regret that he cannot try again.

In the case of Mme. Lehmann, her frontiers as an interpreter of music went to Beethoven on the Rhine and Strauss on the Danube. She sang Mozart, but without great assurance. "My soul is too earth-bound," she told me once. Lehmann was never sure that she could sing anything, as a matter of fact. She doubted her own physical and technical resources; as a woman of the highest musical intelligence she knew perfectly well what she could do, and do better than anybody else in the world, which was to convey the composer's meaning; but she was never absolutely sure that the earth-body, the thing of muscles and glands and variegated organs, would respond to the demands she made upon it. It was a never ending source of surprise to her that this mechanism not only obeyed orders, but gave to the external world high perceptions of beauty. During her professional career in the opera houses—of which the Salzburg great seasons were probably the highest point—she was too busy learning, studying, rehearsing and performing to consider whether or not the actual works, the compositions, were worth it all. She was afraid of every new work without exception. This had nothing to do with harmonic devices, tonal innovations or anything of the sort. It was her usual custom, as she has told me often, to read through a new score and then send it back to the director of the Vienna Opera with a note to the effect that she would be quite incapable of learning it in the first place or singing it after she had learned it. The director—and for most of these years it was Franz Schalk, who adored her and even understood her—sent the score straight back to her with a letter asking her to try again. In a general way this comedy went on three or four times before Lotte finally consented to take a new role. In the case of *Arabella*—I think it was *Arabella*—Schalk wrote her a charming little letter which she has kept and I have seen, saying that the time was short, and would she please read the score very quickly and pretend that she had already read it three times and let him know at once, skipping all the intermediary stages, because Dr. Richard Strauss wanted to know.

She cared nothing whatsoever for the harmonic or rhythmic novelties (and Strauss had plenty of both); she would have sung Alban Berg or Prokofieff without the slightest qualm if their scores had been sent to her by Franz Schalk, Bruno Walter or Arturo Toscanini. The only question she asked was whether or not she could sing and enact (the two were inseparable) the part submitted to her. Her contracts kept her occupied from one year's end to the next, and during this working time she did whatever the Vienna Opera (or the London, New York, Berlin and Paris operas) demanded of her, if she felt that she was capable of doing it, if she had time, if the music and the part appealed. She never showed a trace of prejudice against "new music" or "new forms" or "new scales" or anything of the sort; and I rather doubt if she would have known them if she had seen them. It was all simply music to her, good or bad, and the chances are that she would have been a magnificent Marie in *Wozzeck*. Mary Garden told me, only a year or so ago, that she deeply regretted that her career had ended before she had a chance to sing Honegger's *Judith*—and Garden's musical education, after all, under Claude Debussy, was a good bit before Lehmann's. If Garden could have taken Honegger's dissonance, Lehmann could have taken Berg's atonality. What these great stage creators demand above all is a chance to create—they need the musical and dramatic material, and they do not care any more than I do what it is made of or whence it comes. If you can dig a lyric tragedy out of the four-tone scale of the subtropical pigmies and compose it crabwise in dissonant counterpoint, so that it can be equally well played forwards or backwards, it makes no difference whatsoever: the only thing that counts is the validity of the lyric tragedy. This is the only thing Lehmann cared about—or Garden or Chaliapin either, so far as I know.

The fact remains that she, too, never went beyond Strauss in opera. During her final years before the public she was restlessly exploring the song literature, which she suddenly perceived was quite vast, stretching far and away beyond the classic-romantic fortress. Even within nineteenth-century German music the number of good songs which seldom or never have concert performances is large. In Lehmann's last seasons she made some discoveries even in German—the number of beautiful ones by Felix Mendelssohn, for example, very generally neglected—but her excitement over the world of French songs was the greatest. She sang them with more voice than they usually receive, and they sound very much Lehmann's own as she does them; but the recordings prove that she had genuinely moved into a new realm of beauty. ("*La Vie Antérieure*," by Henri Duparc, was a fine example.)

Salzburg did what was right and proper, it seems to me, for the time and place. Certainly the opportunity to hear great work greatly performed was enough for me. It is only in subsequent years—and by the remarks of captious friends—that I have even noticed the absence, from those memorable seasons, of anything strictly contemporary. The very young, who can hear anything and everything nowadays, may find it difficult to realize that such was not always the case—so much has changed throughout the musical world in a bare couple of crowded decades. You can actually hear today, as I have, somebody of musical taste and intelligence remarking that a certain concert (or seasonal repertoire, or series of concerts) contains "too much Mozart." I doubt if that precise combination of words ever hit my ears in the *Fidelio* seasons at Salzburg. "Too much" we never had; "too little" was what we had known before we went there.

9

Hitler's annexation of Austria was about as inevitable as anything could be: he had never made a secret of his intention; he was Austrian after all, and his entire theory of the "greater Reich" depended on the bringing together of all the German-speaking peoples as a nucleus for the new world order of the "racially pure." This may all have been a pack of nonsense, and was, but if you had read *Mein Kampf* and followed Hitler's course of action you could see that he was going to do it unless forcibly prevented. The possibility of forcible prevention disappeared quite early—let us say at the latest in 1935—and it was plain enough from then on that he would carry out his declared program until it produced catastrophe.

After the event everybody in Austria and elsewhere said all this. "I knew all the time," says X, and "I expected it from month to month," says Y. Actually it is astounding to reflect how few among the nonpolitical really did calculate with any precision on the development of the situation. In the year of the Anschluss (1938) both Lehmann and Walter had firmly declared their intention of returning to Austria for the summer in Salzburg. I know that both had that gloomy premonition, that nervous anxiety, which permeated every mind in Austria toward the end of the pre-Hitler period. The preliminary moves toward annexation of Austria, or its absorption into the Third Reich with subjection to all the Nazi laws, were blatant enough, but it is the habit of people the world over to disbelieve the immense disasters until they have actually arrived. Toscanini, who always seems to have had a political sense keener and broader than that of other musical artists, saw what was coming and made his decision well in advance: he would not return to Salzburg. The Anschluss itself had to come along before some of the others followed his example.

And it was not only musical artists who continued to hope to the end and beyond. I retain with considerable amusement a recollection of a Nazi party member, so-called, who had a great outburst of confidence one evening in Salzburg in the autumn before the Anschluss took place. Encouraged by some good Austrian beer he told me that he was a member of the Nazi party because it was excellent for his business, protected his family in all their activities and gave him some standing in his own particular community. It was quite harmless, he assured me, because the whole purpose of the organization was to take over Austria peaceably (in legal elections, I gathered) and thereafter come to an amiable agreement with Germany for common action. Any such ideas as war, for instance, or a bloody persecution of minority communities, was quite out of the question —he rejected all that with what seemed to be sincere horror. In fact, the mere notion of any such thing was "foreign propaganda." It was proof of my own incurable Anglo-Saxon credulity that I could consider such possibilities.

Whether there were any number of such idiots among the members of the Austrian Nazi party or not is beyond my power to guess; I know by experience that there were some. Most Austrians of my acquaintance were unable or unwilling to see what was coming; they could not, above all, imagine the disappearance of Austria as a separate unit in the life of Europe. When I went to Vienna shortly after the Anschluss I was quite dumbfounded at the sourness of so many ordinary, nonpolitical Austrians to whom I spoke—their irritation at every condition of life—since good humor under all conditions has been their chief characteristic ever since I first knew them. I think now, with the perception of the backward glance, that it was sheer astonishment, disgruntlement, disappointment at the failure of all their own previsions, which governed their minds during the first months of the Hitler dictatorship. They had not believed it was coming and it came just the same, with all its rigors and discomforts—the prohibition of whipped cream; the necessity of driving to the right of the road; such tremendous revolutionary severities—and that was enough to sour them. They did not know (or believe) the horrors which were actually going on at that very time; all the worst things took place at night and it has been an Austrian gift to disbelieve what is not actually seen. My own sympathy with most Viennese at that period (the summer of 1938) was exceedingly limited; the muddle-headedness which always had been a part of their congenital charm was now in full charge. Nothing would happen to the Jews; that was all "foreign propaganda"—this they could say when thousands of Jews took the road to Dachau every night. And there would be no war, whatever happened, because "the Führer would not permit it." This is the kind of thing they said in the summer of 1938, and although they paid for it dearly afterwards, it is hard to forget: hard for me, in particular, because in my own profession of political journalism I was obliged to know the truth which these strange ostrichlike Viennese hid from their own eyes.

So the dark forces engulfed an old Danubian culture in which music had found, for some two hundred years, the friendliest and most fertile soil. The very muddle-headedness of the Viennese character, by blurring all the outlines of possible antagonism and occasions for strife, may have made it easier for music—a supra-political pursuit—to flourish. In this multiracial, multilingual city of the Hapsburgs, where Flemings, Poles, Maltese and Venetians were all equally Austrian along with innumerable varieties of Balkan Slav and South German, there were certainly no barriers of the kind our contemporary world has come to know so well. An immigrant like Beethoven, filled with the most reprehensible revolutionary fancies and with boorish manners to boot, was made more welcome to the Viennese palaces than most of the native-born. The prevalence of music-making in the house (chamber-music), although known to us chiefly in the aristocracy, went through all the rest of society as well; Mozart's friends, with whom he had his regular evenings of music-making, were ordinary enough folk. And the whole thing was held together for centuries by an imperial court which, up until only a few decades ago, was as international as any known to history: when it was inexpedient to speak French, German or Italian, we may remember, they usually depended on Latin, at least in writing.

If music is, as I think, above politics, race or religion, it must have found itself most at home in the Vienna of the past. Whether, after the slicing away of all the historical conditions which made it possible, the Vienna of the future is to offer any such refuge or encourage such hope, must remain (until further proof) a little doubtful, although even today the aftermath of such a prolonged historic experience can be felt in the very air of the land. Perhaps Vienna and Salzburg may still do for further generations what they did for us and for the generations before us. And even if that is not to be—even if there is a fading of the forces which, taken all together, made music of every origin at home here—the long flowering that did take place comprises very nearly the whole of our heritage. In some important respects we shall probably always hear *Fidelio* better in Vienna or Salzburg than anywhere else.

7 : The Troubled Times

Powers destructive to life and art are common enough. They lie all about us even in the best of societies. The most destructive of all are those which work from within—that is, inside one person or one social organism—the worst being, no doubt, the dark forces of a single soul. Dr. Jung and many other psychologists have taught us that these frequently exist on two planes at once, inside and out, and the example most in view during our time was Hitler's Germany. An artist may be destroyed by himself more easily by far than by any external force, however hostile, yet they seem to be linked by a fatality in which one brings on the other, makes it worse, invites its culmination. Mussorgsky in music and Edgar Allan Poe in writing are two ready examples (there are many) of artists who, by destroying themselves, asked for the external catastrophe.

You might think that if this were true the tremendous social cataclysms would be those in which art of all kinds had most to suffer and to lose. War, revolution, the uprooting of whole populations to transfer them elsewhere—these things we have seen on an enormous scale in our own period. The war which began in Poland in 1939 and ended, after a tour of the world, in Berlin in 1945, must have been one of the most intense convulsions of its kind in history. In every way which can be weighed or measured it certainly employed the greatest force, the largest numbers, the biggest of everything in the biggest way. It can be shown that it came from within and exploded into all our lives, strewing the wreckage of human beings up and down the planet.

The paradox, then, which we behold ten years later is indeed surprising: it is that all the arts seem to flourish in the warm sun of general appreciation, none has vanished, the treasures of the past are almost all intact and the artist himself is about as well off and highly regarded as at any period. This seems to me true of the whole range, but my observation is that music in particular is in high estate just now, reaching a greater and greater public, written and performed in more and more freedom. The rewards of individual artists are always variable, and we can all think of some good ones who do not share in the universal bounty, but I think it would be difficult or impossible to claim that this time in which we live, after the worst of all wars, is unfriendly to art or artists; it is on the contrary the world-friendliest—that is, the world over, which is not fifteenth-century Florence or third-century Athens, but in a planetary culture—so far in time.

It is a little disconcerting to reflect that the greatest of wars did no harm to the arts in general; it would be one jump from that realization to the old Fascist argument that war was "good for men" or "good for the soul," as Mussolini used to contend. What I want to suggest is something different: it is that men in general are a little better, anyhow a good deal more civilized, than we used to be able to see in the midst of the conflict. The arts have survived, quite simply, because men preserved them. They are flourishing now because mankind wants and needs them.

The evidence of Europe as a whole ten years after the end of the great conflict is that two things simultaneously occurred: first, those who were threatened tried to preserve their art treasures, and, second, those who could have destroyed them made conscious efforts not to do so.

In 1945, when the war in Italy was swiftly approaching its end, I made an inquiry at the Allied Headquarters in Rome on this subject and learned a number of pertinent facts. In the whole savage campaign from the south to the north of Italy, with bombardment from the air and by artillery raking the hills and valleys, a few master-works of painting and architecture were either badly damaged or wholly destroyed. The Eremitani chapel in Padua, with the paintings by Mantegna, was destroyed by our bombs from the air— Padua was a railroad marshaling-yards for the Germans. The Camposanto at Pisa, with the paintings by Benozzo Gozzoli, was irreparably damaged on two sides but the rest was under restoration. The bronze doors of the cathedral at Benevento were ruined. Among the great masterpieces which abound throughout Italy it is staggering that so few should have been sacrificed during this long campaign (1943-1945) in which millions of tons of explosives were used. I found that the art services of the Allied Headquarters had come into Italy with detailed lists of every painting, sculpture or work of architecture which mankind at large has learned to value, and although some of these things were damaged—I have not named them all—an overwhelming proportion of such work was intact and had been precisely located. Some things had been carried off to Germany but every such one had been tabulated and was afterwards recovered. In the attacks required by warfare it is difficult always to mark a precise pinpoint and say, this spot must be avoided, must be saved if possible; but to a really astonishing extent it was done. I had—in the Air Corps—a little acquaintance with the way in which careful preliminary work could save a given point (such as the Cathedral of Monreale in Sicily), but I never did know, because it was not within my province, how much care was taken by the whole army in such matters.

Furthermore, some similar work had been going on all this while on the other side. I knew that the great museum at Naples was empty when we entered that city and I asked about it. The art service at Allied Headquarters replied that the contents of this museum had been removed by the German army, in trucks, with an exact inventory, and had been delivered *en bloc* at the Vatican with the request that the Papal authority should keep it safe until the war was over. The Allied experts on arrival in Rome had examined the works, with the German inventory and our own, and were satisfied that with one or two exceptions (the whereabouts of which had been determined) everything in that huge museum was then (1945) safe in the Vatican. It has since, of course, all gone back home to Naples. I was somewhat surprised that the Germans in their retreat had taken such trouble about works of painting and sculpture; I was told that they possessed an art service more or less like our own doing more or less the same things. There were, of course, certain Nazi potentates, such as Hermann Goering, who claimed pictures as war booty, but even these have been tabulated and (so far as I know) all returned to their owners since the war.

The whole doctrine of war booty, or loot, seems to have changed completely in the past century. Some amount of looting cannot be avoided: if a company of soldiers on entering a ruined town finds a cellar full of wine . . . But the doctrine of the legitimate prize of war—that the conqueror had the right to definite booty—was advanced only by certain Nazis (Goering the chief), and, in another respect, by the Russians. The Russians amalgamated, as I understand, the old "war booty" practices with those of modern "reparations": to make up for the devastation of large parts of Russia they were prepared to loot any amount of machinery, petroleum or heavy goods of that kind, but they never extended this principle to works of art. (Those they did "borrow" have been returned, we hear.)

Napoleon Bonaparte thought he had a perfect right to carry off a painting or a piece of sculpture if he wished to do so: it was the reward of conquest. Nowadays that doctrine is as dead as Bonaparte himself. There may have been a little looting here and there of minor art objects (never of the great ones) during the past war, but it was not done *as of right*. It was a surreptitious proceeding, forbidden by our own rules of war, and I can only remember one or two attempts at that kind of thing—not, I believe, successful. I remember one Allied officer (British) who took a fancy to a small picture in the palace at Caserta and actually did have it in his own quarters for a while, but I doubt very much if it went any farther. It was his favorite joke—"my loot"—but hardly more.

The respect paid by modern Western armies (the only ones I know well) to works of art is not perfect: how could it be? It is too new. Never before have troops been totally fed and equipped from their own homes so far away, as ours and the British were. It used to be normal procedure, up to very recent times, for an army to "live off the country," as Sherman's army did when it marched through Georgia. If you had to get your food and shoes and everything else from the conquered inhabitants, there was not much sense trying to tell the troops to respect paintings and architecture. Our very strenuous rule against looting (the penalty for which is death, or such other punishment as the court martial may direct) seldom had to be applied, because looting, such as it was, was too trifling. My own general impression was that vandalism might have been a greater danger, although that, too, was severely discouraged. It might have been more serious because too often our soldiers were in a hurry and if an object of art got in the way it suffered. I myself saw some youths of our Signal Corps, directed by a second lieutenant, stringing wires through the great pillars of the Temple of Neptune at Paestum. He had to get his wires up within half an hour, he said when I protested; and what was this "old temple" anyhow? It was already a ruin. Our soldiery made a neat distinction in that area (at the Salerno landings) between what they called the "old ruins" and the "new ruins." The old ones were great Greek treasures of the fifth century B.C.; the new were the ones we ourselves (or the Germans) had just now made. There was great temptation toward vandalism under the circumstances, but scarcely any toward looting. In the devastated and starving areas which we usually entered as conquerors the looting was in the opposite direction—that is, our soldiers looted our own government and taxpayers by giving away their belongings to Italian or German children: rations, mainly, but also every other sort of movable object of government issue.

Vandalism was much commoner among the Russians than among Western troops because, at times, it served political purposes, created intimidation and obedience, etc., etc., as well as satisfying the exuberant impulses of a primitive people in the moment of victory. I have seen the family portraits of a certain very old Austrian clan which were cleanly cut in great X's by Russian officers (not ordinary soldiers) during the occupation—that is, not just in the hour of triumph but quite cold-bloodedly two or three years afterwards. The general tendency of one's experience would be to show that Russian official doctrine had very little to do with the behavior of Russian soldiers. By doctrine they also disapproved of looting except as "war booty" (i.e., reparations), yet they did nothing to stop it. Vandalism was that of which they accused their enemies and friends, with horror, too, but scarcely noticed when it was committed by their own troops.

The behavior of Russian troops bears so little relation to that of Western troops that it hardly enters into the general situation I am attempting to describe. We all have heard innumerable stories of this strange behavior but since I, at least, saw none of it at the time and have seen few evidences since, I must leave it to one side of the argument. There is a curiosity I am tempted to put down because it was well authenticated: it came in a letter not long after the war from a friend in Berlin, to Miss Dorothy Thompson in America, and I have seen the letter. This lady described a Russian officer, fond of music, who entered the house of a pianist in Berlin who was known as a Bach scholar and performer. The officer, possessing no German or other Western language, drove the old man to the piano and shouted "Bach!" at him, meanwhile brandishing a revolver. The Russian officer kept the revolver trained on the pianist and made him go on playing for a very long time, meanwhile weeping copiously. This, needless to say, is a special pattern of military behavior not to be found (so far as I know) in the American forces.

Good luck played a part, too—in some cases, great good luck. I have seen photographs of the tomb of the Empress Galla Placidia, at Ravenna, an irreplaceable work of Byzantine mosaic, with the bomb-hole beside it made by one of our B-17's. The tomb was undamaged. The cathedral at Cefalù in Sicily, as I saw to my amazement a day or so after it happened, was also intact although bombs had fallen quite near on two sides. Bombing from the air, even with every effort made toward precision, is dependent on so many calculations and circumstances—including the bombardier's nervous system, the instruments, the wind, the visibility and so on—that what astonishes me most is not the mistakes that were made but those so very much more numerous that were avoided.

Now, of course, there is an unanswerable objection to all this. I am trying to say that mankind is not so bad after all; that efforts were made on both sides in this war, and remarkably successful ones on the whole, either to preserve, or to keep from obliterating, the treasures of the past; that most of the arts (particularly music) "had a good war" and a better peace afterwards, and that the state of culture after the war is about as healthy as before, here and there even healthier.

The unanswerable objection comes from the direction of Tolstoy and Gandhi, who would undoubtedly say that if you have set out to commit the horrendous crime of killing your fellow creatures, it is no use claiming credit from the Life Force because you saved a few odd sticks and stones out of the mess. You cannot mitigate violence or compromise with it in any way, according to these sages: three days before his death Gandhi told me that violence was always wrong, "at all times and places."

To this argument there is no reasonable reply because everybody in his heart knows that it is true. All one can say is that once war has begun and is being prosecuted with all the resources available in the last one, the preservation of civilization is problematical, and yet it was done.

If anybody (even Tolstoy or Gandhi or their most literal followers) should think that no progress has been made in man's respect for his own hard-won civilization, it ought to be enough to recall a little of the destruction, vandalism, looting and "confiscation" which was ethically respectable in the wars even of the nineteenth century. Not so long ago, as the history of this race goes, every soldier was normally expected to be a freebooter, and much of warfare was simply land piracy. Remember what Field Marshal Blücher said when he had his first view of London as an honored guest from atop St. Paul's Cathedral? *"Was für Plunder!"* said he—what loot!

2

While the troubled years were at their height not many of us were able to take such a cool view, just the same. I should define the time of greatest trouble as roughly between 1937 and 1947. In the years just before the war, when Hitler came thoroughly into view as a man who believed his own monstrous doctrines and intended to carry them out literally—a man capable of the deliberate, final holocaust—there was so much individual suffering, through the successive annexations, the persecution of the Jews and the abolition of liberty, that it was in its own way a kind of war. It was a one-sided war because, unfortunately, he was unopposed in his designs. Then, after the war ended in 1945, it took a year or two for the smoke to clear away (smoke which contained the dust of human cremations). It was at least 1947 before we could more or less get a view of the landscape, see where we stood and where we had been before. In that rather surprising dawn I, at least, was always being astonished to find that Such-and-Such, whose trace I had lost in Spain or Italy or Czechoslovakia or Austria, was (in some form or other) still alive somewhere. The methodical savagery of the Hitler machine at times seemed to be annihilating everything one had ever known or valued; and, moreover, as his conquests progressed, more and more of the world was cut off from our view. And yet, such is the tenacity of the human race that some of his victims refused to be sacrificed. It must have been in 1947, at least (maybe later), that I got a post card from Buenos Aires from an old Salzburg friend whom my imagination had surrendered to the flames long since. The decade of nightmare contained so much indiviual tragedy of every kind that any survival surprised; to call it simply a "war" seems inadequate.

What it did to all the arts and particularly music was most visible to us earlier, before the war began. It so happens that a great number of musicians, especially among composers, string-players, teachers and singers, were Jewish (or half-Jewish or one-quarter or married to somebody who was). The Nürnberg laws defined a Jew as any person with one Jewish grandparent, and a lesser proportion (one Jewish great-parent, for example) became a *"Mischling."* I actually knew one man who became a *"Mischling"* (which means mongrel) without knowing that he had ever been eligible. It was a dreadful rigmarole but it was applied with the utmost barbarian seriousness. It is easy to imagine what havoc such legislation could cause in such a cosmopolitan city as Vienna, for example, where so many people were, in fact a mixture of different strains. Moreover, a person of the purest "German-Aryan" ancestry all the way back to Siegfried and Brünnhilde was guilty of *Rassenschande,* or shame to the race, by being married to another person belonging to one of these Nürnberg categories. It all sounded so insane, when explained clause by clause, that any American's first impulse was to laugh at it: but from late 1937 onward it became deadly serious and rapidly evolved into the immense historic crime now so fully recorded and known.

Orchestra players have always seemed to have, for various reasons, a national or group hankering after certain instruments. Wood winds, for example, have been a great speciality of French and Belgian players for a century or more, and although all these divisions are less marked now than before the war, it still would be a little hard on some of our great orchestras to do without the French and Belgian contingent. North Germans are good at the brasses (so are Americans, especially young ones); Italians often excel at the strings. It happened, for what reason I cannot say, that a considerable proportion of the finest players of violin, viola and violoncello in the orchestras of central Europe were Jewish. Berlin, Munich, Leipzig, Vienna—it was the same everywhere. The most eminent of these were also teachers with pupils who used to come from afar to study.

Here, of course, I am speaking only of the special aptitudes involved (and the crippling of the orchestras which came when they were removed). There were actually Jewish musicians scattered through all the desks of these big orchestras. I was once told that something like one-third of the Vienna Philharmonic in 1938 was either Jewish or somehow punishable under the Nürnberg Laws. All suffered alike, but the orchestras themselves suffered most from the loss of the string-players. Furtwängler in Berlin clung onto five of his long after it was forbidden, and by means of tactics both devious and courageous, but even he gave up in the end.

The orchestras are only one example. The persecution of the Jews actually struck at music in practically every way, through the conservatories, the music schools, the musical business organizations (such as agencies), and even through the public. Well-to-do and cultivated Jewish people have long been one of the principal elements in the best musical audiences of all those cities, as they are in our own. Quite aside from all the human suffering, the innumerable civic injustices (forced sales of property and so on), the public humiliations and, eventually, the concentration camp, what I am trying to indicate here is that music itself suffered greatly. And that, of course, involved a great many musicians who were not Jewish at all —who could have stayed on forever if they had been able to endure the spectacle.

It was all going on when I was in Vienna in 1938 and it would be impossible to forget the horror and also the bewilderment it occasioned. The greater horrors were yet to come, but even in that summer there were nightly raids and nightly shipments to Dachau. (At that period they were secret from the general public: I followed them closely through the Jewish Kultusgemeinde, which the Gestapo held accountable for all Jews.) There was plenty of horror but there was still, also, a great deal of bewilderment and sheer unbelief. It did seem hardly possible; we learned later on that the limits of the possible had nowhere near been reached.

Musicians who were not Jewish did not know all that was going on, of course. The specific events (arrests, shipments of prisoners) were never reported in the newspapers. But the music world is small and word gets about; besides, the blank desks, the constant changes, all the indescribable atmosphere of uncertainty, could be felt by the most unpolitical of creatures. According to my own observation, musicians are all unpolitical, nonpolitical or totally apolitical—they are what the Greeks would call idiots, *idiotes*—and if any one of them ever thought he had a political idea, it was a mistake. Some of these men, of course, meekly put on the Nazi button because "times had changed," but a great many did not. A considerable number of the best and greatest were plainly revolted by the whole Nazi view of the world, shown in great and small things, in the entire conduct of ordinary life as well as in the monstrous crimes. Such was the case of Mme. Lotte Lehmann, for instance, a "German-Aryan" of incontestable "purity" whom the Nazis not only admired but actually wooed. When she first had her tiff with the Nazis (shortly after their seizure of power) they were still a fairly respectable gang of ruffians, highly favored by a great many eminent persons in Western countries as well as by some of the greatest in Germany. Every monstrosity they afterwards carried out was implicit in their doctrine—and fully explained in *Mein Kampf* —but they were still trying to conciliate the world they intended to subdue. Many great and wise men, including the late Thomas Mann, were taken in. Thomas Mann told Benedetto Croce that the dangers of the Nazis were exaggerated, that persons in power always forgot their earlier theories, etc., etc., and that he for one intended to see it out; six months later he was a fugitive. As for the West, a general benevolence toward Hitler was quite general up to about 1937. *Mein Kampf* had never been translated into English or French (Chamberlain had not read it in 1938).

Lehmann, on recital tour in Germany in 1933, was surprised to find herself summoned to Berlin for a consultation with Hermann Goering. He sent an airplane to fetch her, and the anxious director of the Berlin Opera met her and took her to lunch with the plump Petronius of the regime. He offered her fabulous terms and immense privileges to sing at the Berlin Opera; as the greatest German singer of her day, it was no more than her due, but she thought it was all very funny, especially as he had his pet lioness introduced after lunch. Lotte, whose risibilities could never be controlled, actually petted the lioness instead of being (as expected) frightened into gibbers. That was the end for Goering. She never sang for the Nazis: she had laughed at them.

It is worth mentioning also that at the time of Lehmann's clash with Goering in 1933, the persecution of the Jews had not yet begun, although it was fully implicit in every word of Nazi doctrine. There were a good many Jewish artists actually singing in the Berlin Opera and playing in the Berlin Philharmonic. Many (probably most) Jews in central Europe still thought Hitler did not mean quite what he said. Lehmann's attitude was not based upon the injustices done to Jewish friends and colleagues. And certainly it was not based upon political theory; I truly believe she has never had a political thought in her life. It was merely the sovereign instinct of a great artist.

Music, as Shakespeare has pointed out in a number of notable verses known to all, does really do something to its practitioners and its lovers. It may make idiots of them (in part, that is true). It soothes the savage breast, yes—it even soothed Hitler's, although I understand he caught up on a good deal of sleep in that box at the Berlin Opera—but if it is something more than ear-deep it does more than soothe. Music-lovers like Hitler and Stalin are the enemies of music because to them it is ear-deep and brain-deep:

The man that hath not music in himself
Nor is not moved with the concord of sweet sounds
Is fit for treasons, stratagems and spoils;
The motions of his spirit are dull as night
And his affections dark as Erebus.
Let no such man be trusted. Mark the music . . .

William James contends (*The Principles of Psychology,* in that famous chapter on "Habit") that if you are neither a performer yourself nor musically gifted enough for intellectual participation in the performance, the habit of "excessive indulgence in music" is likely to fill you with emotions which pass without an expression in life—"without prompting to any deed." He is talking, naturally, to students of the Department of Philosophy at Harvard College, and since the book was published in 1890 he must have delivered the original lecture during earlier years. To these young men he says: "The remedy would be, never to suffer one's self to have an emotion at a concert without expressing it afterwards in *some* active way. Let the expression be the least thing in the world—speaking genially to one's grandmother, or giving up one's seat in a horsecar, if nothing more heroic offers—but let it not fail to take place."

My contention about Lotte in her private war with the Nazis is not in the least that she did anything heroic. She was supreme on a very wide field, in fact the widest in music; she could go anywhere; Vienna, London, Paris and New York were hers; she did not need Berlin. It was Berlin that needed her. But what I do contend is that she followed out James' injunction. She had music in her soul, and when she told Hermann Goering and the Nazi government what she thought of them—which she did by her laughter—she was in fact speaking genially to her grandmother (Euterpe) and giving up her seat in the horsecar.

There were other artists in different categories who made the same refusal in different ways and for different reasons, although generally at a somewhat later date. It seems hardly necessary to mention Toscanini, who of course never returned to Germany after Hitler came to power and would not have done so if they had offered him the entire national treasury. He loved Bayreuth and his seasons there have remained vivid in innumerable memories, but according to my information he steadfastly refused to meet Hitler, even there, even before Hitler came to power and even though Frau Siegfried Wagner wished it. Toscanini's case is a little special because he had already learned how the usurpation of state power may affect the culture and soul of a people. Igor Stravinsky is another special case: he is a born intellectual and he undoubtedly knew the meaning of the Hitler avalanche before it descended. Then there were the notable

composers and teachers whose actual theory and practice were condemned by the Hitler regime as being "degenerate" or "Western"
or "formalistic" or something else nonsensical—the kind of label
which musical illiterates like Hitler and Stalin distributed so lavishly
all through these years. What they meant, really, was that they did
not, personally, enjoy music in which experiments were made with
our old scale of seven-and-five, or with our old rhythms, or our well-
known old chords, and they did not understand the imperative necessity which drove so many of our best contemporaries into this un-
explored field. Probably the most famous German composer in this
category was Paul Hindemith, who was not only lucky to get out
alive, but whose whole work was strictly forbidden throughout the
time of the Nazi power. (I need hardly say that Hindemith's work is
now being performed constantly throughout central Europe.)

Hitler's musical taste seems to have gone as far as Richard Strauss,
but just barely, and even that old man was allowed to hang on in
his mountain village through this terrible decade mainly because he
was so relentlessly famous. Hitler made him "president of the German
Chamber of Culture," more or less the way a Hindu wears a sham-
rock on St. Patrick's Day, but there is no evidence that the meaning of Strauss' work at its best ever got beyond the dictator's ears.
Indeed one short work the Nazis did produce in Berlin—*Friedenstag*
—in its praise of peace and freedom looks rather like a joke played
on them by the old fox. In spite of being so very old, famous and
inspissatedly German, Strauss, too, was too "modern" for Hitler.

The artists of other countries subjugated by Hitler outside central
Europe had more or less the same responses and the same fates. If
they were Jewish they could go to the crematorium; if they were not
Jewish their souls revolted against all the obscenity and nonsense
and horror anyhow; and in many cases their work, being "modern,"
was itself condemned as well as their persons. How could Hitler like
Honegger's *Judith?* (And, besides, was Judith herself not a Jewish
heroine?) And all that South American rhythmic coloration in Darius Milhaud was obviously "degenerate," a part of the Anglo-
American plot somehow to defeat the inevitable supremacy of the
master race. Such, like Stravinsky and like all the Viennese, like
Martinu from Prague and like Béla Bartók from Hungary and like
innumerable less distinguished musicians, were condemned by bell,

book and candle. In the "New Order" of the "New Europe" they had no place.

Now, of course, some few musical artists of quality did remain under the Hitlerite yoke and continued to work all this time, but I submit that they were very few. They fall into such groups as that of Herbert von Karajan, who was an extremely young man just getting his start when Hitler came to power; indeed it was even 1936 or 1937, I believe, before Karajan received his first important appointment, as general-intendant of the opera and orchestra at Aachen. (I remember it well and took part in his celebration of it at Salzburg.) Such a young man had nothing to expect outside his own country, everything to expect inside it. Even though his wife, as I believe, was Jewish, he somehow managed. There was one much older artist, famous and respected throughout the world, who also stayed: Furtwängler. In Paris the most notable opera singer, Mme. Germaine Lubin, became an enraptured believer in the "New Order." (She was an extremely foolish woman who had been in love with German music, particularly Wagner, all her life, and easily confused Hitler's flapdoodle with the *Nibelungen Ring*). There were the very old and the very young and there were also a number who could not have escaped if they had tried. There was, for example, old Hans Pfitzner, the composer of *Palestrina,* who stuck it out somehow (in the main they ignored him—he was neither Jewish nor "modern"). All of these I should like to return to at a later stage when I get to the years after the holocaust: there is much to be said of them.

It was, any way you look at it, about the most disruptive thing that had ever happened to music in Europe. There have been almost countless wars in Europe and the musicians have paid little attention to any of them—nor have the great soldiers on their white horses paid any attention to the musicians, either. A man like Beethoven, full of passion and prejudice in political matters, is the exception that proves the rule; up to Hitler music had been permitted to flower like a tree, and if a musician was killed it was an accident—such an accident as could happen to a tree.

And in the result, of course, there was the formidable migration. It is still too early to know what will come of it, but a really notable section of the musical culture of continental Europe was transferred to England and the United States during the period to which I refer. They got there in all sorts of weird ways, and every single one of them has a story to tell. When the smoke had blown away—as I have said, I put this date at 1947—we in America looked around and what did we see?

Schönberg and Stravinsky were in California, Hindemith at Yale, Darius Milhaud was at Mills College in California, Ernst Krenek was in St. Paul, Minnesota, Erich Korngold was working in Hollywood, Ernst Toch was at the University of Southern California; Alfred Einstein—the musicologist—was at Smith College; Herbert Graf was the principal stage director at the Metropolitan Opera in New York; Béla Bartók, unfortunately, was dead, but before his death had been teaching at Columbia. Lehmann and Toscanini were still very much with us, and so was Bruno Walter; the orchestras from Schenectady to Dallas, and from Fort Worth to Seattle, had been enriched by players of quality; hardly a college, university or music school in the country was without some valuable accretion from the European disaster. Some had paused in England and some had gone on to Argentina or elsewhere, but by and large the United States received most from this world tremor. If it does not in due course have a significant effect upon composition itself, as well as upon standards of taste, performance and comprehension, there would be occasion for surprise.

3

Every complex moment has its currents of force which flow both ways, clash and go on. When this decade of turmoil began, it was quite easy for most people to travel if they had the money to buy their tickets. Passports were seldom refused, and such persons as singers, violinists, pianists and conductors in particular, who were in demand everywhere, were more or less constantly on the go. The congealing of all the circumstances into what became a kind of icy wall took a little while, but bit by bit—even before war broke out—it was taking place. Mussolini may have been the first of the dictators to seal up his itinerants, to make them stay at home as a deliberate policy, although of course the Russians had been doing this since the 1920's. The Russians did it in simple self-defense: they lost so

many of their best by allowing them to go abroad—best in every art—
that the time came when they locked the door for musical artists and
threw away the key.

Mussolini followed their example in 1939 and a number of the
best Italian opera singers were forbidden to leave Italy. These included performers under contract to the Metropolitan in New York
and elsewhere in the United States, and a great deal of replanning
became necessary on our side of the ocean. Whether it was a good
or a bad thing need hardly be considered, but it was important in
its results to the ensuing seasons. Not only did it promote some
young American singers to leading parts which they might not
otherwise have attained for years, but it actually changed the choice
of works to be given and it was partly responsible for the introduction of "star" conductors to the Metropolitan. There were more
internationally famous conductors within reach than there were internationally famous singers: thus Bruno Walter, Sir Thomas Beecham, Fritz Busch, Georg Szell and others took their turn at the
opera house and conferred upon it the brilliance which was sometimes not present in the singing casts. Those casts, however, although at times inexperienced and subject to incomprehensible substitutions and changes, were brought up to a high level by this
sudden influx of powerful musicians at the podium—and, too, by
the rehearsals upon which they insisted.

In the German repertoire it had just so happened during the 1930's
that a whole crop of fine singers from Scandinavia came to America,
and Wagner's works could be given—often were—without a single
German in any important part. This was the period at which Wagner was the most popular of all opera composers in the United States,
thanks to Flagstad and Melchior. It ended rather abruptly in 1940
when Mme. Flagstad, having flown home to Norway, decided to stay
there. This was at the time a terrible blow to the management at
the Metropolitan, which was again forced into extensive substitutions
and improvisations. Mme. Flagstad was not only a singer whose appearance on that stage would automatically sell every seat in the
house; she was also a whole repertoire, small but vital, and without a
proper replacement for her it would be out of the question to do
these operas over and over again, as had become the custom. The
American *hochdramatisches* soprano, Helen Traubel, whose enor-

mous and very beautiful voice was at its climactic best, had not received much encouragement from the Metropolitan up to this point,
and was comprehensibly reluctant to take over the entire burden all
at once without proper preparation. Mme. Traubel gradually did take
on the heroic roles, one after the other, but it was really the Metropolitan's fault that they had not asked her to do so a little sooner.
By the time she was fully in control of the heaviest Wagner parts,
a few years later, she was no longer singing their higher and more
difficult notes. Those who heard her first concert appearances in
New York with Toscanini—the finale of *Götterdämmerung;* the first
act of *Die Walküre*—realize that it was the Metropolitan that missed
the boat. It is quite possible that her capacity for tragic impersonation was not or never could have been equal to her tremendous
voice, but all one can say, on the record, is that the truly fair trial
was not made until it was too late.

The whole Flagstad episode caused much passion and fury, much
accusation and recrimination—not to speak of a deluge of black ink
on white paper. I never did see any reason why a lady should not
go home to her husband in troubled times and stay with him at
home, even if he were a Nazi sympathizer or collaborator. It would
seem to me a somewhat private matter. We missed Mme. Flagstad's
flood of gold. My guess is that anybody who ever received that flood
of gold in his ears (even once!) will always miss it. However,
voices come and go; music goes on forever. By what reasoning it
came to be supposed that Mme. Flagstad had "betrayed" us I
never really began to guess; she was a perfectly free adult woman, not
in peonage to the Metropolitan, and so long as she did not help
the Nazis in their monstrous schemes (as I believe she did not) it
was her own business what she did. Actually she owed the Metropolitan some debts of gratitude, but I believe she had already repaid them and continued to do so after the war was over. She came
to us at a very modest fee, became within a few weeks the most
phenomenal magnet of popular attraction since Caruso, and continued to sing for some seasons at the same modest fee—not just a
few times each year, but practically twice a week every week. She
cheerfully learned and sang, in no time at all, the most difficult
parts ever written for the female voice, and her courage stopped at no
exertion, at no effort that was demanded. She probably earned

more money for the house than any other single artist since Caruso because (unlike Chaliapin, whose fees were always monstrous) she never exaggerated her financial demands. If she became a trifle exacting in some other respects toward the end of her reign—such as in her attitude toward conductors—it should be accepted as an evidence that she, too, was human; such a success as she had was bound to go to some part of the head some of the time.

The management (chiefly Mr. Edward Johnson and Mr. Edward Ziegler, both my friends, whom I saw often at this period) could not be blamed either. They had learned to regard Flagstad as being something more or less like the floor, walls and ceiling of the house, and her defection threw them into the utmost consternation. If they had guessed her intentions they might have been ready for the grave difficulties which followed. They might have been urging Mme. Traubel on for several years, instead of leaving her with Sieglinde or (worse) some springtime popular-priced opera in English. Managers, too, are human. It seems that it is only the public, especially when it gets excited over wartime accusations and suspicions, which can rise above such weakness.

There was one wartime defection which seemed serious at the time to Johnson and Ziegler, especially the latter ("Ned"). They dipped into their slender resources for a new production of *Alceste*, designed for Mme. Germaine Lubin. I remember Ned telling me that it cost $30,000, which was a great deal more then than it would be now. Whereupon Mme. Lubin, too, sent her cablegram announcing that owing to the events of the war she could not come to America. It was utterly impossible to lose the $30,000, which had already been fully spent—the sets and costumes were actually completed—so they gave the opera with Miss Marjorie Lawrence, the Australian soprano, also from the Paris Grand Opéra, who did not have Mme. Lubin's special adaptation to the part and could not make the same impression. I was especially sorry for Ned, whose special project this was, but at the same time I could not be sure in my own mind what Mme. Lubin would have sounded like or looked like in the Metropolitan. She was wonderful in Paris toward the end of the 1930's, and more or less rejuvenated the Opéra—I had also heard her *Alceste* two or three times, as well as her Wagner performances with Furtwängler, in German. But this highly schooled, musicianly voice was not "great" in any sense, and to a public accustomed to Flagstad I do not believe it would have sounded sufficiently noble. Moreover, in Paris, with an inferior chorus and orchestra, bad fellow principals, mediocre settings and an unmusical audience, Mme. Lubin stood out with planetary brilliance. In New York, where any new production (as distinguished from ordinary repertoire) was on a high level, and where the audience for our first *Alceste* would have drawn heavily upon a musical public of international quality, Mme. Lubin might not have seemed equal to the almost hieratic majesty of that creation. The settings were not lost, however; they were used in the next few seasons, and later on—after Ned Ziegler had died—they served for Mme. Flagstad's memorable last performances at the Metropolitan, the most beautiful, I think, I ever heard even from her.

The incidents of disruption due to the war could be strung out almost indefinitely. I have named some of the chief ones at the Metropolitan, but it happened in the same way in the concert halls of the country. It worked both ways: certainly, as has been emphasized, we gained many composers, pedagogues, conductors and others, however awkward the loss of some performers might have been. Then, too, some performers who were working on our side of the ocean refused to go back the other way after the war (even the "phony" war) had begun. I was at the Maggio Fiorentino in 1940 and remember well how the director complained to me because Mme. Zinka Milanov, then at the Metropolitan, had refused to carry out her contract at that festival. War, like a doctor's certificate, is the one excuse no director in his right mind can refuse to accept.

Whether we lost or gained by the interruption of free communications is, of course, arguable; practically everything is. Some American singers would say that it was a fine thing the war gave our own people a chance; certainly it was good to see so many first-class conductors working in the United States in all our orchestras and concert halls and universities. But music is also a little like science or mathematics in one respect, that it flowers best in its own field on its own terms. Any interference from alien categories of thought is likely to blunt or dull or efface these special aptitudes. The mere bewilderment which interference causes (to put it no higher) is a handicap to musical expression and beclouds or chokes the art which ought to be the most natural of all.

We never had, in the countries which remained free during this decade—England and America were the only ones for most of the time—any direct political influence upon what kind of music could be performed or by whom. There was the general notion (not originating in the government at Washington) that it would be best not to perform *Madama Butterfly* during these years because of the cruelty wreaked by an American upon a Japanese girl in that story. It was a foolish inhibition because the real cruelties of the score (such as the use of the Star-Spangled Banner to emphasize the young man's declaration that his real wife would be an American) generally escape the notice of the audience, which, like most of Puccini's audiences, is awash in sentiment without thought. I am not able to remember any other work of any kind which was dropped out of the current musical lists; Wagner flourished; no changes were to be seen in the concert lists; German songs never stopped being performed for a moment. When Lotte Lehmann sang for vast audiences of soldiers in training, as she did a considerable number of times, they actually yelled for German songs and could never get enough of them.

One wartime variation in repertoire was, perhaps, political in origin, but if so it gave an element of freshness to the concert programs: it was the popularity of modern Russian—Soviet—music. This was beginning before I was engulfed into the Army; I had full notice of it during the years when I was in Africa, Italy, India or China; and twice, on missions home to America, I had a chance to see the thing in operation. A general sense that the Red Army in its 1942-1944 phases—that is, before it had come to seem dangerous to ourselves—was a vital ally in our own struggle: this was, I suppose, the basis of the popularity of Russian ideas and people, arts and crafts (and of Russian War Relief, too, the biggest of all those organizations for collecting money). In music it resulted in a general unfurling of the Soviet orchestral literature before American audiences: not only Prokofieff and Shostakovich (who would have been performed anyhow, and had been well displayed before the war), but also Miaskovsky, Khatchaturian, Kabalevsky, Shebalin and others took their turns. On one of my two visits home during the war I was present at the first performance of Shostakovich's "Leningrad" symphony in Carnegie Hall: it was a very grandiose occasion with more gold braid on display, from both Americans and Russians, than I have ever seen at a musical gathering.

The Soviet composers were, of course, not working in freedom: they were subjected to the most vexatious kind of uncomprehending, pettifogging criticism, some of the worst of which came from the highest source—Stalin. However, it was generally not *musical* criticism. As a rule they were exhorted to write "for the people" and "about the people." In other words, their fetters were mainly in subject matter. Stalin's favorite composer was Tchaikovsky, and it was indeed fortunate that the most copiously gifted of the younger Soviet composers, Shostakovich, was himself a kind of Tchaikovsky; if he had strayed very far away from the tradition of full Russian expressivity he might not have had such a long and brilliant career. The kind of creative experiment which we associate with the names of Béla Bartók and Alban Berg would never have been possible in Russia because the dictator would not have liked the sounds produced; if he had not liked the sounds produced he would have obliterated the work (as he did with Shostakovich's *Lady Macbeth from Mzensk*) and possibly also the composer. There was a moment not long after Prokofieff's return to Russia (1935) when his rhythmical and stylistic inventions brought upon him a terrible reproach: he was "formalistic." This word, which was never fully explained in the Russian publications translated in our countries, seems to have meant something like what we mean by new combinations of musical form, not necessarily in scales or modes or tonalities—which would have been too daring for the Soviet ear at any time—but simply in rhythm and harmony. Prokofieff reformed, although his musical vocabulary remained much the same, and his choice of subject matter made him respectable again to the time of his death. In the war period, when patriotism—that is, not to the "Soviet Fatherland" but to "Holy Mother Russia"—was the predominant theme of every Russian expression, composers entered the freest period they had yet known: beyond a doubt the patriotic subjects were at the time those they felt most deeply and were most willing and eager to write. Their country had been attacked and invaded to the depths: the subjects they were commanded to write were the ones they would have chosen anyhow.

Among all this Russian patriotic work hardly anything but Shosta-kovich and Prokofieff is likely to last in our musical life (and even Prokofieff's beautiful *Alexander Nevsky* was written before the war, under his own steam, so to speak, and without official prodding). The old-fashioned taste, if it can be called taste at all, which prevails in Soviet graphic arts—the Victorianism of painting and sculpture, the out-of-date Americanism of the architecture—and the closely related prudery of subject and style in literature, have been felt in music, too, but it is the prerogative of music to inhabit its own special language which very often cannot be understood by the layman or even, until much time has elapsed, by the musician. A composer is not always fully aware of what he is doing—the half-instinctive process is not brought into "scientific" alignment by any theoretical harness, in the twentieth century or in any other; otherwise anybody who learned (say) Alban Berg's method could have composed *Wozzeck.* These con-siderations may indicate the larger and deeper reasons why such a work as Prokofieff's Second Violin Concerto might be at the very same moment traditional enough to be accepted in Russia at the court of Stalin, modern enough to arouse keen interest in the West, bril-liant and melodious enough to excite common-or-garden audiences the world over. There are not many such works at any period, but it was an observed fact that during the decade of the great troubles the Soviet Russians did send us quite a few compositions which were equally welcome to us and to them, regardless of musical theory or political verbigeration.

So we gained and we lost, on the whole, and it will be for the fu-ture to decide which was heavier, but one thing I can state with as-surance is that I never took keener pleasure in musical performances of all kinds than in that period just before I went into the Army, the few that came my way while I was in the Army, and the period just afterwards—in fact, this whole decade which I have called "the troubled times." It is probably a general truth that we enjoy best what we think half-lost; the *Figaro* or *Rosenkavalier* of 1941 probably seemed to me best of all because I could not count on hearing either of them again; the Beethoven symphonies (Toscanini did a festival se-ries just then, First to Ninth) had never made their utterance so irresistible; every violinist and pianist played better than before, every song sounded better. In my own case, owing to the passage of time and much frequentation of musical centers, I had by now rather an extensive acquaintance among music-makers, which added to the direct musical pleasures another which is hard to define but which all who live or have lived in such circles can identify. It is perhaps best described as "kitchen" pleasure. We have long enjoyed the dishes and relished the sauces and argued about the order or combination; now we are allowed into the kitchen and at very high moments may be permitted to fight with the cook. Music and the theatre are both encrusted with persons appreciative of the kitchen pleasures; with some, probably, the kitchen really more or less replaces the dining room.

It never did with me. Backstage corridors and dressing rooms and alley entrances have their appeal, now as always, and indeed I think I have learned a great deal about music itself from the kitchen-talk; but I never did give up my status as a member of the general public and always took my place, by preference, out in front. Without naming names, which might lead to unseemly brawling, I can say I know a considerable number of musicians and near-musicians, relatives and friends of musicians, writers on music and persons connected with the music business, who scarcely ever listen to any performance all the way through from the point of view of the ordinary public. Opera—because it is so long and to most musicians and singers so boring through excessive familiarity—is the worst sufferer from this. I have sometimes asked highly accomplished singers, conductors and other musicians concerned how long it has been since they heard any one opera all the way through, and you would be astonished at the answers: five years, ten years, fifteen years. It was my privilege only last year to accompany Miss Mary Garden to a performance of *Salome* at the Metropolitan, and although she had herself performed it several hundred times in Europe and the United States during about twenty years, she had never seen or heard it before.

Well, greatly as I have enjoyed the smells of the dressing rooms and the perils of the corridors, I never wanted to hear or see anything from the various perches back there, nor yet on the loud-speakers in the various offices. The exiguous footpaths at the Metropolitan or the more comfortable highways backstage at the Scala might arouse a certain romanticism (literary and adolescent) but they could never beguile me from my place: I belong out front.

4

The Army not only took your mind off the war, but it took your mind off everything else too. Of all abstractions from ordinary life it was probably the most successful because it substituted a whole new structure for the old: something to do (however trivial) and an entirely new set of worries, a *dramatis personae* of such startling novelty that you sometimes thought they had all been summoned into existence only the moment before, and, with all this, a new language on several concurrent planes at once, ranging from the jargon of the War Department to the jargon of the G.I., with touches of Newport and Hollywood along the way from the private store of fellow officers. Under these circumstances it was an excellent holiday from music as from everything else of importance in existence. The Army was frequently duller than any form of life that has come under my observation, and it was occasionally downright dangerous (depending on where they happened to put you), but intellectually it was one long rest.

Even those years, just the same, were punctuated with a few episodes in which "real life" (as the G.I.'s often called it) was sharply recalled to mind. If you happened to be in one of those places where the special services sections had a full supply of books—they were in paper-backed editions prepared by a committee of American publishers and furnished free to the troops—you could dig up all kinds of things, not merely the crossword-puzzle books and infantile stories cherished by the young soldiers, but also books with a direct address to the adult imagination. I remember reading *Moby Dick,* for the first time in many years, in a very cold tent in some dripping woods near Naples; it helped keep me warm and dry. Every once in a while something equally surprising happened in a musical way, although this was more a matter of accident. With some exceptions, the musical fare provided for the troops tended to be restricted to headquarters (such places as London and Algiers, or later Paris and Rome), and my opportunities to hear any of it were few and far between.

One fact that did impress me in every theatre of war was the eagerness with which music was received when it was offered. I never happened to be in any of the areas where great artists, such as Yehudi Menuhin, played for the troops, but I did hear about these occurrences. In the final stages of the war I crossed the trail of Lily Pons a number of times, both in Germany and in the Persian Gulf; in Cologne she had sung while the west bank was being shelled from the east, and at Abadan when the temperature was 130 degrees Fahrenheit; the troops not only flocked to hear her, but talked of it for days afterwards. Her husband, André Kostelanetz, had a remarkable trick all his own (so far as I know): whenever time permitted he got together an orchestra made up of soldiers, and with whatever kind of rehearsal the available hours permitted, he conducted and Lily sang with them. They had just done this at Abadan when I passed through—one of the dullest and saddest posts in the whole war, comparable in its sodden infuriating heat with the awful wetness and grayness of the Aleutian Islands or the white wastes of Iceland.

However, such highlights were not in my own direct experience: I mention them because they did occur and are worth remembering. The musical observation which seemed to me most surprising in the war was the way in which Italian opera flourished in our army. There were actually several G.I. opera companies, that is, companies of Italians performing entirely for the American soldiers in theatres to which civilians were not admitted. We had one in our headquarters at Caserta—the little theatre in the Royal Palace, built for Maria Carolina and her oafish Ferdinand in an epoch so utterly different. Rococo Naples and Capodimonte porcelain were just about as far from G.I. reality as it would have been possible to imagine: ancient China could not seem more remote. And yet that was the place where the troops took to opera not only enthusiastically—they did that everywhere in Italy—but also more intimately than anywhere else I ever saw.

The size of the little royal theatre may have helped; it was packed to the uttermost limits at every performance, and so many soldiers with an excellent view of the stage were bound to take some part in the performance. I was highly diverted one evening when *Il Barbiere di Siviglia* was given and the approval of the soldiery was almost as vocal as anything on the stage. The Rosina was shamelessly flirting with them all, as I am certain she did in Rossini's own day; she was a pretty, plump little girl, *"grassotta"* as Rossini says she ought to be, and she had very expressive eyes as well as a charmingly flexible voice. The G.I.'s never interrupted her when she was on one of her vocal flights, but when she paused to give them a chance they filled the air with whistles of delight. The little fat girl reveled in it: she had never had and never will have a more appreciative audience. If you can imagine such a thing, it was rather as if Victoria de los Angeles were singing for the G.I.'s and flirting with them at the same time. They listened ecstatically when she was actually singing, and her phrases of vocal display drew audible sighs of pleasure, but when she stopped singing it was her eyes and hips that held their attention. (Mlle. de los Angeles is perhaps too great a singer and beauty to be used as an example—this little girl was merely an effort in that direction—but all who admire de los Angeles will understand). The performance of *Il Barbiere* on that night was one of the liveliest I have ever seen anywhere, and I have the moral certainty that Rossini would have enjoyed it as much as I did, whatever the technical defects.

The only other performance I saw in the little royal theatre was one of *Madama Butterfly,* complete with the baby waving the Star-Spangled Banner at the end. The G.I.'s listened with an intentness I have seldom encountered in larger and "better" houses. Their applause, when it came, was thunderous. They were especially taken with Butterfly herself (I think it was the same little fat girl who had sung Rosina), although she never glanced at them during this performance, but did her part with the utmost seriousness. They showed no sign of being nationalistically or patriotically offended; indeed they booed Lieutenant Pinkerton heartily when he took his curtain calls. Again it was an evening of genuine freshness in the opera theatre: the performers realized that this was an audience to which the over-familiar work was brand-new, and they acted and sang as if it had never been done before. That anxiety over "how it turns out," which is wholly missing from the opera houses of the world, was magically restored.

There was a regular season of opera for the Army in Naples, not at the San Carlo itself, which had been damaged, but at a large theatre formerly used for films; the American conductor and writer Robert Lawrence was in charge. At Bari and in a few other places in the South performances were frequently given for the Allied armies or under their direction, although, as I remember, some civilians were also among the audience. The Eighth Army (General Montgomery's, in case anybody has forgotten) sponsored a number of these productions, and I was able to note that the British Tommy and the American G.I. were exactly the same in their responses. The one I remember best from Bari was *Lucia di Lammermoor,* which I thought fantastically funny but enjoyed more than I ever have enjoyed that work in a more "serious" house. The Scottish décor and costumes were funnier than words can say; I have heard in subsequent years that the men in the chorus wore their sporrans over their backsides instead of in front. I do not remember this and must regard it as legend—one of many Eighth Army legends!—but the truth was quite funny enough. I think the Highlanders in the audience must have laughed themselves sick. Through it all a very intent little Italian girl twittered and squeaked away with the utmost virtuosity, achieving such trills, runs, leaps, glissades, staccati and kindred tricks as would startle an oyster. After her Mad Scene the army gave her an ovation—and I think of all the ovations that were ever ovated in my hearing this was the greatest.

Obviously the Army liked the popular Italian operas very much indeed. The reason why so much opera was given was that the higher authorities had tested the response—more or less by accident—and knew, quite early, that a paradox was in being: our soldiers would rather go to the opera than to the movies. It may not have been true of all of them, but it was true of such a very large proportion that the opera theatres were packed to the limit at every performance for some two years or more. There were contributing circumstances, such as the fact that any form of entertainment by living persons had a high premium put upon it by our bored young men. They lived almost entirely out of tin cans—food, drink, medicine, clothing, entertainment and literature—so that whenever a living creature came along and tried to amuse them they were extravagantly appreciative. Bob Hope disrupted the Army routine for days wherever he went; the boys not only told his jokes to each other (and to me!) for weeks afterwards, but also wrote them home, our squadron censor told me, as being their own. Much less inspired comedians than Hope, much less gifted singers or dancers than some of those we got, could have delighted the G.I.'s. Furthermore, in the case of opera, it may be that they were a little influenced by the fact that they were in Italy. (In Italy you go to the opera—it's like eating spaghetti—but at home you don't: that is the form of thought.)

Allowing for all such considerations, there still remains the fact that they thronged to the opera and loved it. Where are they now, I wonder? Unless they happen to live in New York they can get very few opportunities to hear the tuneful tragedies of Naples. They may be among those eighteen million people who are supposed to be listening to the Metropolitan Opera's radio broadcasts every Saturday afternoon. I hope so. But wherever they are, they are my living proof that opera is not merely an aspect of dementia, a hobby for cranks and crackpots, but an art-child intelligible to all who give it a chance.

5

When we got out of those elegant uniforms and resumed our usual humdrum appearance, most of us wanted to know what was new and for a while could not discern it. There was what James somewhere calls the "chaos of the *Durcheinander*"—no clear landscape anywhere. Actually during the war idols had fallen, landmarks had quivered and sometimes disappeared, new voices were endeavoring to be heard; it took a little time to see and hear again with any approximate clarity. We had, as citizens of the republic of music, two administrative necessities: first, to bury our dead, and second, to feed the living, even though we might first have to dig them out from the ruins. If we could then go on to enjoy music again—or rather to live in it—the war would really be over.

I regarded all the Star Chamber justice that was dispensed after the war (this is what I call "burning our dead") as a ghoulish vendetta. I am proud to say that I never took any part in it. I refused to sign the petition which was circulated, even before the war, to keep Furtwängler from conducting the New York Philharmonic Orchestra. I never would sign anything opposing any musical artist on political grounds; if there were on earth any musician who was sincerely a Nazi (which I beg leave to doubt) then all I could do would be to pity him for deficiency of intellect and heart. Performing musicians— as distinct from composers—are far too specialized to have any time for abstract thought: the affairs of the state are not theirs. Sometimes they put the button on and sometimes they take it off, but their reasons in either case are intellectually negligible, morally nil. This is not to deny the moral responsibility of the musician as a human being—not at all—it is to transfer it to another and in some respects a higher plane. If Gieseking had ever permitted Adolf Hitler to interdict the music of Debussy from his own piano, this would have been a moral crime of the highest order known to the laws of Gieseking's being. But this, of course, never occurred: Gieseking (and he alone) continued to play Debussy's music. To take a lesser but still offensive crime in this category: if Gieseking had composed an elaborate pianistic fantasy on the Horst Wessel Lied and played it throughout Europe during the years of Hitler's empire this would have been lamentable and in fact disgusting. But this, too, did not happen. All that happened in the case of Gieseking was that he was a member of the Nazi party, along with practically every other German who was not in exile. The same was true of every German artist; you could not have a public career in Germany without it; it was Gieseking's misfortune—like Furtwängler's and Karajan's—to be so famous that it got noticed. They could, of course, have gone into a corner and quietly starved to death, but this is difficult even for musicians.

The uproar over the return of these and other valuable artists to our music world left me cold indeed, but in the period immediately after the war I could put it down to the hysterical aftermath of a great convulsion. Most of those who carried banners in front of Carnegie Hall or demonstrated outside the Metropolitan Opera had never lifted a finger against Hitler and had never heard a shot fired with lethal intent. They were the disputatious stay-at-homes, the fireside litigants with pains in the income tax; a disproportionate number, in every such demonstration I saw, were women. My guess—impossible to prove—is that most of them knew and cared nothing about music. These vengeful people, be it never forgotten, robbed us of Furtwängler's services for many long years and forced him to work for Hitler since he had nowhere else to go; and I do not think most of them had ever heard him conduct an orchestra. Up to 1947 or 1948 such behavior was still explicable as human weakness, since it had been, after all, a terrible war. But when it continued year after year one was forced to think that some relentless conspiratorial junta must be pulling the strings—some nonmusical purpose of importance was no doubt being served. By the great good sense of our people these demonstrations, although they still continue, are no longer able to deprive us of the inestimable values they attack.

The only time I ever lost my temper with these antimusical demonstrators was on the occasion of Karajan's first concert with the Berlin Philharmonic at Carnegie Hall, only a year ago. My host let us out of his car in the midst of a bunch of hysterical boys and girls carrying banners which said: "Nazi Go Home!" and other things of the kind. I found one of these objects being shaken in my face by a girl who had probably been still playing with her dolls when Hitler blew up his ultimate bunker. I who had, so to speak, fought, bled and died on every battlefield from Spain to China for twenty years, always and forever against the Nazi, before and during the war and forever after! This aroused that unreasoning fury to which we are so often a prey when our deepest sincerities are twisted and turned against us. (We must all, with St. Thomas Aquinas, deplore the concupiscible and irascible appetites, but we cannot deny them.) I was very nearly seized with a palsy and started shouting at the girl: "Go home yourself! You don't even know what a Nazi is! Go home! Go home!" She stared at me in consternation; I suppose she may have thought I was Hitler's ghost. A firm hand was put upon my arm and I heard the soothing voice of the New York policeman: "Now you just go along in to your concert, sir. Don't pay any attention to these people." I suppose if I had stopped to argue (instead of laughing) I might have been arrested for telling that foolish little picket the truth: she did not know what a Nazi was.

Paris at the end of the war and just afterwards was full of this wholesale and retail vengeance. If only one millionth of the French people who were so anxious to shave women's hair off afterwards had done some one small thing to help us win this war, it would have been over a great deal sooner and left fewer scars. The women's prison out at Fresnes was full of "collaborators" who languished there month after month without being brought to trial. *"La fine fleur de la noblesse française,"* somebody told me, was in prison. I suppose these ladies are all out by now and have grown their hair again but it remains in my memory as a singularly unpleasant episode, not because they were comtesses and marquises and the like (or chorus girls or street whores either) but just because I do not see how anybody expects women to behave during four years of occupation by an enemy army and civilian dictatorship.

Chief among the *"collaboratrices"* was Mme. Germaine Lubin, a star of the Paris Opéra. She was the only real ornament that institution has produced during my thirty-five years of acquaintance with it. As I have already said, she was enamoured of German music all her life, spent all her free time in Germany, studied German well enough to sing it admirably, and it was relatively easy for her to fit Hitler into the Wagnerian mythology. She was, in a manner of speaking, Hitlerian before Hitler came along. She had been an eminent and admirable exponent of German art for years, and it was only natural that Hitler should go to see her when he went to Paris after the conquest. Visiting her dressing room after the performance (it was *Siegfried*) he told her that if she would name any wish within his power to grant, he would grant it at once. She asked for her son, who was at that time a prisoner of war in Germany. Hitler released the son immediately.

Now, this crime is, I have often been told, one which no French woman could forgive, because millions of them also had sons in German prison camps. I could not help wondering if many or most (perhaps even all!) would not have made the same answer as Mme. Lubin if given the chance.

At all events, Mme. Lubin was not forgiven. After a very long time in prison she was eventually released, but of course to a form of nothingness as compared to the life she had known. She announced her intention to reappear in concert on two or possibly three occasions but canceled each time.

Now, what is the meaning of such a case? Is it not obvious that everybody concerned behaved foolishly? Mme. Lubin is herself, by definition, a foolish woman, because she thought Hitler could win the war. Any person in the twentieth century who thinks that anybody can win a war against the United States is by definition lacking in good sense. But it is equally foolish to lock up the best singer you possess and rob yourself and your country of irreplaceable gifts. What good did Mme. Lubin do the French people by spending those years in jail? She should have been robbed of her national honors, gratuities and pensions (as she was), but she should have been condemned to *sing*. Considering how very few people in France have ever learned how to sing it seems absurdity itself to silence the only imposing and mature vocal instrument in the country. Lubin was an artist who could make even the dull Paris Opéra seem to be a musical institution; although there was nothing in the house that came anywhere near her level, she somehow jerked it into a semblance of time, tune and performance. Without some such influence it always relapses every time into the same showy, meretricious provincialism, called "the Paris tradition," full of glitter and spun glass and waterfalls and ballet girls in inextricable confusion, bearing no relation to drama or music as elsewhere understood.

There have been so many of these cases that even the professional revenge-seekers are getting tired of them now. The healthy response of the general public to anything good has, in almost every case, won out in the end. If a man can play the violin as David Oistrakh can, says the public, what does it matter whether he is a Communist or a Seventh Day Adventist? If I could just once more in my life hear Gieseking play the Debussy preludes he might wear Nazi buttons all over his coat and I doubt if I should even see them. This is not disputing either the citizenship or the moral responsibility of the musician: it is merely putting first things first. I do not take my political opinions from David Oistrakh or Walter Gieseking; I would as soon attempt to play the violin or the piano in Carnegie Hall myself. Let them think as they please so long as they play as I please.

There was a wise Communist named (I think) Fischer who had the cultural ministry in Vienna just after the war. He called a meeting of all the members of the Opera and the Philharmonic and made a speech to them, which several of the musicians told me about a year or so afterwards. He said to them, at much greater length, something which I shall paraphrase as follows: You are all Nazis and there is no use denying it because if you had not been you could not even be here. Whether you were Nazis just for a ration card, or to support your dying mother, or to keep out of jail, makes no difference to this government. Moreover, we don't care whether you secretly hated them all the while or whether you were foolish enough to believe their talk. None of that matters. We expect you to do your jobs as

members of this institution. If any one of you has actually de-
nounced anybody to the Gestapo, or otherwise taken part in Nazi
dirty work, we shall know it sooner or later because we have all the
Gestapo records. Such persons go out of the institution and will be
dealt with in the courts. But otherwise, whatever kind of button you
had in your buttonhole last month, just go to work and forget it, and
don't bother us with stories about yourselves or each other because
we don't care.

6

The second part of the task—to feed the living—has been carried out
by the natural operation of time and musical appetite. It ought to
be quite easy to prove, statistically, that the public for music is
greater now than it was before the war; seasons for concert and
opera in every country certainly seem to be longer and more crowded
than they ever were. The war may have had something to do with it
—sunshine after storm—but the degree to which new generations are
given the habit of listening by radio and gramophone must be even
more directly responsible. There demonstrably is an added mass,
wherever it came from, in the public which is eager to hear the best
work, and under these circumstances, with a demand which is ever
on the increase, all the new artists of quality have been quickly absorbed into the general international pool. Within five years after the
war was over there was a wholly new crop of conductors, virtuosi and
singers whose talents had somehow (willy-nilly) come to fruition during the decade of turmoil and were now ready for the eager public of
the waiting world.

Some of the treasures of the past had to go, of course; we shall
not hear Lehmann, Toscanini or Walter again. What comes is not
always equal to what goes, but there are always compensations, and
among the most recent acquisitions to the international list are some
artists who are likely to wear long and well and unfold in increasing
beauty of achievement. Moreover, although many are "new" to us because of the way in which our world was for so long divided off into
compartments, they are not "new" in any other sense, and the
astonishment of discovering fully trained, fully accomplished musical athletes fit and ready to carry the torch has been one of the joys

of the (more or less) reunited Western world. Art is long and time is fleeting, says the poet, and although this is rather a gloomy thought for the practitioner of any art or near-art, it has its consolations for the lover of music: it means that although time is indeed forever bearing away on its flood much that we held dear, it is also forever bringing on the new.

8 : Music in the Air

The only two "farewells" which made much difference to me in the world of music were those of Lehmann and Toscanini. Indeed I can call to mind few others; perhaps most musicians are never quite sure of their decision in a matter which, to every one of them, must be all-important, and perhaps also "farewells" were too much abused in the past to be much favored in the present. A year or so ago, in the course of work, I looked at the New York newspaper announcements of concert and opera for the 1880's and 1890's, in which "farewells" abounded. Adelina Patti's last regular seasons in New York—at the Metropolitan Opera in its international spring series under Henry Abbey—were all announced as farewells, year after year, and she was not the only one. Outside of New York the "farewell tour" was a usual device for famous performers; it was either just that—a device—or it was, as with Paderewski, so pathetically true that the audiences wondered why it had been so long delayed.

Both Lehmann and Toscanini belonged to a different category from the virtuosi of the past, and it could be taken for certain that any decision either of them announced would be final. Both, however, hesitated until almost the last minute, and for those of us who had, in effect, spent our entire lives in music under their stars, it hardly seemed possible that so drastic a word would one day be spoken.

Lehmann's farewell recital in New York took place on Wednesday night, February 16, 1951, and Toscanini's last performance with his orchestra was on Sunday, April 4, 1954.

Lehmann had been on the brink of this decision even before she came to New York that year to begin her last tour. I had letters from her in California which sounded distressed and unlike her. She had been beset by a hoarseness which she had never known before, and the throat doctor she consulted told her it was either "psychological" or the result of an allergy: there was nothing wrong with her vocal cords or her throat. For the first time in her life, as it seemed, she was distrusting her own voice, her own work; and this was, for an artist of her caliber, sufficient warning of the end, although I refused to believe it. I might not even have come down to New York (from the Vermont farm) for her first recital of the season if something in her letters had not seemed ominous.

She prefaced that recital—one of her regular Sunday afternoons in Town Hall, which she had made into a fixture for about ten years now—with a brief speech in which she said she was out of voice and must apologize to the audience. After that she sang her program, Schubert to Wolf, very beautifully indeed, although it is possible that in sheer volume the voice had somewhat diminished. Time, as Hardy says in a poem somewhere, "part steals, lets part abide." I could not believe there was anything the matter and yet when I went back to see her after this performance she told me it was all over; she was determined to retire. Her brother asked me if I would attempt to argue with her, which I did, then and the next day and the next, but her mind was made up, and no doubt she was right: a truly great artist could not be wrong in such a matter. She went away to fulfill various engagements—Washington and Montreal, as I remember, among others—and came back about two weeks later for the farewell recital. It was not so announced; but one glance at the program would have given anybody a broad hint: it was a sort of retrospective glance at everything she had valued and had herself enhanced in the song literature, including even Wagner's *"Träume,"* which I had never heard her sing before, as well as many songs we all most closely associated with her work. It looked like *les délices d'un adieu*. After the interval Lehmann herself, in a brief and very lightly delivered speech (cool, friendly, rather amused she seemed) told us that this was the end, said that she had been before the public now for forty years and reminded us of the words of the Marschallin: *"Jedes Ding hat seiner Zeit."* The howls of protest did not disturb her. She had Toscanini's orchids—he sent her orchids for each song recital, year after year, since she was "the greatest artist in the world"—and her mind was quite made up. She sang her program through faultlessly, and indeed she was in exceptionally good voice that night, but at the end, when she had to do something as an extra for the excited and protesting crowd, she sang *"An die Musik."* As she said when she came to the piano for the last bow, "I will *try* to sing '*An die Musik.'* " Under the circumstances it was the only thing she could do (I had known all along that she would do it) but it was an ordeal for her, and at the very end, when the words *"ich danke dir"* come for the last time, she could not pronounce them.

Lehmann's final performance for this audience was the termination of her second career, that of the *Liedersängerin,* in which, if such a thing were possible, she had expressed the meaning of the work in hand even more completely than in opera. The first time I ever heard her sing *Lieder,* with Bruno Walter at the piano, she was still by no means in full possession of that form. She still used a book of words (although she relied on it seldom) and her voice, so rich, big and warm, sometimes still seemed too sumptuous for the material. That was over twenty years ago, in Salzburg, but within a very few years she had grown into this subtlest and most intimate of all arts, so that each person in the audience had the conviction that he was himself addressed in the inner realm of his being. With all the opulence of her voice she could take such a song as Hugo Wolf's *"Auch kleine Dinge können uns entzücken"* and make of it something so close, tender and true that it was like a whisper in the heart. Great songs or great cycles—Beethoven's *An die Ferne Geliebte* and Schubert's *Winterreise*—brought from her such a range of emotion as one has not otherwise heard. As her appearances at the opera grew more rare and finally ceased, she devoted herself more and more to this song literature, so that there had grown up in the preceding ten or twelve years an audience devoted to the point of fanaticism, not only in New York but throughout the country. I followed this second career of hers very closely, of course, and as it happened I was able to hear her—when I was myself on lecture tour—in many parts of the United States. Her own immersion into the mood of the song was reflected back by these audiences, wherever they happened to be, in a manner I have not seen equalled. She had as many moods as the huge and extremely various literature demands— the full, free and absolute range. Hardly any song-singer ever possessed such range and variety; most of them are best in one mood or another; only this winter the greatly admired Mr. Fischer-Dieskau gave a recital of *Lieder* at the Piccola Scala in Milan in which every song was gloomy and tragic in significance. Except in the single case of the *Winterreise,* which is composed as a unit, Lehmann never did this—and even in the *Winterreise* there are some lighter moments, of course. My own memory goes back to Elena Gerhardt, whose mastery of the literature was great, but whose sad contralto was incapable of real lightness; and also to Elisabeth Schumann, whose exquisite soprano was incapable of real heaviness. Gerhardt could sing the *"Sapphische Ode"* and Schumann could sing *"Gretchen am Spinnrade"* to perfection, but the point is that Lehmann could do both.

One of her elements of abstraction—of communication with the composer—which I valued highly was the simple fact that she paid no attention to the applicability of words or meaning to her own situation: she simply sang what the composer had written. Sometimes this might be addressed by a man to a woman, sometimes by a woman to a man; it made no difference. Beethoven's *An die Ferne Geliebte* is obviously by a poor and deeply unhappy man dreaming of an unattainable far-off love; Lotte absorbed herself into it to such an extent that when she sang it she *was,* somehow or other, Beethoven's dream. The *Winterreise* is also supposed to be a "man's" cycle, although a good many of the songs do not make it obvious. This past winter the lovely young soprano (and superb musician) Mme. Irmgard Seefried, of the Vienna Opera, sang Schumann's *"Frühlingsnacht"* at her Milan recital, and when she came to the end she said *"er"* instead of *"sie."* Unable, I suppose, to realize the meaning of the song as written—"she is thine, she is thine!"—this admirable artist changed the words to suit her own personality and sang *"Er ist deiner, er ist dein!"* In all the times I heard Lehmann sing this lovely song she never did that; she sang it for Robert Schumann, not for herself. As it always seemed to me, she possessed a communication with these particular composers (acquired by long absorption in their work itself) which made her in every case the voice not of a particular human woman called Lotte Lehmann, but of the intention of a music-master gone. There were times when with Hugo Wolf, for example, the sense of communication of which I speak (her communication, that is) was almost uncanny. There is nothing in my very large experience to which I can compare it.

2

Toscanini's departure took place under circumstances which, although still recent, have already given rise to a certain amount of dispute and some conflict of testimony. I have reason to believe that he had very nearly decided upon retirement a year before, and that his final decision was only delayed by concern over what would become of his beautiful orchestra once he had left it. His eighty-seventh birthday was March 25, 1954, and for a conductor, subjected to intolerable nervous tension and severe physical labor, such an age seems to have overpassed the possible by a good margin. (I have often reflected that ten minutes of such work would have brought me to exhaustion at any age.)

In the spring of 1954, therefore, there would have been regret everywhere in the Western world, but no surprise, if his intention had been announced. It was not: on the contrary, assurances were given that he was expected to return for the next season. There were many uncertainties involved in this momentous retirement, first of all for his wonderful orchestra, created entirely for him, which could hardly be expected to go on existing afterwards at vast expense to the National Broadcasting Company. There was also a backlog, as they say, a store or reservoir, of recordings made by him but not yet issued to the public, which, in theory at least, would lose some of their desirability on his withdrawal from public life. (A false theory, I believe, but held by many.) His own taciturnity on the subject was by no means the least of the considerations involved. When in doubt, be bold and certain: this is a fairly well accepted principle in business, I believe, and the N.B.C. followed it out. To the very day which ended with the announcement (April 4, 1954) the Maestro's retirement was confidently denied.

Pro memore, let me recapitulate: at the time of the triumphant Salzburg seasons I have dwelt upon in the *Fidelio* chapter, Mr. Toscanini had left the New York Philharmonic and was without a fixed base of operations. He had, of course, any and every orchestra he chose to conduct; he had remarkable results with such very different bands of musicians as the B.B.C. in London, the Vienna Philharmonic, and the Orchestre Symphonique (the one M. Cortot founded) in Paris. The New York Philharmonic, which he had shared for three seasons with Mengelberg, had been all his own from 1929 to 1936 and he had done wonders with it. It might have seemed even then (twenty years ago) that he had had an extremely long and full career; above all, it seemed most unlikely that anything *new* was likely to come his way, since he had already done everything and been everywhere.

It was left for the National Broadcasting Company to think of the "something new" which seemed so unlikely. The idea may have come to several persons at once; I have always had an idea that probably Samuel Chotzinoff was one of the early dreamers in this case; but David Sarnoff, then president of the N.B.C. (now president of the Radio Corporation of America), was beyond a doubt the prime mover. It was a deep, dark secret for a long time; the plans, projects and negotiations were so well concealed that on the day the Maestro finally signed his contract, in Salzburg, I had never heard a word about them. I remember the day well because that evening David Sarnoff and his equally enthusiastic wife, Lisette, bought some excellent champagne for my wife and me and a number of other friends at the Mirabell in Salzburg to celebrate the occasion.

At the time the idea was so startling that it was hard to imagine how it could work at the artistic level Toscanini demanded. American radio was the concern of private industry, governed by public taste, supported by advertising—its whole organizational structure was totally different from that of the state-owned or state-controlled radio systems of Europe. Furthermore, at that time I had listened to very little radio music and entertained a poor opinion of its possibilities.

An orchestra of the absolute first class devoted exclusively to radio
and to recordings did not seem possible in America—even though
the B.B.C. had shown that it was possible in England—and I
thought with anticipatory discomfort of the miseries the Maestro
would have to go through in the way of exact timing, commercial
interruptions, public demands in the way of programs, and similar
trammels upon his cherished freedom.

How wrong I was! The next seventeen years gave the American
public a revelation of excellence in this field; for at least an hour a
week during the music season the entire country could listen to
superb programs; an unequaled library of recordings was built up;
the freedom of Mr. Toscanini to do as he pleased was untouched
except in such matters as time and technology. In these respects it was
the Maestro himself who was the surprise, because there never was a
more willing collaborator with the radio engineers and with the time-
clock. He seems to have understood their necessities from the start,
and later on, when I used to go to rehearsals and recording sessions,
I was constantly being amazed at his good humor in these respects,
his tireless effort to produce what the medium demanded. Any radio
engineer, it seemed, could say anything to him. Once in the recording of the *Missa Solemnis* there was a rather tricky passage for cellos
and pipe organ which did not come through very clearly to the boys
in the control room (the organ at Carnegie Hall is at the right,
behind the cellos, and perhaps that had something to do with it). The
aged and supereminent conductor, whom I never was able to speak
to without stammering, stopped and started, over and over, at
each word from the control room. When it was finally "caught" one
of the boys up there drawled out, over the loud-speaker, "That
sounded pretty good, Maestro." I laughed helplessly; so did the entire
orchestra; finally Toscanini himself—after a moment's bewilderment—broke down and laughed too. It was quite an accolade.

Another misgiving I had had, to begin with, was over the absence
of audience: were we never to hear this extraordinary music-maker in
life again, but only over the air or through machines? This notion,
too, was proved wrong. He always had an audience: for years it was in
Studio 8B, in the R.C.A. Building, which could accommodate some
sixteen hundred people. Admission to these concerts was by invitation, but thanks chiefly to David Sarnoff (or sometimes to

Marcia Davenport or Mr. Chotzinoff) I went to a great many of them. Later on they were transferred to Carnegie Hall, to an even larger audience, and there, too, the great final recording sessions (extremely private) and the rehearsals (semiprivate) were held. In recent years I think no musical experience has been so rewarding as these various kinds of work by Toscanini and his orchestra, culminating in performances of incomparable effect.

The rehearsal of Saturday, April 3, 1954, was of particular interest to me not only because it was for the final concert of the year (with the persistent feeling, in spite of denials, that it might be Toscanini's last), but also because it was made up entirely of Wagner excerpts: in these famous and familiar concert versions (*Meistersinger* and *Tristan* preludes, *Tannhäuser Bacchanale* and so on) Toscanini was always in that particular vein of his own in which precision and fury were inextricably mixed. I made sure of my invitations from N.B.C. and repaired in good time to Carnegie Hall, accompanied by a lady equally interested.

Strange it is to think that this program of so short a time ago—two years—has gone out of my head, when I can remember others from the same conductor and orchestra in every detail from much longer ago. The reason is that in this rehearsal the Maestro broke down into the most terrible rage I ever saw, a terrifying rage in which I was afraid for his life; and, trembling and helpless, he left the stage in the middle of the *Tannhäuser Bacchanale* and went home. All I can remember is the incident itself, an electric storm from which even I (safe in the hall, in front!) could not recover for hours. Many stories have been told of this day and the next, and since they do not agree very well, it may be simplest to tell my own just as I remember it, with no attempt to fit it into others.

The earlier part of the program was played very beautifully, I believe, and with few interruptions for rehearsal. (What happened afterwards has obliterated the memory of the preceding detail.) Then came the *Tannhäuser Bacchanale,* and so far as I could tell it was sweeping along on its usual tempestuous course when the Maestro stopped the orchestra and shouted, rather hoarsely, at the brasses. They had, it seemed, made a wrong entry. I thought they looked extremely puzzled. He shouted the number "Thirteen" at them in English and in Italian. Up the baton: they tried again: again he stopped them. *"Tredici, tredici!"* he called out in that very hoarse and somehow despairing voice. I heard somebody in the orchestra say "Twelve" and the Maestro shouted "Thirteen!" in English. By this time he was already a prey to that extreme nervous exasperation which afflicts conductors who know exactly what they want and cannot get it. He had begun to tremble and mutter; they tried again.

Suddenly, after the third failure, the whole atmosphere of the hall became electric with (for me at least) plain fear. After the third failure the Maestro was clearly quite out of his own control: he was visibly trembling and his voice was downright awful in its raucousness and some note of (no other word will do) horror. He said *"Tredici!"* once or twice more and then, quite loudly although in the same unearthly croak: *"Mi vergogno di loro! Mi vergogno! Mi vergogno di loro!"* (I am ashamed of you; I am ashamed; I am ashamed of you.) I could see his frantic effort at control, but apparently his arms would not obey; he lifted them once, let them fall and walked off the platform.

I had already whispered to Agatha beside me: "I can't stand this; I'm scared to death and I think I'll go." Then he walked offstage and we sat in a rather stunned silence for several moments. There were probably three hundred invited guests in the hall, besides the orchestra on the stage and all the radio technicians in their various posts. Those few minutes seemed long. Then a voice came through a loud-speaker: "This will conclude the public part of the rehearsal and the guests will please now leave; the orchestra will remain."

I had seen Toscanini in rages before, but never anything like this, and my chief concern was that he might not survive it; I had dreaded seeing him collapse on the stage, which at one moment seemed likely. I also suspected that "thirteen" was the wrong number. We repaired to Agatha's house for the medicinal refreshment which in such moments of shock becomes necessary; after about an hour I telephoned the N.B.C. to find out what had happened. I was told that Toscanini had walked straight off the stage and into his car and gone home to Riverdale, where he was, at that moment, incommunicado, but would still—they hoped—conduct the broadcast concert the next day.

My feeling that this was the end was absolute: the end, that is, not only of a career without a parallel, but of what had been for me the longest sustained and highest of musical experiences. I had no desire to go to the concert the next day or even to listen to it on the radio. When the announcement of his retirement was made public that evening it certainly was no surprise to me.

I have both heard and read a number of versions of what happened on the Sunday, the day of the concert. It was cut off the air for a brief period—a matter of about half a minute or a few seconds more—and it has been very frequently stated that a confusion arose in the orchestra which was thought to be due to a failure of memory on the part of the Maestro. So far as I could tell from the accounts, this must have been in the same place, an entry of brasses in the *Bacchanale*—probably at that same number, alas, thirteen, or (if in fact Toscanini's memory had gone wrong for the first time in sixty-five years) at another number. The mere fact that it had occasioned such a terrifying breakdown on the preceding day no doubt made it a difficult moment to surmount, both for him and for those brasses. I know how they must have been dreading it.

However, it seems that those in Carnegie Hall itself did not notice anything wrong at all. The recovery was so quick—and the orchestra was so superbly aware of its music—that nothing was perceived even by very knowledgeable listeners. We have two quite authoritative accounts. One, by Mr. Samuel Chotzinoff, concerns the moment as it was experienced in the radio control booth, up in the wings some-where above the orchestra, where they cut the music off the air; the other, by Mr. Irving Kolodin, concerns the music as heard in the hall itself. The degree of anxiety felt in the control booth, after what had happened on the day before, was naturally very keen, and any sign of confusion would have been detected at once by all those whose work it was to watch and listen. (There also is a dispute about where the confusion came in the *Bacchanale;* by common sense reasoning it seems likely that it occurred just where it had occurred the day before.)

Whatever the imperfection, it surely was one which any lesser conductor would have regarded as one of the hazards of the profession. How often, indeed, both in symphony concerts and in opera, do these imperfections arise! I have heard scores of much worse ones, even from the greastest musicians. However, Toscanini's standards never were of the ordinary world. He said he would not conduct again, and has never done so, in spite of the most importunate pleas from America and Italy in particular.

This conductor aimed so very high that it was difficult or impossible to attain his ends. I know from his own family that after his retirement he spent a great deal of time playing his own records and deploring what he felt to be their various and detailed failures, audible only to himself. One night at the Sarnoffs' house a few years ago after a concert of Mozart pieces, Mr. Toscanini arrived late and in a state of appalling gloom and misery which even his half-bottle of champagne could not alleviate. Vladimir Horowitz told me the reason, even before the Maestro arrived: an E-Flat clarinet had made a premature entry—I think this is in the clarinet quintet—probably the faintest possible toot, and then stopped and made his proper entry later. Horowitz asked me if I had noticed: of course I had not. He took a plebiscite then and there among the persons in our corner of the room. They were all attentive listeners (the Heifetz sisters, Mrs. Chotzinoff and Mrs. Behrman, were among them as I remember). Not one had heard the false entry, and yet it had the power to plunge Toscanini into something resembling despair.

Of course I do not want to belabor the meaning of this perfectionism *à outrance*: it has been well known for many years and stories about it are current in many countries. I might perhaps add one more tale to the long list because it has had a practical result of unexpected rigor. It has to do with the *Missa Solemnis* of Beethoven, which had prolonged private recording sessions in Carnegie Hall as well as the public performance in that last Toscanini year. I went to two of the recording sessions as well as to the rehearsals and the performance of that masterpiece, which I (for one—and I am not alone) actually prefer to the Ninth Symphony. For a long period of time this wonderwork as then recorded could not be released to the public, because Mr. Toscanini had not yet given his permission. (No record made by him can be released until he is satisfied that it should be; and he has held up some of them—such as his recording of the finale of *Götterdämmerung* with Traubel— for as much as four years, while technical details are, when possible, smoothed out or brought up.)

In the case of the *Missa Solemnis,* which seemed to me as good as any performance could be, I was at a loss to understand the delay and made some inquiries. There were a number of points, of course, but the main one which gave the Maestro trouble was the violin solo!

This was so disconcerting to me that when I first heard it I laughed. The fact is that the violin solo had seemed to me beautiful beyond words as played by M. Louis Gilet, the *konzertmeister* of the N.B.C. orchestra. It had moved me deeply in rehearsals, in performance, and, I think, most of all afterwards in the recording session, at which Toscanini had allowed it to pass without a word. On my way out from that session I did something I have never done in my life before or since: I stopped in front of M. Gilet and shook his hand and thanked him for the beauty of the solo. It is presumption on the part of an ignoramus like myself to speak to any player, but I could not help it. M. Gilet was grateful; in that darkened hall where only four or five other persons besides myself were in front of the orchestra he probably thought I was a musician too; he might even have thought I was David Sarnoff. But alas! and alas and alas! He had to do that solo over and over and over again afterwards. Toscanini did not like it when he heard it—the very thing that had most especially aroused my enthusiasm—and I never knew precisely why. He did not have to give his reasons. In thinking it over I came to the conclusion that probably what has stirred me most (its special singing quality as solo, its distinctness from the rest of the composition) was probably what was wrong. My guess is that the conductor wanted it more severely composed into the rest of the work: he may have wanted *less* expression in the bowing; he was probably trying to get it to sound less like a solo rather than more. How can I tell what it was? All I know (and it still makes me smile to think of it) is that what I liked best was what he liked least, and his perfectionism again, in this as in so many other cases, was almost beyond understanding.

The departure of this conductor from the realm over which he had been sovereign for such a long time was felt by many generations older and younger than my own. I have talked to persons who recall with vivid appreciation work he performed in Milan during the early part of this century, or in New York before 1914, or in Bayreuth thirty years ago. Also very young persons who knew his work only in the last few years felt bereft. It so happens, however, that my generation is the one which lived its entire musical life in the light of his effort. I came under his spell in my twenties, and I was in my fifties when he went away. It is difficult to become accustomed to so great an absence.

3

After the war was over—and the San Francisco conference and a few other aftermaths—I settled myself into a farmhouse in Vermont for half of every year and all of some years. There were journeys, of course, since I am a journeying man: two or three lecture tours, visits to India, one of them stretching into a *Wanderjahr* around the world; but the farmhouse in the green hills was the point of return, the place in which such belongings as I have accumulated were disposed in their various lodgments, the place where (as the poem says) if home there be, is home.

And these years of approximate although intermittent tranquillity happened also to be the ones in which the gramophone, or phonograph (and I do not know the difference), went through so many transformations, as a result of technological advances, as to become a different instrument from what it was twenty-five years ago. I had never been greatly addicted to the radio, except for news, but ever since I can remember I had a weakness for listening to recorded music. It used to be pretty bad, as the middle-aged will recall: it was scratchy and tinny and unmusical to a high degree, but it served to put you in mind of what it was supposed to be—it gave a notion. You had to supply the rest of it yourself, and when I was growing up this demanded a good deal of imagination. Long ago I found out the trick of following the music with the aid of printed scores, which were and still are a powerful reinforcement to the musical imagination, as well as a corrective for the error abounding. But along about 1947 or thereabouts great things began to happen to the machines themselves. If I attempted to explain what I do not myself understand the result would be nonsense; all I can do is say what happened in my own case. In that year I acquired a good radio-gramophone of moderate price, which made the kind of noise I thought adequate in the room where I put it. New inventions and technological advances were occurring every moment, although I did not know it, and sometime toward the end of that summer (1947) or possibly the next one (1948), they swam into my life through the ministrations of a young genius in our village. This was Ely Culbertson's son Bruce, who came up for a few weeks from (I think) the Massachusetts Institute of Technology, inspected my radio-gramophone and told me that for a very small sum of money he could bring it not only up-to-date, but somewhere near two or three years ahead of the commercial products then being sold. For some reason I believed this, found the requisite sum of money, and told him to go ahead. An alarming period followed, during which the apparatus was reduced to a chaos of small, indistinguishable parts, all over the living-room floor. At times Bruce would vanish with some of the viscera for a day or so at a time —he had a laboratory in his father's house in the village. Finally he stuck it all together again and triumphantly showed me that the thing could now play records at three different speeds (the old ones at seventy-eight revolutions a minute, the little ones at forty-five, and the big new ones at thirty-three and a third). It also sounded better than before, could be made both louder and softer than before, and gave off a great deal less of the scratching and fuzziness called "surface noise." It has served amazingly well ever since, since whatever he did to it appears to have made it equal to every demand and susceptible to genuine control.

This machine proved a bottomless pit in many ways because no matter how many records I had it seemed to demand more. At the time when these great technological advances in recording were made, I had already acquired and lost a fair number of libraries of records. Ever since I have had any sort of habitation of my own I have had them. In our house in Ireland we had a good machine and a library of records; they went when we went—I think we gave them away. We had another machine and another library at St. Margaret's Bay, in Kent; we had another machine and another library in our apartment in Paris. Still another was in the house we inhabited in Bronxville, near New York, which a maleficent fate burned down one night. There may even have been others, since we lived in many places. But of them all, the machine which seemed most voracious of recordings was the stepped-up "souped-up," ultra-regenerated monster in the Vermont farmhouse, which positively exacted new blood as a condition of its being. Consequently during these years I acquired records of all sizes and shapes, in addition to those I already possessed, so that there was in formation such a mass of the things that, in addition to the thousands of books which clung to the walls, there might soon have been no room for human beings.

In this oddly shaped room during the years between (say) 1946 and a year or so ago I found out that you do not even have to stir out of your chair to derive some kind of special apperception from the performance of music. At the outset of the matter it might be well to make two confessions: first, that the best of all recorded performances cannot possibly equal the effect of living creatures doing the same thing; and second, that the power of the recorded music over one's mind or imagination (I think) is far greater with known than with hitherto unknown music. There may come a day when I can hear a new composition (new, anyhow, to me) on the gramophone for the first time and feel it precisely as I might have felt it in a living performance, but that day has not yet arrived.

Those two limitations may be set aside because I suppose most persons would readily agree with them—they seem obvious enough —except the few who are genuinely addicted to machines and prefer to hear all music through them. What it amounts to is this: the recording devices preserve, perpetuate and disseminate what we might like to hear in a living form, but know we cannot. One would have to go to every concert given in New York for twenty or thirty years, indefatigably, day after day and night after night, to hear even a sizable part of the music I can hear at will on the machine in my sitting room in Vermont. The enormous repertoire and the variant performances, the freedom of choice, the suiting of music to mood, the ability to draw on resources no longer available in public halls, the access to work which is rarely or never heard in the concert hall—all these things enormously enlarge the boundaries of a small room so that it can come at times to be as large as the earth itself. And to hear it *absolutely* alone and unobserved (so that you can conduct it yourself if you will, or follow it with a score or simply yield to it) is a rare and special form of living through music.

When I am told that Oswald Spengler spent his last years in Munich, after *The Decline of the West* had more or less faded into the past for him, playing Beethoven records to himself alone, I do believe that I understand how and why.

It was through this discovery that I found a certain historical imperishability in the work of my most admired friends among the music-makers. During the thirty years (almost exactly) during which I listened and deeply responded to the work of Lotte Lehmann on both her stages, opera and concert, and in many countries, I never really grew fond of her recordings. They always seemed to me to be lacking in some essence which was distinctively Lotte and never could have been anybody but Lotte. Her voice is instantaneously recognizable on even the very worst of records made in the worst of studios long before she was known outside of Vienna; I have heard a good many of these (she has some in her own possession) which are not publicly available any more, and there is not one in which the quality of her voice does not make itself known in the first three or four notes. Even so, to recognize is not always to receive in full, and I thought for some years that Lehmann's recordings were like photographs, and bad photographs at that—the resemblance was there without the living flesh. The very notable exception was that famous recording of the *Rosenkavalier* excerpts made some twenty-five or more years ago in Vienna under the direction of Robert Heger (with Schumann, Olczewska and Mayr) which has fortunately been preserved in the old form and reissued in the new. This I always did regard as one of the great triumphs of recording for voice and orchestra, and in this work I thought Lehmann's art was well, although not completely, represented. The sense of performing the drama may have carried her and the others on into a more fluent and unconscious or semiconscious form of characterization by the voice than is possible in rigid studio recordings into a microphone.

The strange thing that has happened to Lehmann's records since her retirement is that they sound better all the time, not only the very modern ones of the latest years, and also reissues on the newest devices, but also very old ones made at a period when the recording and reproducing machinery was (by contemporary standards) almost primitive. One of these which has never failed to delight me in recent years is a German chorale of about the seventeenth century, and it must be very old because there is nothing on the other side of it.

Toscanini's records always were technically about as good as the machinery permitted, even in early days; but how magically they have come out under the improved conditions of engineering! Every recording library I have possessed had a good many of the earlier records made with the Scala orchestra or (more) with the New York Philharmonic. I never would possess a gramophone at all unless I could play Toscanini's recordings of the Beethoven Third and Seventh Symphonies, at the very least, and with them the First Brahms. In recent years new recordings of a very great part of his repertoire, including a good many operas, have come forth with every advantage of the most erudite technology. Much has also been done with Bruno Walter's repertoire, and as for Mme. Flagstad . . . ! The matchless brilliance of her singing (as, for example, in the *"Dich, teure Halle!"* record) comes through on these machines almost as if she were near at hand. Marian Anderson is another: the music she recorded fifteen or twenty years ago, and would be most unlikely to record again today, is preserved with a richness, warmth and sincerity which very nearly transcend the machine and all other technological transferences: she seems to be actually in the room, and often I can see her plainly.

These are the great artists of my life. But even before them there were others whose talents were withdrawn before I had the fullest opportunity to appreciate them. In these last years I have heard again on the gramophone some others of an earlier moment in the long pilgrimage. There is one by Frida Leider of *"Ich sah das Kind an seiner Mutter Brust,"* from *Parsifal,* which belongs to an earlier stage of sound engineering, and yet, to my ears, possesses a tenderness and comprehension which have never been otherwise equaled in this music. One can forget the scratchy, fuzzy noise made by the record itself because the loving voice can still be heard. I have already said, and will repeat, that Mme. Leider was the greatest Brünnhilde and Isolde and Kundry I ever heard because she truly knew what she was doing and fully understood. Mme. Flagstad was the greatest singer and the greatest voice I have ever heard. Mme. Lehmann (who did not sing any of these roles) was incomparably the greatest artist I ever heard. Now, at last, in these few years after the war, and when I could be there to do it, I played their work on the strangely augmented machine in the small sitting room in the Vermont farmhouse, and I found them all supremely good, with a kind of ideal equality—an ideal correspondence, almost, in their very different ways—which never had occurred in life. Perhaps it is thus that one can come to understand at last the splendid promise: "In my Father's house are many mansions."

Thus was it brought home to me that the gramophone, which has been a convenience ever since I can remember, is also an instrument of the high purposes of music. The separate and quite distinct excellences I had admired, the special contributions of special talents, all fell into their places as offerings upon the altar. This is a phenomenon which could hardly occur to anybody, so far as I can imagine, with *new* singers in *new* works, or with new orchestras or virtuosi. It is what the gramophone has to offer in the twilight. It can show you how very good each was and can not only correct your memory but enhance it immeasurably by plain material proof of the fact, which you may have suspected before but never could be sure about, that the great are all great, no matter how different.

It may be worth pausing for just a moment to consider what these three dramatic sopranos have to teach us by means of the gramophone. Mme. Leider's work has been insufficiently preserved, so far as the public is concerned—it is necessary to search in recondite places and pay double prices to obtain her records—but there are still a few. I have mentioned her exquisite Kundry record. There is also, naturally, the *Liebestod,* and the recordings from the second act of *Tristan,* with Melchior. In what there is, technically inadequate though it may be, there shines through to this very day a comprehension of Wagner, and an ability to transmit it, which are beyond comparison. Mme. Leider not only knew every word and note of her own part, and had the voice and heart and soul to give it to us, but she also knew the whole opera in every case—she knew the other parts too; she knew Wagner. I doubt very much if she would have gone onto the stage without knowing as much about the whole work as she did about her own part of it. She was a truly Wagnerian singer.

Mme. Flagstad was in some respects the daughter of God, and it would be a gross and uncouth ruffian who ever denied his gratitude to her. Hers was the most beautiful voice any of us have heard—and in this I may say I have the agreement of Mme. Lotte Lehmann—with such splendor as mankind has actually never deserved to hear. We really are not good and brave and true enough for that. She never failed us, she was always there, on the tone and in the time. However, up to the final moments of her career, Mme. Flagstad barely knew her own parts and nothing else in the works of Wagner. She tells us herself that this is so. Her very brief career (five years in all) was consumed in learning the parts she was supposed to sing. When she was on stage and not singing she listened avidly (so she tells us) to what the others were singing, because she had never had time to learn what it was! On her knees before Wotan in the last act of *Die Walküre,* as his penitent daughter, she listened to Friedrich Schorr with passionate interest, to the extent that she even forgot the audience, because she had never before learned what it was that the Father of the Gods had to say to Brünnhilde. She sang the Brünn- hildes in New York without a single rehearsal on that stage for any except *Götterdämmerung,* as a tryout some months before she actually had to perform it. She learned Kundry in eleven days, she tells us—not eighteen days as it says in most reference books—and quite obviously had no time to study or even to read any part except her own. In her autobiography she acknowledges her deep gratitude to the prompter, who must indeed have been her most devout adherent during those first seasons in New York. Studying Kundry for eleven days, and Kundry alone, with no time to absorb or even to read all the other parts (and Kundry's part is a fraction of the length of some others), how in the name of common sense could she encompass the meaning of *Parsifal?*

The monumental phenomenon of Flagstad's career consists in her having sung parts she did not understand, in a language not wholly familiar to her, in operas she had never had time even to skim through as a whole, and which in some cases she had never seen or heard before. Doing this without even a rehearsal—as used to be the way in the dear old Metropolitan—and with the further handicap of not being able to hear what was going on around her (since she was almost deaf for the first two seasons) she nevertheless became, for that brief period from 1936 to 1941, the idol of the populace and the most successful heroic soprano of modern times. In a way, one can compare her only to Helen Keller, for there is nothing except some inner heroism of will and determination that could have enabled Mme. Flagstad to do what she did; she was, in a way, deaf, dumb and blind, but she gave out some blazing gift which was not in her but came from God. She repeated this miraculous subterfuge at Covent Garden and in a few other places during the five years of her opera career; then came the six years of her retirement to Norway during the war, after which she returned to the West in concert and finally for one season in her old parts at the Metropolitan. She was persuaded (by Rudolf Bing, who could persuade anybody to anything if he tried hard enough) to add five final performances the following year in Gluck's *Alceste,* in an English translation as *Alcestis.*

This aftermath—the last Isolde and Brünnhilde and the final Alcestis—was what I most highly appreciated in all the opportunities I had to hear this unique singer. By the time she stopped singing Isolde, which she performed 182 times in her career, she certainly did understand it. She no longer made mistakes in German (just for one small detail) and she no longer treated the first act as a singing lesson. There were depths and colors in her magnificent voice which had not been there years before. Her concept of rage, for example, or of sexual passion, or of revenge, always seemed exactly what she says it was, a result of some girlhood lessons in Dalcroze as taught in Stockholm: that is, she had *"plastique"* according to fixed physical principles and she used it relentlessly. (Rage: clenched fist and five steps downstage in a majestic manner; sexual passion: hands clasped on breast and head turned away; revenge: ferocious frown accompanied by three strides in any convenient direction with the clenched hands stiff at the side). Her *"plastique"* was just the same at the end of her career as at the beginning, and I have no difficulty believing that everything she ever did on the stage was (as she says) dictated by her Dalcroze lessons in Stockholm. But what is one to say of the voice . . . ? By the time Flagstad finished she had attained a nobility and grandeur which illumined every corner of the music, touched every single note she sang with heavenly magic and even spilled over onto the other participants and to the orchestra. Those who sang with her in *Alcestis* have never sung so well before or since—particularly the chorus of the Metropolitan. And I remember very well the last Isolde I heard from her: it was the one before her final one, and Fritz Reiner was conducting. Mme. Flagstad always did tend to conduct her conductors, of course, as everybody knows, and in the old days she used to do it with her elbows. (One-two-three-four, elbows counting up and down, second act of *Parsifal*, for example. She continued to do so to the last, but somehow during her years out of opera she had learned to do it with her voice. It was fabulous to me how she could slow Fritz up when she wished, just by that golden flood of her incomparable, irresistible voice. She never looked at him, of course—she never looked at any conductor and could not have seen him if she had, since the lights blinded her—nor could she hear what was going on, since her deafness was conveniently all directed toward the orchestra. She could hear only those who were singing directly to her on the stage most of the time, and to those she listened closely.) In the second act, in order to take the two high C's with some comfort and a sufficient vocal result, she strode over to the darkest corner of the Metropolitan stage (stage right, house left), which was more or less like the Black Hole of Calcutta. Tristan ambled along afterwards, rather undecidedly, because this was something she did for her own reasons and probably was different in each performance. I was standing as close to her as it is possible to get, not many feet from the dark corner where she elected to sing her high C's. Fritz was undoubtedly bathed in sweat by now from the crown of his head to the tips of his toes (he sweats mightily when he is working), because the singer had slowed the orchestra down simply by her golden voice. When she got to the darkest corner she slowed them down even more by those old familiar wiggle-waggles of her incredible elbows. There was nothing in this world that Fritz could have done except follow her tempo, which he did. (That or go home!) But then, when she had it all arranged to her satisfaction, she sang her two high C's. Never have I heard anything like that nor do I expect to hear any such thing ever again. The two phrases were in perfect time (having been put into slow-motion by her) and consequently it sounded exactly as it should sound, each note in the correct relation to each other one, and over the two phrases came the two brilliant notes, perfection itself, something like what you might expect from the trumpet of the

Archangel Gabriel. She sang these notes straight into the folds of the dirty old curtain which hangs at the farthest right-hand corner (stage right, house left), in a Cimmerian gloom from which she must have been invisible to almost everybody in the house except me. However, she was not inaudible to anybody in the house or probably anywhere else within several square miles. Having accomplished this Herculean task, she turned back to Tristan and permitted him (and Fritz) to resume the tempo. She sang every single note of the part exactly as written, to the best of my knowledge and belief, with no other sign of strain or trouble except in this one place. She is the only Isolde I ever heard in my life who could do this, and even in her own most triumphant days, twelve or fourteen years before, she had never sung those high C's with such shattering splendor. (Mme. Leider yelped them and Mme. Traubel omitted them; Mme. Flagstad generally got them in and out quickly in the old days.)

If I have made my point, it is that Mme. Flagstad's wondrous voice never felt at home in its own great music until she was on the eve of departure. She learned all her parts too late, and her great American successes were made in music unfamiliar to her. This was, I thought, obvious during the years of her reign over us. Her revenge came when, after years of absence, she was able to show us that she really did know (or had learned) the operas of Richard Wagner and not only how to sing them. To this final triumph she added one thing of lustrous beauty and irresistible human tenderness, the unforgettable Alcestis.

In a sitting room in Vermont with a very fine "souped-up" recording machine, what came out of all this was something slightly anticlimactic, really, which was that these singers *were all superb*. They were not rivals in any proper meaning for that word, because they had special and separate and individual gifts which did not resemble each other in the slightest degree. Not a single note of Flagstad's voice ever sounded like Lehmann's; Leider never at any moment sounded like either one of them. No doubt all I am proving is my own stupidity, but I really did have to hear them in this other fashion, all alone in a remote place, over and over and over again, before it actually dawned on me that they were not rivals but equals, not antagonists but associates, in the never ending labor of art, life and

love. To one who had spent some decades hearing acrimonious discussions of the respective merits of these and other artists, it was quite
a discovery.

4

Here were all what might be called "primary" performers in one
sense: that I had heard them very often across many years, so as to
regard them as fundamental contributors to musical experience.
They usually had long seasons in one fixed place at a time, so that it
was possible to hear Toscanini (for example) many times in one
year, conducting more or less everything you can think of between
Bach and Debussy.

There was another race of music-makers, fervently admired and
esteemed, with whom neither I nor any other listener could have
such a sustained relation across the footlights. These were the violinists, pianists, violoncellists, the players of the string quartet or other
chamber music, and even some singers, who, by and large, were
rarer birds, because they were forever on the wing. Opportunities to
hear Artur Rubinstein or Vladimir Horowitz, Jascha Heifetz or
Yehudi Menuhin, do not occur every year; they are essentially
wanderers, and since I am also something of a wanderer, my chances
to hear them at all have been erratic. I have been fairly alert about
seizing such opportunities, but the fact remains that I know them
much better from their recordings than I ever could from the occasional recital that comes my way. And combinations of these rare
birds are—so far as I know—for the gramophone alone: when was it
ever possible to hear Heifetz, Rubinstein and Feuermann play the
Archduke Trio together, except on the record? Thus the solitary
session with the machine in an otherwise empty room can vastly enlarge, as it did for me, the boundary of experience on the side of
virtuoso performances, solo or in combination.

It is also true—obviously—of chamber music of all kinds, which
sometimes seems to have been written for the needs of the recording
machines. It sounds almost perfect in a room and loses less than any
other sort of music, it seems to me, by the mechanism through which
it comes. More and more, during those years in Vermont, I grew

addicted to such music, not only for its content but because it did actually emerge so beautifully; and it was a high moment when I found out that Casals was recording more or less his entire festival at Prades for just such purposes. Bach in a dozen different forms seems more at home in that Vermont sitting room than he ever could be in the full blast of a Carnegie Hall performance.

Some genuine oddities have arisen out of the wedding of the gramophone to the music of the past. Just as the piano always recorded inadequately, up until very recent years—with a tinny sound as a rule—the organ has sounded splendid ever since I can remember. I have acquired quite a bit of organ music for that reason, and have been unfailingly amused at the fact that the Mozart processionals—the only music he ever composed for the organ—precisely fit the time allotted for a twelve-inch record of the older variety (before the long-playing devices were invented). These beautiful little pieces were ordered by the Archbishop Hieronymus, to be played while he was getting from the entrance of the Salzburg Cathedral up to his throne by the altar. Hieronymus seems to have had a pretty steady gait, because each of the pieces takes between four and four-and-a-half minutes, which is just right for a twelve-inch record. Neither the Archbishop nor Mozart can have guessed what pleasure this afforded.

You may say, just the same, that chamber music in general, trios, quartets, quintets, organ music and the like (even *Lieder*) are of such special quality that to dwell on their virtues in a room is to beg the question: they were written for the room in the first place. Ernest Newman, after a lifetime of musical experience, has been debating this very point with himself and with numerous letter writers in the columns of the *Sunday Times* this past spring in London. His question is whether the obviously unsuited form—the most unsuited being opera—is able to give pleasure and profit through the gramophone, and his answer is yes. Aside from what he calls "the steady, continuous decline in the art of singing," which is just as deplorable in the theatre itself as it is on the machine, if not more so, he finds that the musical result on the machine is well worth achieving. He does not miss the drama, the color and clash and excitement of the stage, as much as he once did or as he expected to do; his imagination supplies these for him; and he is at times happy to be spared the ungainly forms and awkward acting which are so common among opera singers.

Mr. Newman, of course, is the dean of critics, and there are probably few things in music with which he is not truly familiar. I may think I know *Tristan und Isolde,* and up to a point I do, but I am certain that Mr. Newman knows it far better—better, also, than most of its performers or conductors. It is therefore no trick at all for him to create all the stage business in his own imagination, and to do a better job of it, probably, than could be done on the real stage. *Tristan* is a fairly simple example and perhaps I might be able to do likewise. I am not sure, just the same, that I know exactly where each character is at each moment, or what doing or what wearing, in—say—*Un Ballo in Maschera,* or in a number of others which have been recorded in full for our benefit.

Here is where the score comes in, and with its aid I am able to give myself quite a satisfactory performance of any opera, stage business and all, the degree of vividness depending upon how often I have actually seen it in a theatre. Naturally the familiar comes back best (with the aid of the score), although defects also take on new dimensions in anything we know well. It is a never ending source of astonishment how many great and famous singers cheat on their words, music or both, in the singing of opera. It passes unperceived in the opera house most of the time, but the machinery shows it up relentlessly, and if you read the score while you listen, there will be surprises galore in practically everything, all the way from Mozart to Wagner and back again, taking in the Italians on the way. (There is cheating in all kinds of recorded music—a famous soprano with a very high voice has recorded some Debussy songs with substitute notes, generally an octave up, whenever they go a little low for her! The effect to anybody who knows the songs is decidedly droll, since the melodic line is quite different.)

However, all this being said, I think I must disagree with even so eminent and revered a critic as Mr. Newman on opera as a whole. I think it invaluable to students to have full recordings, and I have immensely enjoyed a few favorites such as *Falstaff, Pelléas, Carmen* and some others, but a whole opera on records is, by and large, too long, too taxing on the attention, too far away from the movement and color which were supposed to go with it. Opera is for theatres. Excerpts, of course, even whole scenes, are in a different category, and I have played such excerpts for hours on end. They are in general the highlights, the most familiar scenes, the best singing, the best orchestral efforts, to be found in their respective scores. They do not contain the padding or the weary stretches where the dramatist and composer have failed to do their best. Aside from a few masterpieces, every opera has such desert areas, and if they seem long even in a theatre, how much longer must they seem in a room? I may say one thing which is fairly conclusive on this point: although I have a good many complete recordings of operas, I should never dream of playing them to anybody but myself unless I had the absolute certainty that the other person wanted to listen and was capable of doing so. I, after all, am a good bit of a fanatic and can listen to practically anything without getting too bored, but an entire opera is an imposition on any ordinary guest. On that same guest I am capable of imposing an entire symphony without hesitation.

All forms, large or small, are suited to the recording machinery in one respect: that is, for study. I am no student, and yet even I recognize how much better I know the music of the great works by making that collaboration of ear and eye which comes by playing the records and following them with a score. The kind of listening which has been my concern throughout this book is, however, not that of the student. It is a form of aesthetic pleasure, like poetry, and to turn it into work (or study) is to change its nature. I am therefore obliged to say that whereas in life—say, for instance, in New York or Vienna—if given the choice I might go to the opera rather than to a symphony concert, other things being equal; in the room by myself in the country I would go to the symphony concert rather than the opera.

These late discoveries of mine—reconsiderations, accentuations, diminutions of value—are probably shared by millions. The development of the gramophone companies and of their lists of records has been fabulous in the past few years. All sorts of mushroom companies sprang up along about 1948 or soon afterwards and started pouring out records of music which in some cases had not been accessible before; the older and more established companies followed suit; the amount of music now accessible in this form is quite beyond the limits of an ordinary collector. You could always have more music in your own room than you could get in years of concertgoing; now you can have more music at home than you can get anywhere else, no matter how long you live or how hard you try. The public has apparently gobbled all this up and asked for more; the sky, they say, is the limit.

Fine and good. There are only one or two rather niggling little criticisms to be made. An eminent and erudite friend of mine contends that every record "goes dead" after you have played it three times. I believe this is roughly true, but I also believe that you can put it aside and take it up again a month or so later and it will live again for three times or thereabouts. In other words, the capacity for repetition is not endless; that is partly why we have so many records on our shelves. And a second observation to be made, more in sorrow than in anger, is that all the recording devices aim at perfection, which means that when human weakness creeps in, the passage involved is done over, and some kind of unnatural excellence is the result—something not quite consonant with what we know to be human effort. As a part of the same stress upon the "perfect product," of course, we never hear the pilgrims to Parnassus, but only those who have climbed to the summit: every artist in every category is a complete, a finished artist, usually famous or at least very well known, and that living pulse of the musical life which consists in watching talent as it unfolds is completely denied us.

Against what we have gained from this new world of music in the air—radio, too, as well as gramophone—the criticisms are valid but minor. Nobody ever thought that the new mechanisms would take the place of concert, recital and opera. Nothing takes the place of anything else, I suppose, in such realms—everything is complementary, each adds something to the other, enriches it where the need is greatest. For the music is not, after all, in the concert hall; it is not on the machine; it is not in the air of the room. It is in you and in me. It was put there by certain agencies, but it is within you as within me to supply what we know very well, in every effort made by man, is bound to be lacking. Only by means of memory and imagination, in fairly active and continuous collaboration, are we able to get out of these partial presentations everything that the composer intended (or anywhere near it). But is this not enough?

A twisted old tree in the back yard of that Vermont house catches the moon in its branches—leafy in summer, bare in autumn—when it is warm enough to sit in the doorway at the back and look at it. The machine at the other end of the odd-shaped room plays with great smoothness an uncomplaining continuity of music for as long as you wish. On those warm evenings I have often sat in the back door and watched the moon in the tree (which, naturally enough, is called Yggdrasil) while sounds of rare magic fill the air. An entire work, the lifeblood of a master spirit, may be played out upon the warm evening before the moon is released from the branches and sails off to illumine a wider darkness. I know of no better box at such times.

Envoi

It is easier to ask than to answer. The questions we asked in the
beginning may not have been answered at all and may not be susceptible of any conclusive answer except in terms not yet evolved, in
the language of some science not yet known. What I hoped was to
shed a little light by the story of one listener's progression, since, as
we all know, the *how* frequently gives some clue to the *why*.

In the end it would certainly be impossible for me to state now,
any more than a year or five or ten years ago, positive consequences
ensuing with logical inevitability from defined causes. Why we listen to modern Western music, in which by definition nothing is required of us except the act of listening, I have only been able to suggest; and what the effect may be upon us in the long run I can hardly
even adumbrate. The "good deed" recommended by Professor William James to his undergraduates does not seem pertinent to music
—that is, if we speak genially to our grandmother, or give up our
seat in the horsecar as a result of listening to Beethoven's Seventh
Symphony, I think we are victims of a wrong connection or associa-
tion. We ought to be able to give up our seat in the horsecar without
holding Beethoven responsible. In my own direct experience, to
which I add a great deal of observation, the person who has really

listened to the Seventh Symphony is far more likely to forget his grandmother's existence, miss the horsecar altogether and walk home in the wrong direction. In fact he is rather lucky if he gets home at all that evening.

James' fear of "inert" listening, and his wish to make it produce a concrete example of good behavior as an antidote to the "inertness," may be puritanism or pragmatism in the philosophical sense, but they do not seem to me to have anything to do with music. I believe that on the contrary no such immediate consequence is to be expected of any aesthetic pleasure, including one's first view of the Parthenon or the Sistine Chapel; and least of all is it likely to come out of the experience of our most abstract and unrepresentational art. Whatever Beethoven is telling us—and it may be different for each of us—we can feel fairly confident that he is not telling us to give up our seat in the horsecar. We do know, just the same, that there is an effect which, near or far, impregnates our modes of thought and feeling, so that after years of musical experience we are no longer the same in those inner regions from which music evolves and to which it is addressed. The true psychological effect, in short, may not come in the horsecar on the way home from the concert but in some unforeseen crisis twenty years later—or perhaps merely in a moment of perception on a hill or in a valley far away in space and time. The wild anemones on the slopes of Attica or Galilee, the white thrust of Shiva's Trident in the high Himalaya, sea spume in the gold light of an Atlantic evening—such rare glimpses over the wide and various earth—may acquire their ability to pierce the heart by a connection, impossible to trace, with the music that foreshadows or echoes them. Any aesthetic experience whatsoever, even if it is the most familiar sunset over the cornfields on an Illinois farm, also contains every aesthetic experience that has gone before it. In this sense music pervades and influences all our perceptions, gives keenness to our days and mellowness to our twilight. Whether it has any direct ethical result at all—whether it ever causes a direct improvement in our immediate behavior—I beg leave to doubt.

Even so, the widening and deepening of our perceptions is in itself a result of value to life, not in any practical sense, but in the inner reality which is just about what we can get out of it in the end. The same may be said of the consolations of philosophy, the offerings of literature and art, but with this difference: that the language of music is above and beyond words, speaking (even when it does also use words) to some faculty deeper and more permanent in the nature of man than the verb-ridden intellect. Shakespeare and Plato both appear to have felt this strongly and the very musicality of their utterance is a form of tribute. The "magic casements" of Keats, the "promise of happiness" of Stendhal, even the "better world" of Schubert in his thanks to music, are all capable of being contained in tone and hence, for millions in the Western world today, more clearly and powerfully than in words.

There remains to be stated the inevitable contradiction: it is not so for all. Nonmusical and antimusical points of view are to be found among the most intelligent of our contemporaries, and every one of us knows at least half a dozen men or women of quality who are frankly bored by anything more than the simplest song or march tune. The complication of development during the past century and a half may have been the root cause: it has made even listening difficult for those originally without inclination to the effort involved. Affectation and pretense have made this alienation more pronounced. I have a very old friend who, for some decades, regarded enthusiasm for music and the ingrained habit of listening to it as a form of pretense—probably because he had encountered some blatant examples of the affectations which, unfortunately, do flourish here and there. One of the greatest of American writers, Sinclair Lewis, was well over fifty years of age before he began to listen to music with any real pleasure; yet when he died he had a huge collection of recordings upon which he spent a great deal of his time. "Red," as we used to call him, regarded music as either a nuisance or a pretense at one period, and in the final period he tended to look upon it as a sort of therapy—it had consolations to offer to his restless temper—but on the last visit I paid to his house in Massachusetts it was plain that it had become to him vitally real. Such transformations of attitude are not unusual, I suppose, and if I read my Freud correctly (especially in *Civilization and Its Discontents*) they may indeed be fairly frequent. To this might be added other minority reports, such as those of the musician who can no longer bear to listen to music (I have known some), and the great artist who will listen to everything except his own or her own recordings.

All these and more, for the cases are endless, would contradict my report, but I still think there are almost incalculable millions who stand with me at the door of the concert hall forever expectant and who go away in some degree satisfied.

This satisfaction may be all there is to it, but I think not. The tale I have tried to tell may indicate what I think modern Western mankind has in this extra dimension of experience: a wider and better being, which does not fail either in the heat of the day or in the gathering dark.

Index

ABOUT THE AUTHOR

While Vincent Sheean is known to the world at large as a
foreign correspondent and author, his friends know his other
great consuming interest is music—the opera and the concert.
The first operatic music he ever heard was at the Chautauqua,
which every summer visited his native town of Pana, Illinois.
There—as a child—it awakened something in him that became
his first and last love. At the University of Chicago he was a
regular attendant, as an usher, at the Chicago opera, then
under the direction of Mary Garden. His time was nicely divided between college classes, drilling for the Officers Training
Corps during World War I and going to the opera. The war
ended before he actually entered service.

As a newspaper reporter in New York, and later as a foreign
correspondent, he was able to see and hear notable performances in London, Berlin, Paris, Vienna, Salzburg, Bayreuth,
etc. He lived two separate and distinct lives, but the two somehow made a necessary pattern for him. He seems to have had
the same uncanny penchant for being on hand at great operatic occasions as he had in his work as a correspondent. He
was working on the *Paris Herald* at the time of Mussolini's
march on Rome. He was in Vienna when Hitler moved into
Austria, in Prague when the Nazis took Czechoslovakia. He
was in France during its tragic fall and got off to England just
in time to avoid capture by the Germans; he was in London
from Dunkirk through all the phases of the blitz. Again, after
a trip to Asia, he left Wake Island just one plane ahead of the
attack on Pearl Harbor. He served in the Air Force during
World War II. In 1946 he was in the garden at Birla House in
Delhi at the time Gandhi was assassinated.

During all these world-shaking events his passion for music
prevailed and has continued to this day. A part of *First and
Last Love* was written in London and the balance in Italy.